THE
LIBRARY OF
DISTINCTIVE
SERMONS

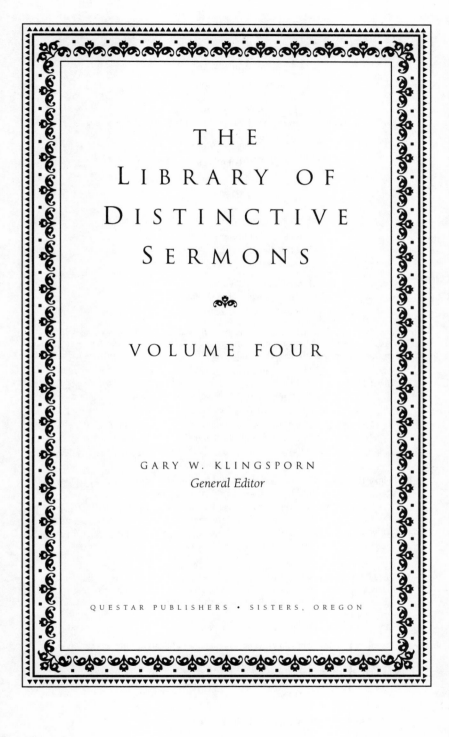

VOLUME FOUR

GARY W. KLINGSPORN

General Editor

QUESTAR PUBLISHERS • SISTERS, OREGON

Executive Editor
Stephen E. Gibson, B.A.

General Editor
Gary W. Klingsporn, Ph.D.

Associate Editor
Mary Ruth Howes, M.A.

THE LIBRARY OF DISTINCTIVE SERMONS, VOLUME 4
published by Questar Publishing Direct
a part of the Questar publishing family

© 1997 by Questar Publishers

International Standard Book Number: 1-57673-146-4
Design by David Uttley

Printed in the United States of America

Scripture quotations are from:
The Holy Bible, New International Version (NIV) © 1973, 1984 by International Bible Society, used by permission of Zondervan Publishing House.

The New King James Version (NKJV) © 1984 by Thomas Nelson, Inc.

The New Revised Standard Version Bible (NRSV) © 1989 by the Division of Christian Education of the National Council of Churches of Christ in the United States of America.

The Revised Standard Version of the Bible © 1946, 1952, 1971, 1973, Division of Christian Education, National Council of the Churches in the USA.

J.B. Phillips, *The New Testament in Modern English,* © J.B. Phillips, 1958, used by permission of Scribner, a division of Simon and Schuster.

Eugene H. Peterson, *The Message: The New Testament in Contemporary Language* © 1993 by NavPress; used by permission.

New American Standard Bible (NAS), The Lockman Foundation © 1960, 1962, 1963, 1968, 1971, 1972, 1973, 1977. Used by permission.

For information:
QUESTAR PUBLISHERS, INC.•POST OFFICE BOX 1720•SISTERS, OREGON 97759

Library of Congress Cataloging–in–Publication Data

The library of distinctive sermons/Gary W. Klingsporn, general editor. v. <4>:25 cm.
Includes bibliographical references. ISBN 1-57673-146-4 (v. 4) 1. Sermons, American.
2. Preaching. I. Klingsporn, Gary W.
BV4241.L47   1996   96-173243   252--DC20

97 98 99 00 01 02 03 — 10 9 8 7 6 5 4 3 2 1

TABLE OF CONTENTS

❧

For all who preach

How beautiful upon the mountains
are the feet of the messenger
who announces peace,
who brings good news,
who announces salvation,
who says to Zion, "Your God reigns."

ISAIAH 52:7, NRSV

The idea of *The Library of Distinctive Sermons* originated in painful practical circumstances rather than in an academic context. A pastor friend of mine went through a prolonged ordeal of tension and conflict with a congregation before he was terminated primarily "because his sermons were dry and hard to follow." As a new, young pastor, he was doing the best he could without the benefit of much experience in ministry. By and large, however, he was not connecting with the congregation in his preaching. The congregation became impatient and was less than compassionate in handling the situation. This led to a bitter parting of the ways.

As a lay person sitting in the pew and aware of the tension, I felt the pain on both sides of the issue. I began to ask myself what more might be done to assist ministers in learning and sharing the insights which contribute to effective preaching. *The Library of Distinctive Sermons* originated from that experience. It is a resource designed to promote vital and effective preaching through the sharing of sermons and insights on preaching by working pastors.

The Library of Distinctive Sermons brings together a collection of powerful contemporary sermons of diverse style and content, along with careful reflection as to what makes each sermon effective, and how each sermon relates to biblical, theological, and practical ministry issues facing pastors today.

It is important to note that we have chosen not to engage in an academic critique of each sermon. No sermon is flawless. We have chosen good sermons and have asked some simple questions: What makes each of these sermons good? What can we learn from the creative elements of style and content in each sermon to assist us in the art of preaching?

Discussion of these questions in the Comment section following each sermon makes *The Library of Distinctive Sermons* unique among sermon publications. We have enlisted only working pastors for the task of commenting on each sermon. While there are many excellent books on homiletics, we discovered that few are written by pastors for pastors. The Comment sections are a means of sharing practical ideas and insights from pastor to pastor in a way that is helpful to pastors of all backgrounds and levels of experience. Our desire is that *The Library of Distinctive Sermons* will enhance your own process of developing new sermons and contribute to the continual renewal of your preaching ministry.

Many people gave of their talents to this series. First, we are deeply grateful to all of the preachers whose sermons appear in this volume. Their commitment to the proclamation of the gospel and their willingness to share their sermons "out of context" with a wider audience beyond their local congregations, have made this series possible. Special thanks go also to those pastors who shared their wisdom, perspectives, and insights in the Comment sections. Appreciation goes as well to the General Editor, Dr. Gary W. Klingsporn, whose special gifts and talents in communication and publishing are reflected throughout the series. Special thanks to Mary Ruth Howes, who, as Associate Editor, kept us all in line with her wonderful editorial expertise in the written word.

In a rapidly changing consumer culture which is increasingly visually oriented, the sermon "competes" as never before with a multiplicity of media and voices vying for our attention. In a culture where the entertainment world sets the pace and celebrities are often the measure of "success," preaching today is subjected to intense scrutiny and is regarded by many as outmoded, especially if it does not "entertain." And yet, since the beginning of Christianity, followers of Jesus Christ in every age have found preaching the most powerful and effective form of communicating the gospel. Indeed, there is something about the gospel that seems to demand this particular expression, this form of communication, and none other. Through preaching, lives continue to be saved and transformed, liberated, healed and reconciled. We pray that *The Library of Distinctive Sermons* will encourage you and help you create new and effective ways of proclaiming the gospel of Jesus Christ in today's world.

Stephen E. Gibson
Executive Editor

INTRODUCTION

Welcome to Volume 4 of *The Library of Distinctive Sermons*. As we did in the first three volumes of this series, we are pleased to offer here another twenty outstanding sermons with comment.

Much has been written on the subject of preaching. Seldom, however, do we find good sermons brought together with commentary on why those sermons constitute effective proclamation of the gospel. Among the literature available today, we can read sermons. Or, we can read about preaching. But seldom do we have the opportunity to do both at the same time: to read good sermons, and to reflect on the art of preaching as it is embodied in those sermons.

The Library of Distinctive Sermons is designed to promote the enrichment of preaching through the sharing of good sermons and careful analysis of their style and content. The purpose is to read a sermon and ask, "What makes this sermon effective as the proclamation of God's Word?" The philosophy underlying this series is that, whether we are novices or seasoned preachers, we can always learn from others who preach. One of the best ways to do that is to "listen" to others, to observe how they preach, and pick up on some of the best of what they do in a way that is natural and appropriate in our own preaching.

Each of the sermons in this volume is accompanied by a Comment section. Here working pastors reflect on what makes each sermon distinctive and effective. To some extent, of course, this is a very subjective undertaking. What makes a sermon "good" or "effective" to one person is not always the same in the opinion of others. Given the subjectivity involved, it would be easy to avoid ever undertaking the task of serious reflection about our preaching. However, in the Comment sections in this volume, the writers have taken the risk of opening the dialogue about what constitutes effective preaching. There is much to be gained in this process: new ideas and techniques, new perspectives on texts, creative forms and structures, new stories and illustrations for preaching.

It is one thing to hear or read a good sermon and to have some sense of why we like it. But how often do we give serious analytical reflection, asking what we can learn from a sermon? *The Library of Distinctive Sermons* provides an opportunity for the enrichment of preaching through thoughtful consideration of why each sermon has been done in the way it is done.

In the Comment sections in this series the writers reflect on the style and content of each sermon. They look at such things as the genre and structure of the sermon, its use of biblical texts, illustrations, literary or rhetorical techniques, tone, and language. They also comment on how the content of each sermon proclaims biblical faith; remains true to the biblical text; reflects sound theology; deals with faith questions; addresses ethical and social issues; and shows the relevance of the gospel in today's world.

The Comments are presented in a fairly nontechnical way. The focus of this series is not on an academic analysis or critique of sermons, nor is the focus on theoretical aspects of communication and homiletics. The purpose of this series is to offer practical reflection aimed at stimulating our thoughts and improving our preaching in very practical ways.

The format of this volume is simple. Each sermon is presented as closely as possible to the original form in which it was preached. Obviously, in moving from the original oral medium of preaching to the written form represented here, some editing has been necessary to facilitate literary style, clarity, and comprehension.

The Comment following each sermon assumes that every effective sermon includes at least three basic elements. First, every sermon addresses questions relating to the problems and needs of the human condition. Second, every good sermon has a thesis and makes an assertion. It proclaims truth from the Scriptures using one or more biblical texts. Third, every good sermon invites people to respond or motivates them to think, act, or believe. These preaching elements can be described in many different ways using varieties of language. In their Comments the writers commonly use the terms Text, Problem, Proclamation, and Response (or Invitation) to refer to these elements of sermonic structure and content.

In the Comments, then, you will notice frequent discussion of the following items which are intended as helpful tools of reflection and analysis:

1) Text. How does the preacher interpret and apply the biblical text(s) in the sermon? What techniques are used? What insights into the text(s) are found in the sermon?

2) Problem. What human problem, need, question, or life situation does each sermon address? How is the problem of the human condition understood and presented in the sermon?

3) Proclamation. How does the sermon proclaim the good news of the Christian gospel? What is the truth or "kerygma" drawn from the Scriptures and applied to the human situation?

4) Response. How does the sermon invite us to respond? What does the preacher invite, urge, or encourage us to believe or to do? What motivation is there to act or to change, and how does this flow out of the interpretation of the biblical text(s), the human problem, and the proclamation of the gospel?

5) Suggestions. Each Comment section concludes with some practical suggestions for thought or discussion, for further reading, or for incorporating some of the insights from the sermon into one's own preaching.

The Library of Distinctive Sermons features a wide variety of sermon styles and subjects. This is important in a series designed for the enrichment of preaching. You will undoubtedly like some of the sermons more than others. You will react differently to different sermons. You may agree or disagree with some of the Comments. But all of these reactions can be learning experiences. So as you read, ask yourself: "What do I think about this sermon? Why do I feel as I do?" Interact with the material! Reflect on your own preaching and ministry as you enjoy this volume. Then the sermons and Comments will become a valuable resource for your own ministry.

It is important to remember that each of the sermons in this volume was preached in an original context, most of them in congregations on Sunday mornings. Each was spoken with the presence and guidance of the Holy Spirit to a particular people in a particular time and place. Each sermon had a life of its own as the Word of God in that specific moment.

While the sermons that appear here are removed from those original contexts, there is much we can learn from them. Whenever possible, the attempt has been made to acknowledge significant aspects of the original context. But now these sermons appear in a new context. God can use them in this context to speak home to our hearts and to create new understanding and possibilities for ministry.

The apostle Paul wrote, "So then faith comes from what is heard, and what is heard comes through the word of Christ" (Rom. 10:17, NRSV). It is in and through the preached word of Christ that God directs us to faith in Christ and imparts to us the gift of faith. In preaching, the wonderful work and mystery of God take place: the living Christ becomes present through the preached word. Bonhoeffer said, "The word of Scripture is certain, clear, and plain. The preacher should be assured that Christ enters the congregation through those words which he [or she] proclaims from the Scripture...."[1] Preaching is a holy calling filled with the mystery and promise of God. We do well to give all the careful time and attention we can to this holy task, while always giving ourselves to God. As Augustine said of preaching, "Lord, give me the gifts to make this gift to you."

Gary W. Klingsporn
General Editor

Note

1. Dietrich Bonhoeffer, *Worldly Preaching*, ed. Clyde E. Fant (Nashville and New York: Thomas Nelson, Inc., 1975), p. 130.

Donald K. Adickes is a retired minister of the Evangelical Lutheran Church in America. A graduate of Gettysburg College (B.A.), Lutheran Seminary in Philadelphia (M.Div.) and the University of Kansas (M.A.), he served twenty-five years as a chaplain in the United States Army and a number of years in parish minstry in Texas, where he continues to serve parishes on a part-time and interim basis.

Dixie Brachlow is a recent graduate of Louisville Presbyterian Theological Seminary (M.Div.) and a candidate for pastoral ministry in the Presbyterian Church (USA). Her professional experience includes college administration, grant writing, public speaking, program development and high school teaching. She is a graduate of the University of Minnesota (B.S.) and Augustana College (M.A.).

Richard A. Davis is Teaching Pastor of Hope Presbyterian Church in Richfield, Minnesota. A graduate of the University of Minnesota (B.A.), Luther Theological Seminary (M.A.), and San Francisco Theological Seminary (M.Div.), Davis has served Presbyterian churches in Minnesota and Belfast, Northern Ireland. He has contributed a number of articles to various publications and is author of *The Prism Project: A Survey of the Bible for Adults.*

Gary W. Downing is currently Evangelism Pastor of Faith Covenant Church in Burnsville, Minnesota. He has previously served as a seminary instructor, executive minister of Colonial Church, Edina, Minnesota, executive director of Youth Leadership, and area Young Life director. A graduate of Bethel college (B.A.), Bethel Theological Seminary (M.Div.) and Luther Theological Seminary (M.Div.), Downing is author of *One Man's Heart,* a book on male spirituality.

Gilbert R. Friend-Jones is Senior Minister of Central Congregational Church (UCC), Atlanta, Georgia. He previously served churches in Minneapolis, Minnesota; Reston, Virginia; and South Paris, Maine. A graduate of Princeton Theological Seminary (M.Div.) and Howard

University Divinity School (D.Min.), he has been active in ecumenical and urban ministries and initiatives against violence and racism. He has written articles for national publications on subjects as diverse as jazz, Chernobyl, philosophy, sexuality, theology, and urban violence.

Marianna Frost is Professor of Bible and Religion at Athens State College in Athens, Alabama. She is an ordained United Methodist minister who has served pastorates in Tennessee and Texas. An author and former newspaper editor, she received the Doctor of Ministry degree from Vanderbilt University.

Gary A. Furr is Pastor of Vestavia Hills Baptist Church in Birmingham, Alabama, and adjunct instructor in New Testament at Samford University. The author of numerous articles and book reviews, Furr is coeditor of *Ties That Bind: Life Together in the Baptist Vision.* He has served churches in Texas, Georgia and Alabama, and is a graduate of Carson-Newman College (B.A.), Southeastern Baptist Theological Seminary (M.Div.) and Baylor University (Ph.D.).

Greg Garrison is Religion Editor and staff writer for *The Birmingham News* in Birmingham, Alabama. A graduate of the University of Missouri School of Journalism (1985), he has written articles for the *National Catholic Reporter, Liberty,* and *Presbyterians Today,* and was a 1996 finalist for the Templeton Reporter of the year Award sponsored by the Religion Newswriters Association.

K. Thomas Greene is pastor of Greenwich Baptist Church in Greenwich, Connecticut. A graduate of Campbell College (B.A.) and Southeastern Baptist Theological Seminary (M.Div., Th.M., D.Min.), he has served churches in North Carolina, Texas and Connecticut with special emphasis on urban and prison ministries and in outreach programs serving the inner city.

William J. Ireland, Jr. is Pastor of Briarcliff Baptist Church, Atlanta, Georgia. A graduate of Mississippi College (B.A.) and Southern Baptist Theological Seminary (M.Div., Ph.D.), he has served churches in Louisiana, Kentucky and Georgia, has served as Moderator of the Atlanta Baptist Association and has written numerous articles for preaching and teaching publications.

Debra K. Klingsporn is an author and former public relations and marketing executive who has served as executive director of marketing for Word Publishing, and as a vice president of Carol DeChant & Associates, a public relations firm based in Chicago. A graduate of Texas A&M University with a bachelor's degree in journalism, she is the coauthor of *Shattering Our Assumptions: Breaking Free of Expectations—Others & Our Own; Soul Searching: Meditations for Your Spiritual Journey;* and *I can't, God Can, I Think I'll Let Him;* and coeditor of *The Quickening Heart* and *The Remembering Season.*

Gary W. Klingsporn is Teaching Minister of Colonial Church in Edina, Minnesota, and serves as General Editor of *The Library of Distinctive Sermons.* He has served churches in Texas and Minnesota and has taught religious studies at Baylor University and Metropolitan State University in Minneapolis. Formerly a writer and editor with Word Publishing, he is a graduate of St. Paul's Lutheran College (A.A.), Oral Roberts University (B.A.), and Baylor University (Ph.D.).

James J. H. Price is Professor of Religious Studies at Lynchburg College, Lynchburg, Virginia. An ordained minister in the Presbyterian Church, U.S.A., he holds a Ph.D. from Vanderbilt University. For several years he has written exegetical/expository studies in the International Uniform Lessons in *The Presbyterian Outlook,* along with articles, book reviews, and exegetical studies in a variety of other publications. He is the coauthor with William R. Goodman, Jr., of *Jerry Falwell: An Unauthorized Profile* (Paris and Associates, 1981).

Peter J. Smith is Pastor of First Congregational Church of Thomaston, Connecticut. A graduate of Trinity College (B.A.) and Gordon-Conwell Theological Seminary (M.Div.), he has served United Church of Christ churches in Indiana and Minnesota and has been active in Habitat for Humanity, the United Church Board for World Ministries, and other ministry endeavors.

Peter G. St. Don is Founding Pastor of Harbour Community Church in Huntington Beach, California. A graduate of Fuller Theological Seminary (M.A.) and McCormick Theological Seminary (D.Min.), he has served a number of churches and is a leader in the National Association of Congregational Churches.

Karen Fisher Younger is Minister to Families and Youth at Faith United Methodist Church, Downers Grove, Illinois. A graduate of Trinity University (B.A.) and Gordon-Conwell Seminary (M.Div.), she won the Gordon-Conwell Seminary Preaching Award and has served as an intern at Park Street Church, Boston, Massachusetts.

WORDS, WORDS, WORDS

JOHN 4:16–26

REV. DR. THOMAS G. LONG
FRANCIS LANDEY PATTON PROFESSOR OF PREACHING
PRINCETON THEOLOGICAL SEMINARY
PRINCETON, NEW JERSEY

REV. DR. THOMAS G. LONG

WORDS, WORDS, WORDS

JOHN 4:16–26

I would like to begin by saying two things to the Class of 1991. First, I would like to express my gratitude to all of you for the invitation that you have given me to be the preacher at this service, your baccalaureate. You have a very fine class; I feel as though I have a special personal relationship with many of you, and I am honored to have the privilege of serving in this way.[1]

The second thing I want to say is that you do not really know whether I just told you the truth or not. As a matter of fact, I did tell the truth. I am honored to be preaching here today, but saying that it is an honor and a privilege and so on is the sort of thing that people in this position are supposed to do. For all you know, my real feeling is that being up here today is a headache and a chore, just one more task to perform at the end of an already too busy year. The words that come out of my mouth are "honor, privilege, and gratitude," but, after all, they're just words. Words, words, words.

One doesn't have to search very far in our world to realize that we live in a culture that doesn't trust words very much. We use words by the bushel. We are the "Information Age." We process words by the billions, but we don't trust them very much. We know that words can be slippery, weasel things. Words can be used to conceal, to deceive, to distort. Words are cheap; people can hide behind words.

When a politician gives a speech, what do we say? "Promises, promises." When the telephone company says, "We'll be by to install your phone on Thursday at 2:00. You can count on it"—we don't. When George Bush spoke boldly of building a "new world order," it sounded vaguely like the "old world order" to us.

We don't trust words. They are sneaky; talk is cheap. Don't give us words; give us substance. As Eliza Doolittle says to her two suitors in *My Fair Lady*: "Words, words, words...Is that all you blighters can do?" Or, as Edgar Guest put it, uncomfortably close to home: "I'd rather see a sermon than hear one any day."

This distrust of words is nothing new. Indeed, it's been in the human spirit almost from the beginning. According to the story of Adam and Eve, the situation began to deteriorate in Eden precisely at the point that the serpent began to raise the possibility that words just might not be all that they seem: "Did God say...? No, you will not die."

Words are a gift from God. They were, in a sense, the first sacramental elements of communion. Whatever else we lost in Eden, we lost the trustworthiness of language. Men and women became afraid, and because they became afraid, they began to hide—from God and each other—behind fig leaves and behind lying words:

"Where is your brother?"

"I don't know. Am I my brother's keeper?"

Now all of this should give us some concern today, since we are sending out this graduating class to do ministry basically with words. Financiers have capital; physicians have medicines; farmers have seed and soil; soldiers have guns; ministers have words. Words, words, words. Sermon words, prayer words, liturgical words. Where there is grief, words of comfort. Where there is injustice, prophetic words. Where there is complacency, challenging words. Words, words, words.

That is why it is important to hear this day the claim of the gospel that, in Jesus Christ, we get our words back, that the words we speak can become filled with grace and truth, instruments of redemption. That is part of what this story of Jesus and the woman at the well is all about. What did Jesus really do for this woman? He did not heal her of any disease; he did not raise her child from the dead; he did not dazzle her by turning the water into wine. He simply talked to her. Words, words, words. But the words he spoke were so radically different from the other words she had heard, words so filled with grace and truth, that she was never the same again.

It is important to note that this story does not begin with words. Quite to the contrary, it begins in silence. Not gentle, tranquil silence, but hard, cold silence because she who came to the well was a Samaritan and he who rested at the well was a Jew. She who came to the well was a woman; he who rested at the well was a man. Between the Samaritan woman and Jewish man there was a wall of silence, built brick by brick with prejudice and hatred, through which no word was allowed to pass.

"Would you give me a drink of water?" said the Jewish man to the Samaritan woman, and the wall came tumbling down. One word, one seemingly ordinary phrase, a quiet word that cut against the grain of the culture, and the wall came tumbling down.

It is amazing to me how often significant ministry takes place in not very dramatic ways. Oh, sometimes there is the sensational confrontation with Caesar or the thrilling turnaround to faith, but most of the time, ministry is something like the speaking of a single surprising word. Like the December day in 1955 when a bus driver in Montgomery, Alabama, ordered four people in a row of seats to move to the back of the bus. It is said that one of these people, a department store clerk named Rosa Parks, spoke so softly that it was hard to hear her voice over the noise of the bus. What she said was, "No," and a wall came tumbling down.[2]

William Willimon of Duke University tells about a young woman named Anne who was a member of a congregation he served. After college Anne had entered pharmacy school, but from time to time she came home and worshiped with her parents. One Sunday evening, after one of her visits, Will received a telephone call from Anne's father:

"Do you know what's happened?" he said. "Anne just called us to say that she has decided to drop out of pharmacy school."

"Really?" Will said. "What on earth is leading her to do a thing like that?"

"Well, we're not sure," he said. "You know how much Anne likes you. We thought maybe you could call her up and talk some sense into her."

Will did just that. He reminded Anne of all her hard work and her achievements and how she should think carefully before throwing all of this away. "How in the world did you come to this decision?" he asked her.

"It was your sermon yesterday that started me thinking. You said that God has something important for each of us to do, in our own way. I thought to myself, 'I'm not here because I want to serve God. I'm here to get a job, to make money, to look out for myself.' Then I remembered the good summer I spent working with the church literacy program among the migrant workers' kids. I really think I was serving God then. I decided, after your sermon, to go back there and give my life to helping those kids."

There was a long silence on Will's end of the line. "Now look, Anne," he finally said, "I was just preaching."[3]

Sermon words…and the wall came tumbling down. When the wall falls down between Jesus and the woman, she seems startled, perhaps even frightened. There's something comforting about a wall. It may hem us in, but at least we don't have to face what's on the other side of it. The woman fires a flurry of words at Jesus in disbelief that the wall has fallen, perhaps even trying to rebuild the wall as a hiding place. Beneath the words, he hears the person; in the windstorm of her words, Jesus hears the woman.

"Why is it that you, a Jew, ask for water from a Samaritan woman?"

"If you knew the gift of God, you could have asked, and he would have given living water."

"Who do you think you are? You haven't even got a bucket. Even Jacob had to have a bucket. Are you greater than Jacob?"

"Everyone who drinks of this water will thirst again, but those who drink of the water I give will never be thirsty."

It was then that the woman said the fatal word, the word that caused the death of her old self and gave her new life: "Give me this water that I may never be thirsty."

"All right," said Jesus. "Go call your husband."

"I have no husband."

"That's right. You have no husband. You've had five husbands, and the one you are with now is not your husband. You told the truth when you said you have no husband."

Now the commentators have raised a lot of eyebrows about this woman, as if she were some sort of merry divorcée, the Liz Taylor of ancient Samaria, trading husbands like sports cars. Women in the first century did not have that option. She has not devoured husband after husband; she has been devoured by a social system that, for whatever reason, has passed her from man to man to man until she no longer has even the dignity of marriage. When Jesus talks about her husbands, he is not so much exposing her sin as he is naming her wound. With a word he has touched the issue in her life.

A former student of mine graduated from seminary and became the pastor of a small Presbyterian church, small enough so that she set for herself the goal of visiting every family on the roll in the first six months. At the end of six months, she had almost done it. She had visited every family but one. "They haven't been here in two years," people said. "Don't bother; they aren't coming back."

She had set her goal though, and so one afternoon she drove out to their house. Only the wife was at home. She poured cups of coffee, and they sat at the kitchen table and chatted. They talked about this; they talked about that; then they talked about *it*. Two-and-one-half years earlier she had been at home with their young son. She was vacuuming in the back bedroom and had not checked on him in a while, so she snapped off the vacuum, went into the den, and did not find him. She followed his trail, across the den, through the patio door, across the patio, to the swimming pool, where she found him. "At the funeral, our friends at the church were very kind. They told us it was God's will."

The minister put her cup down on the table. Should she touch it or should she not? She touched it. "Your friends meant well, I am sure, but they were wrong."

"What do you mean?" she asked.

"I mean that God does not will the death of children."

The woman's face reddened and her jaw set. "Then whom do you blame? I guess you blame me."

"No, I don't blame you. I don't want to blame God either."

"Then how do you explain it?" she said, her anger rising.

"I don't know. I can't explain it. I don't understand why such things happen either. I only know that God's heart broke when yours did."

The woman had her arms crossed, and it was clear that this conversation was over. The minister left the house kicking herself. "Why didn't I leave it alone?" A few days later the phone rang; it was she. "We don't know where this is going, but would you come out and talk with my husband and me? We have assumed that God was angry at us; maybe it's the other way around."

With a word we touch the issues in people's lives. When Jesus named the issue in her life, the woman tried to change the subject:

"I see that you are a prophet," she said. "Now let's see, you prophets like to talk theology. Isn't it interesting that you Jews worship in Jerusalem, and we Samaritans worship on the mountain. Isn't that a fascinating theological difference. Would you care to comment on it? After you do, maybe we can move on to eschatology."

"Woman, I tell you," said Jesus, "the hour is coming, and now is, when the mountain, the temple, it won't make any difference. What will make a difference is you—your worship in spirit and in truth."

"Me? Make a difference? To God? When hell freezes over...when Messiah comes."

That's when Jesus said the best word of all: "I am he." The One who, with a word, breaks down the walls. The One who, with a word, touches the deepest wounds in your life. "I am he." In the beginning was the Word...and the Word became flesh and dwelt among us, full of grace and truth. "I am he." Jesus was the Word, and because she was transformed by that Word, she who had been locked in silence left that place with a word to live and a word to speak.

My Uncle Ed ran an American Oil service station in a small town in South Carolina. He was a wonderful man. He hunted and fished and told loud, uproarious jokes, and people loved him. While he was still a young man, his big heart failed him, and the family gathered for the funeral. I was a young teenager at the time. The minister at Ed's church was on vacation, and despite assurances from the family that he need not come back for the service, he insisted and interrupted his time away to return.

He drove the many miles back, arriving just in time to come by the family home and to accompany us to the church for the funeral. I will never forget his arrival. Indeed, as I look back on it now, it created in me one of the first stirrings toward ministry. The family was all together in the living room of Ed's home, and through the big picture window we saw the minister arrive. He got out of his stripped down Ford, all spindle-legged, wearing a cheap blue suit, clutching his service book like a life preserver. Now that I am a minister myself, I think I know what was going through his mind as he approached the house: "What to say, dear God, what to say? What words do you speak when words seem hardly enough?"

What he did not know, could not know, is how the atmosphere in that living room changed that moment we saw him step out of his car. It was anticipation, but more than that. His arrival was, in its own way, a call to worship. This frail human being, striding across the lawn in his off-the-rack preacher suit, desperately trying to find some words of meaning to speak, brought with him, by the grace of God, the presence of Christ. In his presence and in his words—words, words, words—was the living Word.

Because the Word became flesh and dwells among us...so will it be for you, too. So will it be for you.

Notes

1. This was the baccalaureate sermon for the Class of 1991, Princeton Theological Seminary, originally published in *The Princeton Seminary Bulletin*, New Series, Vol. 12 (November 1991), pp. 314–19.
2. Taylor Branch, *Parting the Waters: America in the King Years 1954–63* (New York: Simon and Schuster, 1988), p. 129.
3. William H. Willimon, *What's Right with the Church* (San Francisco: Harper & Row, 1985), pp. 112–13.

COMMENT

The large number and variety of sermons based on the conversation between Jesus and the Samaritan woman at the well in John 4 suggest to us that there is more than one way to preach on the passage. Yet not all ways are equally sound or effective. This sermon by Thomas Long is uncommonly sound and effective.

The sermon belongs to a particular context: a baccalaureate service at Princeton Theological Seminary where Long serves as professor of preaching. The obligatory expression of thanks to the graduating class for the invitation to deliver the sermon serves as the foil for the theme of the sermon, which is also its title: "Words, Words, Words." Even his own words, Long acknowledges, may be "just words." By casting the first stone into his own pulpit, he at once commands our attention and respect. "We don't trust words," Long declares in the opening sentence of the third paragraph. His original hearers are surely prepared to stay with him the rest of the sermon since they will "do ministry basically with words." By a sensitive treatment of the theological horizons of the text of the Samaritan woman in John 4, Long challenges the graduating class that their words—spoken from the pulpit to those spoken at the bedside of the ill or dying—have the potential to be words of vitality and energy when in the service of the Word made flesh. The sermon strikes one powerfully because of its economy of language, vivid phrases, and the preacher's perspicacious "reading" of both the biblical text and the situation of his hearers. The allusions to Rosa Parks, *My Fair Lady,* Anne the pharmacy student, and Uncle Ed's minister "in his off-the-rack preacher suit" connect with the interests and experiences of many hearers.

STRUCTURE

Long builds the structure around the leitmotif of "words, words, words" in which we cannot trust. He relates the theme of words to the familiar story of the woman at the well to demonstrate that words used in ministry can be "filled with grace and truth" to topple the walls of estrangement. He develops further the word motif in placing the spotlight on the woman's words that request the water that will forever quench thirst (v. 15). This is for Long her "fatal word, the word that caused the death of her old self and gave her new life."

In the final third of the sermon the preacher invites his hearers to note the words that "touch the issues in peoples' lives" by probing Jesus' request that the woman call her husband. With the word about the woman's husband, Jesus "has touched the issue in her life." Two effective personal stories of his former student's words with the parents of the child who drowned and the pastor "in his off-the-rack preacher suit" bringing a word of comfort to his Uncle Ed's family conclude the sermon. Long points to Christ as the living Word who will be present in our words. The "words" leitmotif provides the structure of the sermon.

TEXT & PROCLAMATION

Johannine passages are particularly vexing and challenging to a preacher seeking to be faithful to the biblical text. In this excellent sermon, specifically directed to seminary graduates, Long refuses to imprison the passage in its pristine meaning. He avoids offering to his hearers a mere inspirational restatement of the passage. He refrains from giving them a précis of the fruit of the exegetical labor of the commentaries of the "Triple Bs"— Bultmann, Barrett, and Brown. Yet the sermon manifests a serious exegetical and theological encounter with the passage. Long gives his original hearers and us an energizing word that connects with both the theological horizons of the passage and the fears and faith of those who by their words will call others to faith.

Long recognizes that one way of entry into the multifaceted story of the woman at the well in John 4 is to throw the spotlight on the words of Jesus to the woman and her words in response to Jesus. Such an approach to the passage discloses the theological field of vision of the writer of the Fourth Gospel. The grace and ease with which Long builds this sermon around the trinity of "words, words, words" may conceal his mature encounter with the text. The sermon provides many examples of creative interpretation.

Only in the sixth paragraph of the sermon do we know we are in church when he deftly presents Adam and Eve's hearing from the serpent that "words just might not be all that they seem." Long directs the master image of "words, words, words" to his particular congregation, the seminary graduating class, when he asserts that they will "do ministry basically with words." It is only at the eighth full paragraph of the sermon that he introduces the passage from John 4. He maintains that the conviction that words can be filled with grace and truth "is [a] part of what this story…is all about." Long reminds us that there is more in the passage than he is going to tell in a single sermon. A reader is grateful not only for his honesty, but also for the obvious study in commentaries that were central to the preparation of the preacher (not only of the sermon!) before and during the writing of the sermon. The delicate sauce a chef brings to the table does not directly reveal the separate ingredients of the basic stock, aromatic herbs, tomatoes, garlic, and shallots. Although Long has listened to John through serious study and reflection, he doesn't parade a string of exegetical insights before the congregation.

Note how he helps his hearers to catch the depth of estrangement between Jew and Samaritan and male and female by emphasizing the role of silence. Although not explicitly noted in the biblical text, the emphasis on silence depicts the wall of alienation that will be demolished in the words of Jesus. There are so many striking phrases in the sermon that space would not allow one to refer to all of them. Surely memorable are the words: "there was a wall of silence, built brick by brick with prejudice and hatred, through which no word was allowed to pass." Those words impact the essence of what an informed preacher reads in solid commentaries.

Long skillfully appropriates the biblical text in the final paragraphs of the sermon to explore in a more nuanced fashion the crumbling of the walls through words. Following the story of the collapse of the wall in the life of Anne the pharmacy student through the words of a sermon, Long returns to the story at the well and what Jesus hears "beneath the words" uttered by the woman. He creatively cites the dialogue in John 4:9–14, which particularly picks up the mistrust of the woman for the words of Jesus.

Especially impressive is Long's ability to avoid a moralistic reading of the reference to the woman's five previous husbands. He shows that her life has been placed in a social context where "she no longer has even the dignity of marriage." A single sentence imparts a core conviction of the passage: "With a word he has touched the issue in her life." The sermon moves from the brief reference to the woman's husbands in the biblical text to the story of his former student's words that touched the lives of the parents of the drowned child.

That story in turn provides the bridge to return to the biblical story's dialogue of the woman's changing the subject of the conversation to divert Jesus' question by turning to another subject (vv. 19–20). The dialogue leads to Jesus' affirmation, "I am he" (v. 26). Confronting the Word, she "left that place with a word to live and a word to speak."

The proclamation of the good news is appropriately concluded through the story of the pastor "in his off-the-rack preacher suit, desperately trying to find some words of meaning to speak." Long affirms that "in his words—words, words, words—was the living Word."

SUGGESTIONS

This sermon was designed for a specific congregation of graduating seminary students. One cannot import this sermon in its present form into a typical parish church, but it can stimulate thought, provide images, and offer a model of creative appropriation of a Johannine passage for preaching.

- Some sermons probe the entire conversation in John 4 in a more expository mode while others focus on a specific verse or theme in the story. There are also sermons that combine the two approaches. It is not unusual to read a series of sermons on different sections of this complex passage. One might pick up on the "must" theme, which is not really a geographical must, but a divine must which made necessary according to the will of God, a Samaritan mission (v. 4). The revelation of God in Christ shatters the barriers we erect. Or one might pick up on the "misunderstanding" theme, which warns us that one may miss or fail to respond to the clues to the Word made flesh dwelling among us. In a culture that has little room for ambiguity, the conversation between Jesus and the woman challenges our demand for a God without ambiguity.

- One also might show how the story that begins with the irregularity of a Jew talking with a Samaritan is dropped to take up the deeper question of the identity of Jesus. The social distinction between Jew and Samaritan and the social conflicts that tear the fabric of our society apart lose their power in the presence of the Savior of the world (v. 42).

James J. H. Price

ON MAKING A COVENANT WITH YOUR STRATEGIC SELF-IMPORTANCE

JEREMIAH 1:1–19

DR. CALVIN A. MILLER
PROFESSOR OF COMMUNICATION
SOUTHWESTERN BAPTIST SEMINARY
FORT WORTH, TEXAS

Dr. Calvin A. Miller

On Making a Covenant with Your Strategic Self-Importance

JEREMIAH 1:1–19, NKJV

What's in a name? What's in Your Name?

Do you like your name? Once in a while, as you continue your pilgrimage through life, write your name down. Study it and pray over it, until you can make it a covenant of celebration. Especially in moments of despondency, never forget that whatever your name is, it is important to God.

As the 60s, the hippie era of American history, came to an end, those old rock-and-roll LSD refugees of San Francisco's Haight-Ashbury district began moving down the coast to Santa Cruz. They got married and had children too, though usually not in that sequence. These hippie parents never named their children Melissa or Brett. They gave their children lovely names like Snow Princess, Sea Foam, and Panache. So people around Santa Cruz grew accustomed to having their children playing ball with little "Time Warp" or "Spring Fever." Eventually a lot of children named things like Moonbeam, Earth-Love and Precious Promise all ended up in public school. It was in that era of history that one of the Santa Cruz kindergarten teachers first met "Fruit Stand."

"Fruit Stand" on the first day of school got off the bus wearing a tag proudly displaying his name "Fruit Stand." The teacher thought the boy's name was odd but no odder than many other hippie children. So she tried not to make the boy feel self-conscious about his name.

"Would you like to play with the blocks, Fruit Stand?" she asked. And later, "Fruit Stand, how about a snack?" Little Fruit Stand accepted all her offers but hesitantly. By the afternoon recess, his name didn't seem much odder than Heather's or Sun Ray's or Fairie Queen's. At the final bell, the teacher led the children out to the buses. "Fruit Stand, do you know which one is your bus?"

He didn't answer.

That wasn't particularly strange. He hadn't answered all day. His teacher realized that lots of children are shy on the first day of school. It didn't matter. As a teacher, she had instructed each of the hippie parents to write the names of their children's bus stops on the reverse side of their name tags. Just as she put the little boy on the bus and said, "Good-bye, I'll see you tomorrow, Fruit Stand!" she turned over his bus-tag. There, neatly printed was the word "Anthony."[1]

I've often thought how much like "Fruit Stand" these Bible names must have sounded. Isaac meant something like "Giggles!" Esau, "Big Red"; Jacob, "Grabberboy." Jonah was "Dovey," Methuselah, "When I die, watch out!" Damascus meant "Bag of Blood," Habakkuk, "Babylonian House Plant." Jeremiah means "God Will Hurl." (You could wind up with a horrible inferiority problem with such a name.) Anathoth was his bus stop. So when God yelled down and said, "Hey you, down there! Yes, you...you, God Will Hurl! I've known you since you were in the womb," Jeremiah must have asked, at least once, "Well, for goodness' sakes, why didn't you name me Bradley?"

Of course, that would sound too odd in the Old Testament's table of contents: Psalms, Proverbs, Ecclesiastes, Song of Solomon, Isaiah, Bradley, Lamentations, Ezekiel.... While I don't believe that Jeremiah much cared for "God Will Hurl," still, with a name like that on your I.D. bracelet you know you're no ordinary kid. You must realize how strategically important you are to God.

All of my life I have suffered from inferiority. It took me a long time to come to grips with the idea that I was strategically important to God. The word *Calvin* is related to *Calvary*, which as you know is the Latin translation of the Hebrew word *Golgotha*, which means "place of the skull." This Latinesque *Calvin* more properly means "bald." (I actually think I would have preferred "God Will Hurl.") Like so many, I have never particularly liked my name, though more and more it is becoming my definition! But, for all of its shortcomings, I now take it by faith that my name has consequence. And God who has counted the hairs of my head, has saved me and called me and constantly reminds me that he has called me by name and that my name has significance to him.

Names matter. And the name that matters most to us is our own. Our names matter not because they tell others who we are but because they tell us who we are. Most of us are riddled, at one time or another, with feelings of inferiority. How incompetent and unsure of himself Jeremiah was! He is known as the "weeping prophet." In chapter 1 of his book Jeremiah rises from the mishmash of his own inferiority.

Which of us has not felt Jeremiah's strong feelings of inferiority? Most of us in confronting any great task say something like, "I can't do it. I'm afraid. I'm not adequate. If somehow conditions were better or I were in the right place! If only I had more strength of character, I'd do it."

A cartoon I recently saw pictured a psychiatrist sending his receptionist out into the crowded waiting room with the instructions, "Send the paranoids in first—the ones with inferiority complexes don't mind waiting!" That's not altogether true, however. Inferiority-complexers do mind it, but they feel they somehow deserve it. The inferiority-ridden love their "worm theology," agreeing with Isaac Watts that Christ died "for such a worm as I." The inferior have practically invented worm theology, and they keep it alive. The inferior usually love their inferiority and only feel really good when they feel really bad. They love to sing, "Oh, to be nothing, nothing!" but they rarely sing it out of healthy humility. In fact, they'd rather be singing, "Oh, to be something, something!" But they simply feel they're not worthy.

Inferiority is our common malaise in the ministry. A lot of ministers suffer from it. I was so inferior even the neighbors noticed it and pointed it out to my mother as I grew up. In my late teens, one of my sisters felt led of God to help me get in touch with myself by telling me that in her opinion, which was as inerrant as the King James Bible, if God had called me to do anything, he must have had a wrong number.

When I told my preacher I was called to preach, he didn't necessarily feel that God had a wrong number, but he was concerned that I might have had a poor connection. Still he wanted to help me get started on my calling. He asked me to preach at the Garfield County Old Folks Home. Most of those at the county home were deaf, so it seemed to him a safe place for me to try out my calling. The fact that the sermon would fall largely on deaf ears did not ease my anxiety. The very idea of preaching filled me with terror. I still remember how hard I worked on that very first sermon. I wanted it to be great. I typed five, single-spaced pages of notes. I managed to preach for three minutes! (It takes me longer than that to clear my throat now!) Feeling humiliated, I sat back down and refused to preach for a year and a half. Inferiority nearly destroyed my desire to try again! Yet God had called me to make a covenant with my strategic self-importance.

You as pastors may often lament your small role in a big Christian machine. You may feel that your church negates your special role. But Christianity ought to have magnified you, not reduced you. It ought to have taught you that Jesus is a special Savior who came on a special mission to call specific individuals for specific assignments. You are special. It is easy, and it may seem more spiritual, to sit back and cry, "Oh, to be nothing…nothing." The problem with doing that is that it reinforces what many of your deacons may already think. If you are really obsessed with sitting around and thinking you are "nothing, nothing," you shouldn't do it on God's time. He is counting on your significance, not your nothingness. We are to take up our cross, not to annihilate ourselves but to take meaningful stands for Jesus in a doubting world. Those who crucify their old sin nature demonstrate to the world what their significance to God really is.

In the opening chapter of the Book of Jeremiah, we encounter Jeremiah, the man from Anathoth. Anathoth wasn't much of a town. It was poor and beyond the north walls of Jerusalem. Jeremiah is probably no more than fourteen years old when God comes to him and says, "I want you to bear my word before kings." Can you see why he's insecure? Think how you would feel if you were in the eighth grade and God told you he had a little sermon he wanted you to give to the U. S. Senate. Naturally, Jeremiah says, "Who am I, God? I'm only a boy from Anathoth. Perhaps, God, if I were from somewhere else with a more prestigious name, I could do it."

God said, "No, Jeremiah, your problem is not that you are helpless and hopeless. Your problem is that you've never made a covenant with your strategic self-importance."

We all want to be somebody! We want to be proud of who we are and where we're from. Anathoth was a nowhere place. And so in this great passage, when Jeremiah says in effect, "God, I am nothing," he feels he has geographical credentials to back it up.

> "Ah, Lord God!
> Behold, I cannot speak, for I am a youth."
> But the Lord said to me:
> "Do not say, 'I am a youth,'
> For you shall go to all to whom I send you,
> And whatever I command you, you shall speak.
> Do not be afraid of their faces,
> For I am with you to deliver you," says the Lord (Jer. 1:6–8).

Inferiority always comes because we measure who we are or where we are against those who seem to be more and have more than ourselves. The truth is, God doesn't care about these things. God loves people regardless of where he finds them. Our willingness, not our skill, is the key to God's use of us. As the cliché says, God wants our availability not our ability.

Inevitably, all the great heroes of the word of God began with some kind of excuse. Moses had exactly Jeremiah's excuse. He said, "Lord, I cannot speak." Unlike Jeremiah, he couldn't say, "Lord, I'm young," because he was eighty years of age. Moses had taken eight decades to practice his excuse and get it down! For eighty years of life, Moses had said, "Oh, I'm not much. I can't speak."

When God calls our name, we remain weak while we slink down and hide behind our inferiority. The God of all the cosmos who has redeemed us is waiting to complete us with all that we need to accomplish great things. But we've got all the excuses memorized.

Gideon also cowered behind inferiority. He said, "Not me, Lord. If you want me to do this, Lord, put dew on everything but my fleece, and I'll believe you." Isaiah, like Jeremiah, pleads youth and inability as the cause of his inferiority. "Lord," Isaiah cried, "my lips are unclean!" We all have some reason why we don't want to or can't do God's will, and our denials all too often rise from our inferiority.

There are two or three things that God wants you to know about yourself that will eliminate your feelings of inferiority. One of them is hidden in Jeremiah 1:5: "Then the word of the Lord came to me, saying: 'Before I formed you in the womb I knew you'" (Jer. 1:4–5a).

I really appreciate some of the more Presbyterian parts of our theology. John Calvin taught that in eternity past God picked us out to love us. He didn't just wait till we got here, he acted well ahead of time. God said to Jeremiah, "Before I formed you, I knew you! Before you were born, I called you to be something brand new." This passage leads us to celebrate the creative tenderness of God. With divine creativity, God shapes in the human womb an image and form like his own. Each embryo is a person whom God in eternity past has formed and destined for his own use.

To have been loved a long time before our arrival is one reason for getting rid of all our feelings of inferiority. There is another reason. God told Jeremiah, "Before you were born I sanctified you: / And I ordained you a prophet to the nations" (Jer. 1:5b).

God isn't haphazard in his plans for your life. Long before he formed you in the womb, he not only knew your name, but he had a life-calling all picked out for you. And yet so many of us have only a fuzzy commitment to who we are. When we are confused about who we are, we may also become confused about what we mean ultimately to God.

Before we were ever born God made a decision about our importance to him. God wants each of us to embrace this as our strategic self-importance. In spite of this, we may be living in strategic self-denial. Self-denial can be beautiful, but it can also be ugly! It is all too often the lie that says, "I don't matter."

Jeremiah's calling begins with God's saying, "You do matter." Jeremiah hears from the Almighty who says clearly, "Jeremiah, if you feel inferior, the problem is that your sights are too low. Just look up! I knew you, I called you. You cannot be inferior as long as you are connected. Look up, young man! I have a plan for your life." God knows us and ordains us to live lives that keep us from going nowhere.

If we want to leave our feelings of inferiority, we must listen to Jeremiah.

> But the Lord said to me:
> "Do not say, 'I am a youth,'
> For you shall go to all to whom I send you,
> And whatever I command you, you shall speak.
> Do not be afraid of their faces,
> For I am with you to deliver you," says the Lord (Jer. 1:7–8).

Do you ever find yourself questioning God? "Who am I Lord? What difference can my life make? The denomination is going up in flames and I hardly know who I am. I'm too liberal to be a conservative, and too conservative to be a liberal. I believe every word of the Bible from Genesis to Revelation, yeah, verily, from the table of contents to the maps. But God, give me some noble way to live and die. I would much rather die fighting for Jesus in Burundi than fighting other Christians in the business meetings of America's Bible belt. God, help all the Lutherans in Milwaukee love all the Baptists in Texas, and help all the Baptists in Texas simply love each other. Make all the bad Baptists good and the good Baptists easy to get along with. Lord, handcuff my untried hands to your nail-pierced hands, and send a Spirit Breeze to stretch my banner on the wind. Keep all my Jesus allegiances primary, even if the institutional quarrel drains the coffers.

God, I don't know what else to do! I have no power, no position, I am youth."

Hear God cry, "Do not say, 'I am a youth'...[whatever the denomination does]; you shall go to all whom I send you, and whatever I command you, you shall speak. Do not be afraid of their faces...[or of this boiling pot]...I am with you to deliver you" (Jer. 1:7, 13).

"I'm going to fill up the deficiencies in your personality," God says to the child prophet. "My child, no longer cry, 'God help me—I've got an inferiority complex!' Of course you do and there's a good reason for that. You are inferior. But you're not in this alone. I'm going to fill your inferiority with my strength!" Further, God says, "Not only am I going to do that, I'm going to honor your dreams for yourself."

> Moreover the word of the Lord came to me, saying, "Jeremiah, what do you see?" And I said, "I see a branch of an almond tree." Then the Lord said to me, "You have seen well, for I am ready to perform My word" (Jer. 1:11–12).

This is a tricky passage in Hebrew. The word for "almond branch" in Hebrew is *shaqedth* and the word for "ready" or "watching" in Hebrew is *shoqedth*. God says, "What do you see?" Jeremiah said, "I see an almond branch *(shaqedth)*." And God said, "I'm going to make you ready *(shoqedth.)*"

This "shaqedth, shoqedth" pun is beautiful. It would be like catching up to Jeremiah outside Dallas and saying, "What's that tree, Jeremiah?"

"Why man, that's a Texas Pecan! God *can use you!* As sure as that's a *Pecan, he can!* He can use you and you're as *shoqedth* ready as sure as God made *shaqedth* almonds."

But the almond rod is not the end of his visions. "What else do you see, Jeremiah?" cried God.

Jeremiah replied, "I see a boiling pot from the north, spilling armies and demons down over this whole land."

"Shucks, that's just a typical denominational quarrel, my child. Don't be intrigued by it. Stand still and see what I'm going to do with your life. I am going to honor all your dreams. Now, Jeremiah, you just quit your whining and stand up, son. You're my child and all my children are downright important."

Make a covenant with your self-importance? Why?

"I'm telling you, Jeremiah, 'God Will Hurl,'" God goes on, "you are going to stagger the world because of my importance in your important life.

"Prepare yourself and arise,
And speak to them all that I command you.
Do not be dismayed before their faces,
Lest I dismay you before them.
For behold, I have made you this day
A fortified city and an iron pillar,
And bronze walls against the whole land—
Against the kings of Judah,
Against its princes,
Against its priests,
And against the people of the land.
They will fight against you,
But they shall not prevail against you.
For I am with you," says the Lord, "to deliver you" (Jer. 1:17–19).

God has promised us that we never have to face this world in our own strength. He protects us. He clothes our weakness in the impenetrable armor of life. God is our defense! Our peace!

Last spring I was meeting in a prayer group with five seminary friends. I must confess I like living close to students. I find a richness in watching them as they cope with poverty and slug it out with denominational identity. I like watching them struggle in that furious race to try and get their degrees before their world dissolves. I like them because they are all keeping their eyes on the boiling pot of the North. In some of those existential moments, we'd be on our knees in prayer and one of them would say, "Calvin, I have no idea what I'm doing here!"

I would comfort them by saying, "You too?" But in my heart, I knew better. In my heart, I knew I was here by divine appointment. It was good to put my arms around my young brothers and say, "Come on, Brother, it's time for you to get on your knees and let God tell you why you're here. You're here because God's got a plan for your life. But nothing good is going to happen till you make a covenant with your strategic self-importance."

Some time ago Barbara and I visited Rome. The city is built over a system of soft lava tunnels called catacombs. There are five hundred and twenty-five of these tunnels beneath this ancient city. (The catacombs seem so institutional, so Baptistlike—just miles and miles of dark hallways waiting for bulletin-boards and tract-racks!) Barbara and I descended into that section of those dark, dank passageways known as the Catacombs of St. Sebastian. For only thirty thousand lire our guide told us that these were believed to be the actual rooms where Peter and Paul hid out before their arrest and martyrdom. I was skeptical. Then he showed us a piece of plate glass on a wall that protected a very early ancient etching. Someone, perhaps waiting to be thrown to the lions, had scratched into the soft stone the words, *"PAULE ET PETRE, PROVICTORE."* This is good Latin vocative for "Paul and Peter, pray for us." It may be a mistake to insist that the inscription is first-century. The words could have been put there by a first-century martyr or they could have been put there by Indiana Jones. But I've never been able to forget the words. There must have been a lot of confused Christians down in those sunless tubes, trying to figure out how they were going to answer their world in a desperate time.

When you wander through the catacombs of Christian existence, try to see them not as an alimentary canal filled with denominational enzymes trying to digest your uniqueness, but as the birth canal of a covenant— your covenant with your own strategic self-importance.

I am always amazed at what God can do with those who are willing to be used. I often think back to that day when, as a teenager, I made a covenant with God. And then I preached that first awful sermon and failed. Then, when I was so far down and so deeply depressed I thought I would never get out of it again, I made a covenant with my self-importance. God began to enable me. I got an education. I went to Nebraska where I started a new church. In a quarter of a century I won literally thousands of people to Christ. I tell you this with no sense of ego. I know who I am. I know what grace has afforded me. I would be spiritually lost today had it not been for Jesus. But he was there. And when I see all that he has done, I know that I have been made useful.

The procedure is as simple as it is meaningful. First, see how important you are. Second, surrender. Third, whatever you do, or however major or minor you consider it to be, pronounce it as an issue of relevance to God. Moody's statement is still true. "The world has yet to see what the person entirely committed to God can achieve." Declare yourself. Who knows, maybe your name is "God Will Hurl!" Maybe your bus stop is Anathoth.

Note
1. Luanne Oleas, Salinas, Calif., in *The Californian*.

COMMENT

A young boy was traveling coast-to-coast by air with his grandmother. As the aircraft climbed into the sky and reached a cruising altitude of 30,000 feet, the child turned to his grandmother and asked: "Grandma, when are we going to get smaller?"

When I first heard that Paul Harvey story, I waited for the punch line. But there was none. The more I thought about it, I came to see the event through the eyes of the child. As a plane lifts up into the air, it gets smaller and smaller to the observer on the ground. Why *not* ask, "When are we going to get smaller?"

The humor in most stories comes from an unexpected twist. The listener must make a "leap" to discover the humor. Once we make that "leap," our funny bone is tickled and a belly laugh follows. More importantly, the impact of the "leap" and the humor is longlasting.

Humor often breaks through our stiff formality, our logical world, our ingrained assumptions, and introduces us to a differing perspective. In his sermon, "On Making a Covenant with Your Strategic Self-Importance," Calvin Miller uses humor in a masterful way to reach his listeners with the life-changing truth of the gospel. Miller gets our attention in his introductory story about the youngster named "Fruit Stand." He then quickly moves to the importance of one's name, especially to God. This is a powerful transition that enables the listener's spirit to get "bigger," not "smaller."

PROBLEM

The premise of this sermon based on the call of Jeremiah is that God's redeeming power can use our denials, excuses and feelings of inferiority "as the birth-canal of a covenant with one's own strategic self-importance." Miller effectively describes the pervasive feelings of inferiority. He points out that Jeremiah means "God Will Hurl." However, Jeremiah's early response to God hardly portrays a man who was "hurled by God." Jeremiah denies his "strategic importance" to God in voicing his objections to God's call in his life.

Miller helps us acknowledge the problem of inferiority by revealing his own feelings of unworthiness: "Which of us has not felt Jeremiah's strong feeling of inferiority?" Denial of our strategic importance to God is at the core of the human condition. We refuse God's love. We resist God's call. We make excuses. We feel unworthy and undeserving of God's grace and call. Miller notes that inferiority is a particularly common problem in ministry. Referring to his own experience, he says: "Inferiority nearly destroyed my desire to preach again. Yet God had called me to make a covenant with my strategic self-importance.

TEXT

A distinctive strength of this sermon is that Miller skillfully maintains the centrality of his biblical text, Jeremiah 1:1–19. Scripture is his authority as he develops the problem and presents the solution. In examining the problem of human inferiority, Miller not only follows the commonly accepted approach of focusing on Jeremiah's excuse that "he is too young" for the mission at hand, but he also brings into play the insignificant hometown of Jeremiah, Anathoth. Miller suggests that the prophet uses his lack of geographical credentials to back up his excuse. It's interesting how God uses people from insignificant places to accomplish his redemptive purposes. Jesus of course was from Nazareth. Nathanael said of the town: "Can anything good come out of Nazareth?" (John 1:46). It is the *person* who matters to God, not one's geographical credentials. Jeremiah was God's person. God was going to "hurl" him. Miller strengthens his discussion of the human tendency to make excuses by identifying other biblical personalities who responded to the Lord with excuses: Moses, Gideon and Isaiah.

The solution to feelings of unworthiness and inferiority all flow from the Jeremiah text. Miller uses the following portions of the text to develop his thoughts:

The Lord says to the prophet: "Before I formed you in the womb I knew you."

God continues with the promise: "For I am with you to deliver you."

The Lord inquires of Jeremiah: "What do you see?" The prophet replies:

COMMENT

"I see a branch of an almond tree." God replies: "You have seen well, for I am ready to perform My word." In approaching this portion of the text, Miller describes the similarity between the Hebrew words *almond branch* and *ready*.

The implication is that in dreaming of the almond branch, Jeremiah was ready to commit himself to God's will.

Finally, Miller centers on the Lord's direction to Jeremiah. "Prepare yourself and arise, and speak to them all that I command you.… For I am with you to deliver you."

The theological premise Miller develops is that our God is a hunter God, the "Hound of Heaven" who relentlessly seeks out his people to accomplish his redemptive purpose. Excuses are normal, but God lifts his people above their inferiority and empowers them.

PROCLAMATION

Perhaps the greatest strength of this sermon is Miller's gift of interpreting the gospel for today. Time after time he takes Scripture and theological truths and reinterprets them in easily understandable contemporary terms. He uses humor to accomplish this task by helping us see beyond our small, self-centered world to the bigger world of God. A few of Miller's classic reinterpretations follow:

> Jeremiah must have asked, at least once: "Well, for goodness' sake, why didn't you name me Bradley?" …While I don't believe that Jeremiah much cared for "God Will Hurl," still with a name like that on your I.D. bracelet, you know you are no ordinary kid. You must realize how strategically important you are to God.

Miller explains the etymology of his own name, Calvin. He relates that it is derived from "Calvary—the place of the skull." He points out that in Latin his name could mean "bald." Then he concludes: "And God who has counted the hairs of my head, has saved me and called me and constantly reminds me that he has called me by that name and my name has significance to him."

Miller is good at paraphrasing the gospel message. "Hear God cry, 'Do

COMMENT

not say, I am a youth…I am going to fill up the deficiencies in your personality,' God says to the child prophet, 'My child, no longer cry, "God help me—I've got an inferiority complex." Of course you do and there is a good reason for that. You are inferior. But you're not in this alone. I am going to fill your inferiority with my strength!'"

Miller is a master at proclaiming the gospel in terms people can understand in today's world. In a unique way, he makes the reverent more relevant and the divine Mystery more approachable for us all.

RESPONSE

This sermon calls for the following responses from the listener: 1) Claim the truth that God has known you from the beginning of time, and claim the covenant of your own strategic self-importance to God. 2) Surrender to the redeeming power of God and permit him to "fill your inferiority with his strength." 3) Remember always that "whatever you do, or however major or minor you consider it to be, pronounce it as an issue of relevance to God." Miller sums up the call for a response in the closing phrase of the sermon: "Declare yourself. Who knows, maybe your name is 'God Will Hurl!' Maybe your bus stop is Anathoth."

"Grandma, when are we going to get smaller?" The pressures and problems of coping with everyday life can cause us to feel "smaller"—insignificant and inferior. In this sermon Miller sets forth the amazing gospel truth that by the grace and power of God, we are chosen for a "big" purpose with eternal consequences. Before the throne of the heavenly Father, we have a strategic self-importance.

SUGGESTIONS

- Make an intentional effort to use appropriate and related humor in your preaching.
- Bring the gospel to life by reinterpreting its truths for the experience and understanding of your hearers.
- Explore the root meaning of key words in your biblical texts. This will help reveal hidden truths in the text.

- Use an illustration like the catacomb experience in this sermon to give added dimension to a key sermon point. In Miller's sermon it illustrates how denial and feeling of inferiority can become the birth canal leading to redemption and new life.
- Reveal your own weaknesses, doubts and struggles in your preaching. This kind of openness adds authenticity to your preaching and invites people to request your ministry during difficult times.

Donald K. Adickes

C O M M E N T

WHAT JESUS BELIEVES ABOUT YOU

MATTHEW 4:1–11

REV. DR. JOHN R. CLAYPOOL
ST. LUKE'S EPISCOPAL CHURCH
BIRMINGHAM, ALABAMA

WHAT JESUS BELIEVES ABOUT YOU

MATTHEW 4:1–11

I n the realm of intimate personal relationships, nothing is more powerful than the expectations one has of another. If a person "relates up" to me; that is, sees high potential in my being and proceeds to affirm this and to encourage me to actualize it—to prove it true—such a relationship has a very creative impact on me. It tends to bring out the very best in me. However, if a person "relates down" to me, that is, makes me feel I am inadequate and incapable of much accomplishment—that relationship has a debilitating effect on my spirit and tends to crush whatever potential might exist in me. In an intimate relationship what is needed is a clear understanding of the other's reality, so that we avoid the temptation of expecting either too much or too little. I repeat, expectations are exceedingly potent when it comes to the business of two people relating authentically and creatively to each other.

Against this background, it is therefore not surprising that just after Jesus' baptism, where he was given the task of relating redemptively to the whole human race, the Spirit drove him into the wilderness to explore there the whole question of how he was going to accomplish such a task. First and foremost in such a deliberation had to be this issue of expectations. Precisely who were these creatures he had been called to save? What were their potentials? What were their limits? What would be an appropriate

form of relating that would not expect too much or too little of these creatures so beloved of God? Obviously, the conclusion Jesus came to in the
wilderness formed the basis of his whole ministry. What are we to say
about what Jesus chose to believe about human nature? We are often asked
the question, "What do you believe about Jesus?" I want to turn the question around now and ask, "What do you believe about what Jesus believes
about you?"

The verdict of the last twenty centuries has been a mixed one, to say
the least. Many have concluded that Jesus was mistaken, that he was totally
naïve in his estimate of human potential and therefore expected way too
much of a frail species. One of the more articulate expressions of this opinion is found in the famous section of Dostoyevsky's novel, *The Brothers
Karamazov,* known as "The Grand Inquisitor." Many of you are familiar
with this story within a story. It is a fantasy piece set in sixteenth-century
Spain at a time when the authority of the Roman Catholic Church was at
its height and heretics were being burned daily, "to the glory of God," in the
great square before the Cathedral of Seville.

In the midst of this great Inquisition, Jesus comes to Seville in bodily
form. While he does not speak or say anything openly, the people immediately recognize him, for the same love and compassion that had warmed
and excited Galilee streamed forth once again from his person. Such affection draws human beings the way a magnet draws metal filings. Such
unconditional love is innately healing and restorative, and in the plaza
before the cathedral a blind man recovers his sight, a seven-year-old girl is
raised from the dead, and a frenzy of excitement begins to spread through
the whole city.

Just at that moment, the aged Cardinal of Seville, the one known as
"The Grand Inquisitor," happens to walk through the cathedral square. In
a flash he sees what is occurring, and recognizes who it is that has re-
appeared on the earth. Instead of falling on his knees in celebration of his
Lord's return, however, he quickly commands the cathedral guards to arrest
Jesus and puts him in prison.

That night, all alone, the old Inquisitor pays a visit to the prisoner, and proceeds to level about as devastating an attack on Jesus' belief system as I have ever read.

"Why have you come back to hinder us?" he asks Jesus. Then he goes on to say, in essence, "You were wrong, Jesus, absolutely and totally wrong in your estimate of human nature. You 'related up' to human beings, as if they really were the sons and daughters of God, capable of deciding things for themselves, capable of taking responsibility for their lives and for the world. You saw them as if they were copartners with God, when in fact, they are nothing but slaves and children by nature—weak, vile, rebellious, and unstable.

"What you never could grasp, Jesus, was that human beings cannot be free and happy at the same time. For one thing, they are not good enough to be able to handle freedom. There is a corruption in them that always rises to the surface as soon as the controls are taken off. Anarchy and destruction always result when human beings are allowed to be free. Nothing is more insupportable, either for individuals or society, than this thing that you valued so, the freedom of the individual.

"Nor are human beings strong enough to handle this power. They really do not want the burden of having to decide for themselves or provide for themselves. No desire in them is greater than finding someone to whom they can turn over this burden of freedom.

"You see, Jesus," the Grand Inquisitor goes on, "you really did not love human beings, for you expected too much of them. Where you made your mistake was there in the beginning in the wilderness. Don't you remember how the spirit of this world came to you and tried to show you what would and would not work in this kind of world? Your great mistake was that you did not listen to that wise one. Don't you remember how he said to you, 'Human beings have three needs and three needs only—the need to be fed, the need to be mystified, the need to be dominated'? He suggested to you then that if you would just turn stones into bread, you could make human beings truly happy. There is no crime, there is no sin, there is only hunger. Human beings are little more than mouths and stomachs.

"Again, that wise spirit tried to get you to go up on the pinnacle of the temple and jump off and dazzle the masses. People want to be mystified, they want to be made to feel that things are beyond them, and that therefore it is all right for them to accept blindly whatever they are told to do. He also tried to get you to put on the mantle of Caesar up there on the mountain, for what human beings want more than anything else is to be ruled, to be dominated, to be told what to do.

"You see, the spirit of this world understood human nature, but you would not listen, would you? You with your impossible dreams—that human beings could be sons and daughters of God—that they could exercise freedom and use their gifts responsibly. I can hear you now—'Human beings do not live by bread alone. They are more than mouths and stomachs,' you contended. You refused to dazzle their senses or stupefy them with the miraculous, because you thought they could think for themselves. You would not bend the knee and get involved with the only process that really works in this world—the process of coercion and domination. You held out that human beings deserved to be treated better than that.

"Well, hear this, Foolish Dreamer. We, your church, have accepted the gifts that you rejected on the mountain. For centuries now, we have been about the business of correcting your work. We love human beings realistically, which means that we are willing to treat them as the slaves and children they actually are, and we are not about to let you come again and revive your erroneous ways. Some day we will conquer the earth and rule human beings as they were meant to be ruled.

"Jesus, you were wrong! Totally and absolutely wrong in your estimate of human nature. And unless you leave on your own at this moment, we will kill you all over again and get you out of the way."

Here is about as cogent and penetrating a critique of Jesus' beliefs as I have ever seen. The Inquisitor's argument forces us to face the question: Was Jesus right or wrong in his decision in the wilderness to relate "up" rather than "down" to our human species? As I have said before, it is by no means a simple issue to decide. There is considerable evidence in history to back the assertion that we are more like children than responsible adults, that we are neither good enough nor strong enough to be treated as anything but slaves.

Yet, in the face of all that evidence, look at what came of Jesus' ministry of relating "up" rather than "down." The Book of Acts presents considerable evidence that perhaps it was the Inquisitor, not Jesus, who was mistaken about our human potential. For example, take Simon Peter. The task of transforming this impulsive peasant fisherman into a courageous and incisive leader was by no means a simple process or without its struggle and lapses. But this is precisely what Jesus did by "relating up" to Simon's innate potential, changing his name to Peter the Rock. As you see Peter standing up to authorities and saying: "We must serve God rather than man" or reaching out across centuries of prejudice to embrace a Gentile like Cornelius, you do not see a person who can be dismissed cynically as "having only a mouth and stomach." There was more to Simon Peter than the need to be fed, to be mystified, or to be dominated. Jesus sensed that potential and related up to it in ways that facilitated its emergence.

Look also at what the community empowered by Jesus did with their money and their possessions. The Inquisitor said that as long as people were free, there would never be bread enough for all, but in Acts we find a refutation of that claim. When Jesus' love cast out their fear, in freedom they proved good enough to share with each other. It is simply not true that the only way for all to be fed is for everyone to be enslaved. When the generosity and compassion that are in us all by creation are "related up" to in hope, rather than cynically denied, the possibility of being free and good at the same time is eminently possible.

Therefore, it seems to me that what Jesus concluded in the wilderness was closer to the truth than the cynicism of the old Inquisitor. In choosing to relate "up" to the image of God that is in each one of us, Jesus was not only the most realistic of persons, but also the most creative and redemptive. People tend to rise or fall according to the expectation others have of them, and part of the reason so many have remained slave-like and childlike is that no one has seen in them what Jesus sees and wants to stir into life. What Jesus did for Simon Peter and the early church was just a foretaste of what he has been doing ever since when he is taken seriously.

In the final analysis, you must decide for yourself. You, too, must go to the wilderness as Jesus did, to decide the issue. On one side is the estimate of the Grand Inquisitor. On the other side is the estimate of Jesus. I ask you: What do you believe about what Jesus believes about you?

Well...?

COMMENT

John Claypool understands the impact of expectations. "What Jesus Believes about You" is a creative presentation of the importance of expectations—both in our relationships with each other and our relationship with God. In the unfolding drama between Christ and The Grand Inquisitor, Claypool calls the congregation to participate in the text, inviting listeners to become part of that drama. This sermon is no monologue. There is dialogue here. We join the drama. We enter the conversation.

Claypool sets the stage. The curtains are drawn. The drama unfolds. By cleverly merging the biblical text with The Grand Inquisitor's attack on Jesus in Dostoyevsky's novel *The Brothers Karamazov,* Claypool creates a backdrop for us to examine our own expectations and allow change to take place. It isn't long before all of us find ourselves drawn onto the stage with the key characters.

"Relating up" versus "relating down" is Claypool's central theme as The Grand Inquisitor enters with his "relating down" style. In his cynical monologue, the cardinal insists that Jesus has been wrong to relate "up." The cynic's opinion is that all humanity cannot grasp anything beyond their need to be fed, mystified, and controlled. "Why trouble the church with methods that don't work?" says he.

"People tend to rise or fall according to the expectation others have of them," Claypool contends. He unfolds his biblical text which points to a view opposite from that of the Inquisitor. He cites the generosity of the early church, and Simon whose name was changed to Peter the Rock, as examples of how relating "up" does work. "You, too, must go to the wilderness," says the preacher, "as Jesus did to decide the issue.

PROBLEM

The late Henri Nouwen lamented, "Much of our world is similar to the acting stage on which peace, justice and love are portrayed by actors who cripple each other by mutual hostilities." In this sermon Claypool tugs at the Gordian knot of human relationships, specifically, the manner in which people choose to relate to one another. Nouwen says, "Many ministries and priests who announce peace and love from the pulpit cannot find much of it in their own rectory around the table" (*Reaching Out,* Doubleday & Company, 1966, p.50).

What do you believe about what Jesus believes about you? This question is at the center of Claypool's sermon—and at the center of our faith in Christ.

The Grand Inquisitor knows what he believes regarding "those who hinder the church with an insistence of 'relating up'." In his view, all daughters and sons of God are weak, vile, and rebellious by nature. We are mistaken to give them the freedom to decide and to provide for themselves.

Could this be the central theme behind Jesus' wilderness experience? Might the Church be guilty of taking the short-cut in human relationships through offering food with no bread for the soul? Do mystifying miracles provide the children of God with the answers they need in life? Can this lead to a form of worship that is all about domination? What is the evidence? Do we relate "up" or "down" in our relationships with one another? These are among the questions Claypool's sermon puts before us.

TEXT & PROCLAMATION

If you are the Son of God, tell these stones to become bread (Matt. 4:3). Take care of the need to be fed. *If you are the Son of God, throw yourself down....* (Matt. 4:6). Dazzle others with unexplainable, death-defying miracles. Show them you have no limits. Mystify them. *All this I will give you if you will bow down and worship me* (Matt. 4:9). Succeed by making others submit to you. Relate "down" and avoid intimate relationships. Show them that they are inadequate and avoid the temptation of expecting too much from others.

The Grand Inquisitor has entered the text and counters the heartbeat of Christianity. "Human beings have three needs and three needs only— the need to be fed, the need to be mystified, the need to be dominated." His words rattle with intense staccato. His opinions are pointed. His view of humanity is dim. Claypool has wisely chosen this character to model how "relating down" works. Throughout his attack, Jesus remains silent. The Inquisitor's inhospitable contempt offers no invitation for dialogue. Jesus' silence speaks for itself. No need to impose his convictions upon the cardinal; that would be "relating down."

True freedom is not as easy as it looks. Yet Claypool contends that the early church does give evidence that Jesus was right in relating "up" to those he loved. Expanding on the text, he points to Peter's embrace of the Gentile Cornelius. In the early fellowship of the church, believers related "up" in their generous gifts of money and possessions. By reminding us of these examples, Claypool refuses to get caught up in the Inquisitor's snare.

"Why have you come back to hinder us?" the Inquisitor demands. Claypool concludes, "In the final analysis, you must decide for yourself. You, too, must go to the wilderness as Jesus did, to decide the issue."

RESPONSE

Claypool demonstrates that a sermon does not have to be lengthy to be effective. While quoting at length from Dostoyevsky's novel, Claypool clearly understands the drama and assimilates it into the sermon with skill. His cryptic conclusion leaves the congregation with the probing questions, "How do I relate to others?"

Dare we look behind the curtain of the stage of our own lives? If so, perhaps we will find ourselves looking for the highest potential in ourselves and others. In time, those who receive such honor will prove that in the long run, relating "up" with one another is far more rewarding than "relating down." The key to our response is found in the closing line of the sermon: "What do you believe about what Jesus believes about you? Well...?"

SUGGESTIONS

- It is remarkable that the busy preacher often looks for an easy formula for preaching, finds one, and works it to death. Why does Claypool's sermon work? It works because Claypool uses a creative approach in his preaching. He manages to say it as-it-is, without making the mechanics of preaching stick out. He avoids too much

C O M M E N T

polish and too much grace, without appearing apologetic or artificial.

- Tone and cadence are important in a sermon designed to challenge. This sermon has a prophetic edge. Tension exists between two opposite opinions, yet it is balanced.

- In sermon preparation the preacher thinks, translates into words, and vocalizes. During the sermon, the congregation hears, sees, and interprets with the preacher. They may laugh, smile, yawn or frown. An effective communicator flows with this participation, inviting the congregation to be as much a part of the process as he or she is. This approach to preaching moves one out of an "I, the speaker," "you the congregation" mode. It is helpful to think of oneself and the congregation as participating in a conversation. Preaching should create dialogue between proclaimer and hearers and between hearers and God.

Peter G. St. Don

OUR MOLTEN MOMENTS

MATTHEW 19:16–22

REV. DR. MICHAEL P. HALCOMB
NATIONAL ASSOCIATION OF
CONGREGATIONAL CHRISTIAN CHURCHES
OAK CREEK, WISCONSIN

REV. DR. MICHAEL P. HALCOMB

OUR MOLTEN MOMENTS

MATTHEW 19:16–22

T he drama that unfolds in this passage depicts one of the most tragic moments of Scripture. Here is a wealthy and powerful young man, obviously a high achiever, who wants to do well in life. He has all the energy of youth and is actively shaping a very promising future. Then, with all this potential and promise, he comes face to face with the Lord of the universe. Think of it—all of those gifts and, in addition, a rare invitation to join the inner circle of Christ's disciples. But in the end, the encounter is filled with poignancy and pathos, because the young man draws back. He chooses caution rather than commitment.

Perhaps the young man was afraid of losing prestige and power that go with wealth. Or perhaps his priorities were just confused. We're not told what was going through this young prodigy's mind, but we do know that he missed his golden opportunity to follow Jesus; he walked away from an invitation that had eternal consequences. It was one of those momentous decisions that each of us faces from time to time, when an opportunity to grow spiritually hangs in the balance. C. S. Lewis, it is said, pictured such moments of choice as moments when "the angels of God hold their breath to see which way we will choose to go."[1]

When I began ministry in Detroit many years ago, we routinely took visiting family members and friends to tour the Ford Motor Company. The huge industrial complex known as the River Rouge plant was a favorite place to go because we enjoyed watching the molten metal at one end of the plant become new automobiles emerging from the other. From high above on the catwalks we marveled as the great slabs of steel came rolling out of the furnaces so brilliant an orange that, like the sun, it almost hurt our eyes to look at them. Even though we were far above them, their heat made our skin feel as though it were sunburned. We were told that there were just a few critical moments at which the molten metal was just the right temperature to become pliant so that it could easily be cut and molded into the forms needed to make parts for automobiles. Only in those molten moments when the metal was malleable could it be shaped for its greatest usefulness.

So it is when the Holy Spirit is at work in our lives. There are times when the Spirit of God is discernibly moving in our hearts and minds. God may use circumstances, our conscience or the counsel of the Word to work in us so that we feel a beckoning to act. Those times are our molten moments, when we must decide either to respond to the Spirit or to walk away like the rich, young ruler. Such molten moments may be only a brief season of opportunity, seldom to come our way again. For the Bible warns of a "hardening of the heart" if we are not responsive. But this is not something God does to us. God's love for us does not lessen, nor does he grow weary in his patience. We harden our own hearts through delay, or by denying that something is important, or by diversions that keep us from thinking about those spiritual matters that are of greatest importance. Hardening of the heart begins from the inside, and becomes a creeping paralysis that makes us insensitive, resulting in a callousness of the soul.

The miracle is that if we do respond to the Holy Spirit in these molten moments, our hearts and lives can be molded into unique instruments that God can use to share his peace, love and grace. Each one of us has many opportunities for this to happen.

We have molten moments in our relationship with Christ. These are the times when Christ becomes so very real to us that we sense his presence in a unique way. Some of you may have first felt this inner stirring of the Spirit as a child in Sunday school. Many people tell of God's touching their lives in an unforgettable way in their youth while at a church camp, perhaps around a campfire. As a result, they opened themselves to Christ, deciding to live for him the rest of their lives. Such molten moments are powerful and long remembered.

When I visited Romania not long ago to see the conditions of orphanages and mental hospitals, our guide was a beautiful young woman named Marianne. Something about Marianne's humble spirit touched me. She had a warm curiosity about my beliefs, and asked why I cared about people in mental institutions in Romania. One evening, as the group was discussing the day, I found myself sitting beside Marianne. I asked her about her own spiritual experience. She told me how the government had repressed religion for many years and only old people went to the churches. Her grandmother had taken her to an Eastern Orthodox Church a few times, and she was intrigued, wanting to learn more, but the schools had taught her generation to fear Christianity. Then greater freedom came to Romania a little over six years ago. Finally Marianne was able to get a Bible. She began eagerly reading it every day. With her dark brown eyes focused intently upon mine, Marianne said in her hesitant English, "It was then that...how do you say..." and she made a twisting motion with her hands that told me her life had been turned around. I knew that had been a molten moment in Marianne's relationship with Christ.

The Christian faith is not something we just stumble into or inherit. It requires a decision. It requires that we respond to the stirring of the Spirit. The young man in our Scripture text walked sadly away, but millions of people like Marianne have responded at the time of their molten moment.

We also have molten moments in our families. The few years we have in which to share our Christian faith and values with our children and grandchildren are very precious. If we are too busy, or assume that someone else will teach them, we will miss a great opportunity.

In one of her books, Anne Ortlund, the wife of a Congregational minister, reminds us that "children are like wet cement!" Little hearts are so open and impressionable. When one of our sons was three or four, he broke his finger in a sledding accident. I recall being in the emergency room, holding him on my lap, with his painful finger wrapped in a bloody bandage. With his chin trembling he looked up at me and said, "Jesus can make bad things good, can't he, Daddy?" He was already starting to apply the simple Bible lessons we had been teaching him! It made me realize again that we parents dare not miss even one of those teachable moments when our children's hearts are so tender and receptive.

If we do not actively share our Christian beliefs with our children or model for them a faith that is an important ingredient of our daily lives, trusting Christ will not be a serious option for them. If our children do not see our Christian values in action, they will look to peers or others for guidance that may be questionable. Christianity is always just one generation away from extinction. So we dare not miss those molten moments when our children's hearts are open to receive our guidance and counsel. If we miss those opportunities, our children will walk away from Christ just as did the rich young man in the Scripture. How sad that would be.

There are also molten moments in the life of our churches. When a new minister arrives at a church, that is a molten moment, for new visions to be considered and commitment to be renewed. The dedication of a new building may be a molten moment for a congregation. Very quickly it will be determined whether the building will be used to serve people, or if the people are there to serve the building. I have seen the Spirit move people to use their church building and other resources to reach out into the community, and lives have been changed. But I've also seen congregations act selfishly, turning away from the needs of the community so they could have the building for their own comfort and convenience.

One church I visited worshiped its building and endowments more than they worshiped God. Blinded by the value of the property and pride in past accomplishments, they allowed one opportunity for ministry after another to slip past. After years of existing like this, their numbers dwindled, and finally their minister left. Only a dozen or so older people were left with a large, ornate structure that they knew they couldn't keep up.

Perhaps you think this is the end of the story. And it could well have been. But God, in his grace, gives us many molten moments in which to redeem our failures. He is a God who will help us turn around and begin a new pilgrimage of faith, if we are willing to take the risk that faith always requires. That is what happened at this church. The small group of older people decided they would all constitute the search committee for a new minister. To everyone's surprise, they determined to take a leap of faith by letting go of their precious endowments, which were dwindling anyway, and using the funds to hire a new minister. Later, he told me of his first meeting with them.

When he asked the group to describe their church, one gray-haired woman said, "Well, first of all, it really isn't a church. It's more like a social club."

My friend was so angry at that response, he almost got up and walked away, considering the meeting a waste of his time. But being civil he stayed to talk further with them. More or less in an effort to make conversation at this awkward time, he asked if they were happy. "No," the same woman answered, "we would like to go back to being a church again."

On the basis of that rather tenuous commitment, my friend agreed to be their minister. He sensed that his coming to them could be a molten moment. They began by talking about what it means to be a Christian, and how Christ surely wanted them to care for people. A few started to tell neighbors and friends that they had a vision of becoming a real church again. Tentatively, a few new people began to attend worship. A Bible study group was formed, where they could discuss the problems of their community and the needs of people in the world who did not know God's love. Eventually, the church decided there should be some kind of mission program. Even though they had little to share, they knew that others had even less, and they started to give to missions.

Because I work with missions, I was invited to their church and was surprised to find over one hundred people attending the service. And the Holy Spirit was there, leading and guiding them. Today they have about one hundred and fifty people actively attending, all because a few older people and a skeptical pastor took the risk of faith and responded to a molten moment.

My own experience as a pastor has taught me that molten moments come at the most surprising times. I recall a family showed up at our affluent church, and it was clear at first glance that the parents were both mentally and socially challenged. The husband talked a lot and very loudly, as if he was accustomed to people not listening to him. Then he decided to sing in the choir even though he sang off key. The wife was pleasant enough, but she couldn't control the children alone and they disrupted the services. Each Sunday they drove up in his rusty old taxi, inevitably banging their doors against somebody's new Cadillac. I saw looks of deep consternation on people's faces.

The feelings suddenly came out in a torrent at one of our deacons' meetings. One man summed up the opinion of many when he said, "Pastor, you've got to convince these people to find another church." That made me uncomfortable, but I didn't say anything for awhile, because I was feeling a lot of internal pressure. It's often like that when the Spirit is at work in your life. Molten moments aren't always warm and welcome times. Like metal we sometimes have to go through stress to be made malleable. I felt that God was pulling me one way and the deacon board another. Finally, I spoke up and said, "Some of us have been praying for months, asking God to give us a vision for our church. I'm thinking perhaps this is God's way of answering. It seems to me he's put a whole mission field at our doorstep and is waiting to see how we will react."

"You *would* have to bring the Bible into this!" another deacon responded. I was glad that he smiled as he said it.

As it turned out, a few people started trying to assist this family, helping them manage the little bit of money they had, and finding replacements for the scruffy clothes the children wore week in and week out. More problems came to light, but others saw what was happening and stepped up to help. People started to feel good about helping this family, confident that this was what Christ wanted them to do. Then something surprising happened. Someone asked the question, "Why should this family get all of our help? There are all kinds of struggling families out there and we should be helping them too." Out of that experience came a whole mission program that was aimed at helping families, especially single parent families in the city. Lives were blessed both in our church and outside of it. It took a while to adjust our perspectives, but now we look back and see the arrival of that family as one of our molten moments. We are so glad that we were not like the rich, young ruler and we didn't walk away.

Is there a situation in your life right now that may be such a molten moment? Is God's Spirit trying to work in the life of your church? How will you respond? Will you just walk away? There is a broken heart in every pew. There are people in your community and mine who need to feel the love of God, who need to be touched with the compassion of Christ. We must not let our hearts become cold and calloused when a secularized society needs to hear about faith, when fractured families need to experience forgiveness, when a hurting world needs the good news of Christ. How can we blithely pass by on the other side? We cannot, for the Spirit has taught us that God can plant within the very circumstances that distress us a latent power to bless.

But we must choose. Like the rich, young ruler. In the molten moments of our lives, we must decide. This community awaits our decision. Society waits to see how Christ's church will respond. A hurting world waits. And the angels of God wait silently to see which way we will go.

Note

1. This phrase attributed to C. S. Lewis is quoted by H. Stephen Shoemaker in "A Tale of Two Cathedrals," a sermon in *Pulpit Digest*, Vol. 65 (March/April 1985), p.32. Shoemaker cites the quote from H. C. N. Williams, *The Latter Glory* (Manchester: The Whitehorn Press), p. 2. The exact origin of the phrase is unknown to me. Compare the scene in C. S. Lewis, *Perelandra* (New York: Macmillan, 1944), p. 148.

COMMENT

In our daily lives, we face all manner of decisions with accompanying circumstances that must be weighed. On interstate highways, exit signs indicate the number of miles to the next exit. Should we take this exit? Will we lose too much time stopping now? Should we stop at this hotel or is there a better one down the road? The driver who misses an exit by failing to read the signs correctly, or who miscalculates a refueling stop, or who does not commit to turning off at the proper time, could wind up lost or stranded. In this sermon, Michael P. Halcomb stands by the side of the road with a sign saying "Take this exit!" He encourages others to take the right exit and to know when to serve as signs on the highway of life.

The art of good preaching does not lie in good storytelling, though good storytelling can be employed by the preacher. It does not lie in quoting great writers, though that device certainly can help a sermon. It does not lie in having lived an exciting, eventful life full of anecdotal material that can be mined for great sermon points. Preaching requires an ability to draw on different elements to bring home the gospel message with a lesson appropriate to the audience.

LACK OF COMMITMENT

Halcomb's sermon addresses the issue of a lack of commitment. Needless to say, this will hit the average church audience where it hurts. We all have our comfort zones, but to live our lives properly and productively we have to break out of these zones, to proceed rather than procrastinate, to step forward and take appropriate risks rather than hang back and miss the chance to make a difference. Fear of losing financial security can be a reason for failing to make a commitment.

Halcomb preaches about the rich man who met Jesus and passed on the chance to follow him. "He chooses caution rather than commitment," Halcomb writes. We too can miss our opportunity to follow Jesus, like the man who "walked away from an invitation that had eternal consequences."

Halcomb has chosen a guiding image of "molten moments" to make his point. In his description of a tour of the automobile plant, Halcomb presents an image that he could have easily taken from the Bible: molten metal that must be forged to its intended form. "See it is I who have created the smith who blows the fire of coals, and produces a weapon fit for its purpose" (Isa. 54:16, NRSV), or "For he is like a refiner's fire...he will sit as a refiner and purifier of silver" (Mal. 3:2–3, NRSV).

By recounting a personal experience that relates directly to daily life, at least to anyone who has ever driven a car, Halcomb takes a biblical image and makes a modern metaphor.

Preaching must ultimately achieve the difficult feat of bringing ancient truth into its most modern manifestations in an ever-changing society. Halcomb knows that the best way to do that is to show a biblical truth that he has experienced himself in a very visual way.

That is the molten moment. Whether at the steel furnace of the car plant or in the lives of spiritual seekers, there are malleable moments that must be seized upon.

In relating his experience of visiting the orphanages and mental hospitals in Romania, Halcomb again shares a personal recollection of just such a molten moment. Notice his careful description of Marianne's halting yet effective explanation, finally through hand gestures, of how God turned her life around.

DECISION TIME

Halcomb shines light on a practical truth and a theological truth by taking a broad view of decision making. Decisions must be made at critical times. It is possible to face a moment of decision and miss its opportunity. In relating his experience with a dying church that recognizes it is dying, Halcomb shows another way in which decision can lead to action. Like the rich man worried about giving up his possessions to follow Jesus, this congregation "worshiped its building and endowments more than they worshiped God." But it was willing to face up to its commitment to revitalize itself spiritually.

COMMENT

Halcomb also shares his own experience as a pastor when a poor family began disrupting services, finally prompting the congregation to react. At first with anger, then with a sense of caring, the congregation reached out to this family and then to others. Halcomb demonstrates through these stories that when presented with opportunities for bold, important decisions, individuals and congregations must learn to respond. His personal stories echo the point of the biblical story of the man who failed to follow Jesus, although his layered versions of the story add an opportunity for redemption. The misguided congregation can change its focus. The petty gripes against outsiders' upsetting the rhythm of a worship family turn into a ministry opportunity.

To take these stories back to the biblical premise, it's as if the rich man who rejected Jesus suddenly changed his mind. Certainly it's a scenario Jesus would have preferred. Halcomb does not limit his discussion of molten moments to decisions to accept the Christian faith. He includes teaching moments in families, when parents have a limited window to share their beliefs with their children not just through telling them but by impressing upon them principles through their own behavior. He shares his own experience with his young son breaking a finger, then appealing to Jesus' healing power as he sat in the hospital emergency room. Halcomb was impressed to see that, even at a young age, the basic faith principles the child had been taught had taken hold.

ACTION TIME

The hearers of the sermon are called to rise to the occasion, to meet the moment, to decide properly when they come to a fork in the road. But more than just seizers of the moment, Halcomb urges them to provide their own teaching moments, opportunities for their children to grasp the faith. He capsulizes this challenge ominously: "Christianity is always just one generation away from extinction." It's a reminder that the responsibility falls to everyone to pass on the faith. Failure to do so carries consequences.

SUGGESTIONS

- Only twice in the sermon does Halcomb quote other writers. First, he appeals to C. S. Lewis, not for a quote, but for an image, of angels silently awaiting a man's choice. Later, he quotes author Anne Ortlund, the wife of a Congregational minister, "Children are like wet cement." Everyone has heard of Lewis; fewer have heard of Ortlund. But in each case the use of the literary reference is quick, punchy, and effective. So often preachers will overquote in their sermons, using long-winded recitations of other people's writings. The use of literary allusions and quotations can be effective, but it can also be a trap for ponderous writers and unoriginal thinkers. Note how Halcomb quickly borrows the image of Lewis' angels to hammer home his point, then moves quickly into his personal anecdote. This is no crutch but a tactful deployment of another's wings to lift up an idea. The Ortlund quote fits perfectly into Halcomb's plea for the parental role modeling of Christianity. Think about the use of quotations and allusions in your preaching and don't overdo it.

- Are there times in your life when you have, through personal experience, relearned biblical truths? Can you frame those experiences in such a way that they become points of reflection for teaching and fit into the context of a spiritual lesson? Inserting gratuitous personal anecdotes may hinder a sermon more than help it, but by evaluating and understanding the underlying spiritual meaning of an experience, that insight can be passed on quite powerfully by way of personal anecdote. At first reckoning, recounting a tour through an auto plant could be disastrously boring and pointless, but by capsulizing and interpreting a moment on such a tour, refining its meaning for the listener, this preacher distilled and conveyed powerful spiritual truth.

Greg Garrison

THE
TOHU WABOHU!

GENESIS 1:1–2:4a

REV. DR. GARTH R. THOMPSON
MIAMI BEACH COMMUNITY CHURCH
MIAMI BEACH, FLORIDA

THE TOHU WABOHU!

GENESIS 1:1–2:4a, NRSV

I'm sure you must be wondering, "Where did he get that sermon title, 'The Tohu Wabohu'?" Good question!

Tohu wabohu is the Hebrew phrase for "chaos." It's used in the Old Testament to describe that time when the earth was "without form and void" (Gen. 1:2).

We know, you and I, that chaos is always bubbling there, in your life and mine, just below the surface—the *tohu wabohu,* ready to rise up and engulf us.

A seminary student worked one summer as a counselor at an exclusive camp in Michigan. There he made friends with another counselor. As they walked and talked in the beautiful grounds and woods of the camp, it seemed like paradise—Eden.

Then his friend invited him home to his parents' Michigan farm, a well-kept, impressive place. His host took him to the barn where he opened the door to a secret room that had floor-to-ceiling posters, books, flags, pictures of Hitler, Nazi insignia, and stacks of hate literature, along with guns and weapons of various kinds. "We plan to take our country back from the niggers and the Jews," his friend said.

The seminary student said it was as if the veil separating creation from chaos was drawn back, revealing the waters of darkness and deceit. On a pleasant June afternoon, in a neatly kept barn out behind well-ordered farmhouse walls, when the door opens, we see that things are not as they seem. The *tohu wabohu* bubbles up and creation is imperiled once again.

Or, perhaps, you go to the doctor for a check-up. Though he shows studied, careful, apparent lack of alarm, you can sense it, coming through the cracks in the floor—a silent, foreboding rumble underneath what began as an ordinary, orderly day. It's the dreaded *tohu wabohu*. Your body has betrayed you after you've faithfully cared for it and pampered it for years and years.

Frequently, the chaos is financial. More often it is personal. Your significant other is no longer as significant, or you are not as significant to them. Each of us knows the silent desperation brought on by chaos or impending chaos. We know that we cannot always count on things remaining the same. Life is not always well-ordered. For we live in a broken world.

Not long ago, the Olympics were held in beautiful Sarajevo. But how the scene has changed since then! A man who had been a lawyer was recently seen tearing a small shrub to pieces, in order to burn the twigs to keep his family warm at night. The shrub was all that remained of a garden in front of what was left of a multimillion-dollar luxury hotel. Some call it social dislocation, the byproduct of civil unrest, or an international diplomacy problem. Genesis names it *tohu wabohu*. So did the prophet Jeremiah as he described his time:

> Disaster overtakes disaster,
>   the whole land is laid waste....
> I looked on the earth, and lo, it was waste and void *[tohu wabohu]*;
>   and to the heavens, and they had no light (Jer. 4:20, 23, NRSV).

Jeremiah did not look carefully enough. The heavens did have light. God had said, "Let there be light," and there was light. There is light and there always will be light. A better translation of the beginning of Genesis is "When God began creating the heavens and the earth...." Creation is not something that was fixed or finished a billion years ago. It's going on right here, right now. God never stops wrestling with the *tohu wabohu*. He keeps bringing order out of chaos.

The Jews in Babylonian exile in the sixth century B.C., having lost everything, needed to be reminded that God was still Creator, still bringing something out of nothing, still battling chaos in all its forms. So the prophets Ezekiel and Second Isaiah reminded them of the faithfulness of the Creator God.

Job, having lost all, refused to curse God, for he knew that God could bring order to his life once again, despite his loss of loved ones, health, status, and money. Job encountered the Creator God who restores order out of chaos.

What about us? We wrestle with the fact that darkness is only a telephone call away. Our lives could become chaos at any moment. But we also know from the testimony of others who have lost all, who have been thrown into a pit filled with the lions of grief and loss, loneliness and depression, unemployment and hopelessness, that we may rise out of it through the strength given us by our risen Savior, Jesus Christ. His death pointed to the *tohu wabohu* in all our lives, but his resurrection affirms that death and chaos are no match for God. We're fine as long as we keep close to him.

The only danger we face is that we may allow ourselves to quit keeping company with our Creator, that we will leave his ways and worship other gods. After humans ignored him and began worshiping other gods, libertine lifestyles, evil ways and monetary madness, God chose to let the waters of the *tohu wabohu* rise up once again and cover all except the family of Noah. Noah knew what we need to remember:

God is our refuge and strength,
　a very present help in trouble.
Therefore we will not fear, though the earth should change,
　though the mountains shake in the heart of the sea;
though its waters roar and foam,
　though the mountains tremble with its tumult....
The Lord of hosts is with us... (Psalm 46:1–3, 7, NRSV).

Chaos comes to us. We go to God. Better that we have been there all along, coming to his house, eating at his table.

COMMENT

What do our fellow worshipers bring with them as they trudge into church on Sunday? What is happening in their lives? Every preacher knows the awesome challenge of trying to speak to such diverse life-experiences. On any given Sunday, a congregation probably involves people caught in secret addictions, someone facing a moral decision, a depressed widow or widower, a person with cancer who may or may not know it yet, and any number of marriages on the brink.

Our proclamation can have an air of unreality about them if they do not somehow cross the bridge into the dark and threatening chaos of our listeners' lives. A pastor was once asked by a group of young ministers what he would suggest for them to study that would prepare them for the ministry. His answer was, "Anything that better helps you to understand and deal with human beings." We exegete human lives as well as Scripture.

I love perplexing titles! If you can elicit a "What in the world is he preaching on today?" you've got their attention, at least at the beginning. Garth Thompson does it with the Hebrew phrase which really has a funny sound. That funny title, however, is at the heart of what he preaches.

QUESTION

Life is essentially tragic. To say that life is tragic is not to say that it is utterly evil, or without joy. But it does mean that we acknowledge a tension that cuts through the heart of existence, a struggle between forces of light and darkness, wholeness and brokenness. Thompson captures this tension with the imagery of the waters of the primordial chaos prior to creation.

God's creative act becomes the archetype of all of creation thereafter: the ordering of disorder. "What can prevent the chaos in my life from overwhelming me? How can I keep from drowning in the floodwaters of disintegration that surprise me?"

TEXT

The task of interpretation, known as hermeneutics, is the art of connecting ancient texts and contexts with present reality and problems. Vast philosophical and theological discussions covering centuries of thought have wrestled with this gap between "what it meant back then" and "what it says to us now."

If we jump prematurely to the present, we may violate the meaning of the text and, worse, offer superficial or trivial solutions to daunting problems and sorrows in human hearts. Every preacher must struggle with this gap. Practical concerns demand that we provisionally resolve the tension every Sunday morning. Our theological training however, reminds us inwardly that we cannot permanently resolve the questions.

This is a good tension—it engenders humility and guards against subjective extremes, but it has a risk. We may also get bogged down in explaining a text or resolving some biblical problem of interpretation and never show the relevance of that text for universal human concerns.

This sermon handles the text well. Thompson helps us understand what the text meant, but he also helps us set it against the whole of Scripture. He ranges through the Bible to show us his theme cross-sectionally.

One way to look at a text is microscopically—unearthing words and issues and grammatical nuances that the casual reader cannot catch. Another way, though, is to place a text in the grand sweep of the larger story of the Bible.

I counted all the biblical references and allusions in this sermon. In this one brief sermon we have references to the creation and the story of Noah from Genesis, Jeremiah, Job, Psalm 40, and the exile from the Old Testament. Thompson also connects the theme of chaos and order with the heart of the Passion story by showing it at the heart of the cross and resurrection of Jesus.

This is a good use of Scripture for a number of reasons. First, it reinforces his theme effectively, repetitively showing us his main point—that chaos always threatens but God the Creator can bring order out of chaos.

Second, it exposes the congregation to a wide range of Scripture. Unfortunately, it is often in evangelical churches where the Bible is affirmed most vocally that Scripture is least used. A friend told me once about going into a prominent evangelical megachurch. Upon leaving the service, he realized that he had not heard any Scripture and no prayers except at the offertory. Scripture needs to be at the heart of both our worship and our preaching.

Finally, in a society that no longer knows the biblical story, recitation of the story and larger connections are important. We are teaching as we preach to a postmodern, postbiblical culture.

PROCLAMATION

Thompson makes a powerful gospel affirmation near the end of this sermon when he says, "His [Jesus'] death pointed to the *tohu wabohu* in all our lives, but his resurrection affirms that death and chaos are no match for God. We're fine as long as we keep close to him." "Gospel" means "good news," not denial of reality! Without the darkness of the cross, there is no resurrection. Without the resurrection, the cross is only a tragic death.

Too many sermons say, "Hey, things may look bad, but they're really okay!" That is not the gospel. The gospel looks into the face of evil and sin and says, "There is still a way and it leads through here."

Now permit me a brief aside about the use of asides in sermons! Or, in other words, "When is it all right to chase rabbits?" A man in my church once said, in good Southern hyperbole, that his father used to take him and his brother out to the rabbit trails in the morning and say, "Boys, breakfast is at the other end." Rabbit chasing is acceptable if it has a point, but can be quite frustrating if you never get to eat.

Every sermon does not have to treat everything. Simplifying is a virtue that has to be mentioned again and again. However, there are times when an aside or a brief tangent can be employed effectively. Thompson does it in this sermon. Ethical issues often benefit from just such treatment.

The point of this sermon is, of course, about the chaos that always threatens us and how God can help us order life. One of the first illustrations that Thompson uses, however, is one with ethical implications. It is about visiting a friend who gave every surface appearance of being a decent and good man. When he arrived at the house, though, he discovered that this man was a neo-Nazi. In this illustration, Thompson is able to declare himself and the gospel on the issue of race and prejudice.

Notice, though, that he never says, "Racism is wrong," or "We ought to never hate black people." Indicatives are unnecessary. It is clear in the telling of the story that racism is evil and the preacher is against it.

Ethical issues can be so controversial that sometimes it is better to mention them in small doses. This does not preclude an occasional broadside, but it stands to reason that targets will eventually hide when they see you coming. Thompson's main point didn't get lost, yet he was still able to strike a position that helps guide his congregation on a volatile issue. Best of all, it came up naturally, much as it might in a conversation between two friends!

RESPONSE

Thompson treats an existential theme—coping with the chaos. His prescription is deceptively simple: keep close to God. "Better that we have been there all along, coming to his house, eating at his table." If we stay close to God, God will keep the chaos from overwhelming us. So stay close to God.

What does that mean? It is spelled out in one paragraph in negative fashion (and left to the reader to connect). If we forsake fellowship with God (so seek that fellowship), if we worship other gods (so do not worship other gods), if we live libertine lifestyles and pursue evil ways and monetary madness (so do not pursue these), then the chaos will overtake us (and if not, the chaos cannot destroy us).

We know he is right. The delusion that life is ordered and stable is just that—a delusion. The sermon serves as a warning. Do not pursue the chaos or it will overwhelm you.

SUGGESTIONS

- One of the things Thompson does is to seize upon a striking image in the biblical text. Notice how often Scripture uses visual, aural or other senses to describe spiritual things.

- Become a student of human nature and human problems. Biographies, popular magazines and novels can give us insights. Another fine source of insight can be found in the magazines which target women in the United States. They generally respond to marriage and family issues, relationship problems and many other issues that women in particular struggle with in this country.

- Pastoral care is a great source for preaching—but not necessarily for illustrations! We must take care to safeguard the confidences that others share with us. This does not prevent us from bringing the insights and questions raised in these encounters into our preaching. When Thompson described a check-up at the doctor which brings bad news, he is using pastoral experience to connect with his congregation. He has obviously generalized many individual encounters into a recognizable description. Think back over a variety of pastoral encounters you have had recently. How might you generalize what you learned about human problems there in a way that could be communicated?

- A vast body of literature exists in the field of pastoral care and counseling. One excellent resource that every pastor should have on his or her shelf is the *Dictionary of Pastoral Care and Counseling*, edited by Newton Maloney, et. al., and published by Abingdon Press. It contains hundreds of articles on issues that people struggle with, like "fear" and "depression," etc. At the end of every article is an excellent guide to further readings on the subject. The volume is a fine introduction especially for those who do not have expertise in the field.

Gary A. Furr

WHO PRAYS FOR US?

JOHN 17:9–26; ROMANS 8:28–39

DR. ELIZABETH ACHTEMEIER
ADJUNCT PROFESSOR OF BIBLE AND HOMILETICS
UNION THEOLOGICAL SEMINARY
RICHMOND, VIRGINIA

DR. ELIZABETH ACHTEMEIER

WHO PRAYS FOR US?

JOHN 17:9–26; ROMANS 8:28–39, NRSV

All of us are aware of the fact that when our parents die, our lives are impoverished and diminished. Along with the loss of two persons whom we deeply love, we lose a lot of little things. For example, we lose a large portion of those family histories that have made us who we are. There may be no one alive anymore who can remember where our great grandmother was born, or perhaps what some uncle did for a living. We may be divorced from the hometowns where we grew up, and have no reason to return to their familiar sights and streets. But above all, when our parents die, we know we have lost two people in the world who cared desperately about what was happening to us and what kind of persons we were becoming.

Since the death of my own parents, one of the things that has diminished me most is the loss of the prayers of my mother on my behalf. My three brothers and I never asked Mother if she prayed for us, but we all knew she did. We knew that daily she lifted us up before God and asked his guidance and protection for us. I am sure that those prayers of my mother guided me into right paths that I might never have taken, kept me from temptations to which I otherwise might have succumbed, and blessed me with good that I might otherwise never have received. So my life is diminished by the loss of the prayers of my mother on my behalf.

Yet, I know that there is still someone who prays night and day for me. There is someone who prays night and day for you also. Christ Jesus was raised from the dead to the right hand of God, says our epistle lesson, and there he intercedes with the Father on our behalf. Jesus Christ prays for us. He prays for us to God. Just as he prayed for Peter, according to Luke's Gospel; just as he prayed for all of us even while he was dying on the cross, so too he now sits at the right hand of God in heaven and makes intercession to the Father for each one of us.

Surely that is prayer that is heard by God, is it not? After all, Christ occupies the place of honor at the right hand of God. On the right—that is the place where the most esteemed is seated at the banquet. The one on the right has the greatest power. It is no accident that we talk about our most valued helper as our right-hand man or woman. Christ sits at the right hand of God as his beloved Son of power.

Christ has won that position next to the throne of the Father by his faithful obedience. Christ's prayers on our behalf are heard by God because our Lord Jesus is righteous. "The eyes of the Lord are on the righteous," sings the psalmist, "and his ears are open to their cry" (Ps. 34:15, NRSV). God hears only those prayers that are uttered to him by those who are faithful and true. Certainly you and I would not make much of an impression in the court of a king if we went rushing into his royal presence with dirty hands and filthy clothes. Rather, most likely we would be ushered out quickly and unceremoniously. Surely that would be our fate were we impure worshipers trying to burst into the pure presence of God the king.

I had a friend once who objected to that thought. "There is something wrong," she protested, "when I cannot approach God directly and speak to him without the necessity of having a mediator between us." Well, you'd better believe that something is wrong! Our sin has cut us off from our communion with God. You and I do have dirty hands—stained with all our careless compromises, with our pride and hatred, with our selfishness and our refusal to forgive, with our continual unwillingness to trust God with our future. So our righteousness is nothing but filthy rags, and we have no way we can approach a God who is the opponent of all sin and evil.

But Christ can approach him. Christ was tempted in every way that we are, yet he never lost his trust in his heavenly Father. So we pray every prayer through the mediation, or in the name of, Jesus Christ, because God will listen to his righteous Son. Jesus now is there at the right hand of power, making intercession on our behalf.

Certainly God wants to answer the prayers that Christ utters on our behalf. For after all, it was God who sent us his Son to be our mediator. "He who did not withhold his own Son, but gave him up for all of us, will he not with him also give us everything else?" (Rom. 8:32). When God sent this beloved Son to die for us, he sent his best. He gave everything that he had. And he is in that gift on Golgotha. So now God wants to answer Christ's prayers for us, and he wants to give us "all things" (Rom. 8:32, RSV) through him.

What do you suppose that Christ asks for from the Father on our behalf? When we hear that God will give us all things, that tends to arouse our greedy natures, does it not? As if somehow we have found ourselves in possession of the winning lottery ticket and are about to be granted a twenty-million-dollar prize. If God in Christ will give us all things, then let's go for it all: a promotion on the job, a big salary, a name for ourselves, or perhaps a comfortable retirement and nice clothes. Of course, our Lord Jesus Christ does not know how to ask for such worldly favors. He was a poor man with no place to rest his head, a seamless robe his only possession that those soldiers gambled for at the foot of the cross. He was a humble person, despised and rejected by the powers that be, one so powerless that when they arrested him, he was like some poor lamb led to his slaughter. To be sure, he knows that the things of this world are important to us. He promised us that his heavenly Father would provide us the basic necessities, food and clothing, just as he faithfully provides for the birds of the air and clothes the lilies of the field in a beauty exceeding that of Solomon. Beyond that, our Lord Jesus Christ apparently has little interest in satisfying our greedy grasping after worldly gain.

Do you suppose that as Jesus sits there at the right hand of the Father, he asks for us some satisfying self-fulfillment, some magnification and glorification of our own personalities? Certainly our Lord wants us to be all that we can be, but as he walked in our midst, he made it clear that we reach our full potential only as we offer up our whole selves and glory to God's purpose. "What should I say?" he prayed to the Father, as the cross loomed up before him. "'Father, save me from this hour'? No, it is for this reason that I have come to this hour. Father, glorify your name" (John 12:27–28). Jesus was quite sure that the purpose of human life was not to glorify itself, but to glorify God. So he asked his followers to take up the same cross, the same crucifixion of their own selves, that he took up for us.

Perhaps we think that as Christ prays there beside the Father on our behalf, he asks God to release us from some awful suffering that we now endure. That may be the case, dear friends—that may be the case. Certainly, he shared our sufferings, and he knew all our afflictions. As he moved among us on this earth, he healed and eased countless tribulations—restoring the sick, the troubled, the possessed to wholeness and to health. Who among us does not know of someone who has been healed or comforted by God, the prayers of Christ on their behalf mercifully heard and granted? We also know that God's ways with our afflictions sometimes remain a mystery. Sometimes our afflictions are not healed and our suffering is not done away with. Our Lord himself was not delivered from the suffering of the cross. Paul, with that thorn in his flesh, heard that it would not be removed. "My grace is sufficient for you," his Lord replied to Paul's pleas for release (2 Cor. 12:9).

Surely as Jesus prays for us at the right hand of the Father, he continues to ask for our forgiveness, that we may be counted righteous and acceptable in the eyes of God, that God will receive us back into communion with himself. We were justified and counted innocent before the bar of God on that spring day when the cross was raised on Golgotha's hill, and that verdict was affirmed and sealed by Christ's empty tomb. So now there is no condemnation for us. For "who is to condemn?" Paul writes. "It is Christ Jesus, who died, yes, who was raised, who is at the right hand of God, who indeed intercedes for us" (Rom. 8:34). Our Lord Jesus is not content to let his past act cover all our ongoing sinfulness. No, even now he continues to pray his prayer for you and me. *O Father, forgive.* "Father, forgive them; for they do know not what they are doing" (Luke 23:34). God hears that prayer and answers it, and accepts us back into his company. Every day Christ prays for us. Every morning, his mercies are new. Every evening, his loving mediation makes us acceptable to our heavenly Father. We can approach God's throne with confidence and find grace to help in time of need.

More than that, if our Gospel lesson be any indication, Jesus utters other prayers to God on our behalf. The great high priestly prayer in John's Gospel gives us the content of some of those prayers. "I am not asking you to take them out of the world," Christ petitions, "but I ask you to protect them from the evil one" (John 17:15). Christ prays now on our behalf that God will keep us from the evil one—that some great, grimy hand will not reach out toward us and wrench us free from the loving grasp of our heavenly Father. What is it in your life that threatens to tear you away from God's clasping hand—that lewd immorality, so prevalent in our society, that would do violence to your marriage or your morals? Some selfishness so pernicious that it would defy all laws of love for neighbor? Some deceit so careless for the truth that it would corrupt all your speech and action? Some anxiety so deep that it would destroy all your hope and trust? Our Lord Jesus Christ now prays to the Father that we will not be surrendered up to such evils. God hears the prayer of his beloved, begotten Son.

Jesus also petitions the Father, "Sanctify them in the truth," and then he defines his terms, "your word is truth" (v. 17). Our Lord prays that God will make us holy by his word. We do not think very much about being holy these days, do we? The ideal of becoming what we used to call a man of God, or a woman of God, is no longer held up before us. That is, we no longer want to be good persons, as the Bible would define the term. In fact, we are very likely to call such good persons wimps or squares or nerds—persons who do not realize that anything goes these days, and that therefore they can have it all and go for all the gusto they can get. Oh sure, we stand in awe of a really good person like Mother Teresa, but we make little effort to cultivate such goodness in our selves. Yet, here in our Gospel lesson, Jesus prays for our sanctification, for our growth up into the measure of the fullness of his stature, for our day-by-day, gradual transformation into the image of his goodness. Why? Because he knows that the good person has real life and has it more abundantly. The good person has Christ's peace that the world cannot give or take away. The good person has Jesus' joy in the midst of all tribulation. Jesus prays to the Father for our growth up into goodness through his word. And that prayer is answered by the Father.

Jesus also asks the Father for something else on our behalf. "Father," he prays in our Gospel lesson, "I desire that those also, whom you have given me, may be with me where I am, to see my glory, which you have given me because you loved me before the foundation of the world" (v. 24). In short, Jesus Christ prays to the Father to grant us eternal life in his kingdom. He prays that we too may finally stand there with him at the right hand of God, enjoying eternal life in the Father's house, which has room for us all. That, finally, is the greatest gift he could give us. To know that all our joys, all our work, all our lives in this life, do not finally end in the dark meaninglessness of the grave, but are taken up by God and perfected and preserved forever.

What is the meaning of human life, good Christians, if it finally ends in nothingness? Where is the reward for faithfulness, where is the blessing for service? What goal is there for our personalities if they are but small phrases in a never-ending story that goes round and round, leading nowhere? What is the meaning of life if it is only a story of birth, of struggle, of suffering, and finally of death and void, a cyclical story of countless, futile generations, living out their lives, for no purpose at all? The New Age religionists try to tell us these days that it is all just a merciless fate, one unending wheel of karma on which we suffer in every new reincarnated life for the evil we have done in the last one. But no, Christ prays to the Father, forgive them for all the wrong they have done. Then bring them, dear Father, to live with us here in the glad eternity of your kingdom. God hears that prayer uttered by his beloved Son, and he promises that he will heed and fulfill it.

Christ is risen and he now sits at the right hand of the Father, and there he continually makes intercession for you and me. He prays to God for our forgiveness and for our protection from the evil one. He prays to God for our growth in goodness and for eternal, joyous life for us all. God hears the prayers of his Son, and God answers those prayers.

So, good Christian, if you trust Christ, is there anything that can defeat or destroy you? Death cannot do it. So is there anything in life of which you need to be afraid? No, oh no! For I am sure, with Paul, that neither principalities nor powers of the evil one, nor anything that happens in the present, nor things to come, nor height, nor depth of any circumstance, nor anything else in all this creation, will be able to silence Christ's prayers or separate us from that wondrous love that he pours out there for you and me, night and day, in his intercession before the Father. Amen.

COMMENT

PROBLEM
The Trials and Tribulations of This World

As ministers of the gospel of Jesus Christ, we are constantly threatened by the trials and tribulations of this world; by power struggles within the church; by unceasing (and often unrealistic) demands upon our time and our resources; by insufficient means to meet our own mental, physical, spiritual, and emotional needs; by internal struggles with doubt, fear, depression, and despair. The needs surrounding us are real. Our own resources are often painfully inadequate for the task at hand.

Elizabeth Achtemeier's sermon provides the reminder we need of the greater source of power for the living of our days as servants of our Lord Jesus Christ. He prays for us day by day, hour by hour, minute by minute. Jesus Christ is praying for us from a position of power and influence with our Creator God.

TEXT
Draw the Listener into the Sermon

Achtemeier draws us into the sermon immediately by sharing memories of her parents. We identify with her loss. We remember our own parents, whether dead or living. She shares poignant memories of small losses, and they become our own losses. After calling to mind little things we have lost, she leads us into the recognition of a far greater loss. The power of a mother's or a father's prayers on behalf of a beloved child is something most precious, an irreplaceable loss.

By drawing us into the sermon, Achtemeier helps us become participants in the sermon. Her loss becomes our loss, her memory our memory. We are "in" the sermon with her. Good preaching involves the listener in the proclamation of the good news. This is good preaching.

Achtemeier's style is conversational, deeply theological, yet intimately personal. Her language is clear and easy to follow. The sermon feels like a talk between good friends. We are hooked, listening intently as the sermon becomes the confession of a trusted friend. "I never asked...but we all knew.... My mother prayed for us." We sympathize in Achtemeier's loss. Not only of one she loved so dearly, but of the mother's prayers for her daughter's well-being. We yearn to believe our mother prayed for us, prays for us even now from earth or heaven. A parent does not have to be deeply religious or spiritual to need and seek help from a higher source in raising children. What mother has not prayed for her children?

The rhythm of the sermon moves us as memory surrounds us. It is a shared journey, an intimate experience. Then ever so skillfully we are reminded there is yet One whose prayers for us are even more powerful and effective than the prayers of our mothers or our fathers. That one, Jesus Christ, raised from the dead to the right hand of God, prays for us. Yes—for us!

Achtemeier reminds us of things we know in a poignant way that make a clear and lasting impression on us. She uses biblical images to remind us of who we are as Christians. She uses subtle repetition to weave a pattern of remembrance.

A good sermon is one the preacher remembers on Monday morning. Hopefully, members of the congregation will also remember it. This is a good sermon. It places a marker in our memory in clear and direct language. After hearing or reading this sermon, we will not forget that Jesus Christ is praying for us.

PROCLAMATION
Jesus Christ Is Praying for Us

The good news is that Jesus Christ is praying for us and in us and through us. Whether we are clergy or laity. Whether we recognize the power available to us through the prayers of Christ or whether we are feeling depressed, desolate, and abandoned. The prayers of Jesus Christ for us are real. We hear in and through Achtemeier's sermon the importance of remembering our invisible alliance with the power of the risen Christ through his prayers for us.

COMMENT

As ministers of the gospel, we are in constant need of replenishing the water in our well. When the well goes dry, as it will now and then, we need to be reminded of our Lord's constant love and care for us. What better example than Jesus' praying for us without ceasing? What better picture to visualize than that of Jesus at the right hand of God interceding for us, each and every one of us who choose to follow him, to call ourselves Christian?

Achtemeier's sermon creates vivid visual images: a filthy beggar dressed in rags intruding on the splendor of a king's court; "some great, grimy hand" reaching out to threaten our well-being; the poverty of our Lord as he died on the cross. Strive to create visual images in your preaching. People are more inclined to forget what they hear and to remember what they see. Let pictures tell the story and proclaim the gospel.

RESPONSE
Convince without Condemnation

Achtemeier draws most of her illustrations from the Bible. They are familiar to the practicing Christian. Yet she takes the familiar and makes it particular. We can see ourselves rushing into the king's presence with dirty hands and filthy clothes. We are reminded of our sin in a way that convinces us rather than condemns us. We see, feel and remember our greedy nature. But we are not left to flounder in our sin. We are not condemned for our faults, failures, shortcomings.

There is forgiveness, hope, and reconciliation so necessary for our well-being. This is the good news. There is hope because Jesus Christ is praying for us. He prays for our forgiveness. He prays for our protection from evil. He prays for our growth in goodness, even though holiness is out of vogue. He prays for us to have eternal life with him.

Achtemeier's message has well-defined and clearly developed points. The sermon does not deviate from the direction she has chosen to pursue. She knows what she wants to say, and she says it well. The sermon begins by drawing us in, then leads us in a logical and convincing progression:

Mother prays for us.
Jesus prays for us.
Who is Jesus?
Why is his prayer most effective?
What does Jesus pray for us?
  Forgiveness for our sins.
  Protection from evil.
  Growth in goodness.
  Eternal life and joy in Christ.

Achtemeier calls us "Good Christians." We may not deserve it, but we all want to believe it. She is preaching to our need in a way that encourages us to hear and respond to the expectations of the best that is in us. A good pastor preaches to the need of the Christian in the pew, whether that need is recognized, unknown, or denied. The pastor in the pulpit may be uncomfortably aware of the sins of the congregation, but he or she must beware of being like Jonah and wanting vindication and judgment upon the sinner. We all sin and fall short of our potential for goodness. Hold forth the good news of forgiveness for sins, of the power of good and right living, of our deliverance from sin and evil. Preach the good news.

SUGGESTIONS

- Pray daily. Establish a disciplined prayer life. As preachers and pastors, we are expected to be masters of prayer. Chances are we came to hear and respond to our calling through prayer. But the demands of pastoring a congregation erode and intrude upon a pastor's prayer time in subtle ways. I am reminded of a cartoon where the preacher is kneeling in prayer. The church secretary opens the door and says, "Oh, while you're not doing anything, pastor...." Church folk who want and expect us to pray are likely to believe we should be "doing something" rather than spending time alone with God-in-Christ. We too often equate busyness with productivity. We feel we should be doing something, and God knows there is plenty to do. After all, we are called to be about our Lord's work, are we not? There are people to see, sick folks in need of attention, meetings to attend, youth to guide, reports to send, finances to review, correspondence to answer, and of course, a sermon to write every week, among other things. "Lord help me. It's Monday. And Sunday's a-comin'." Most preachers are phenomenal workaholics. Prayer time is the most likely to suffer from overwork. Jesus is praying for us. Sometimes he needs our undivided attention, so pray daily! Prayer determines action. Action becomes the prayer.

- Preach often on prayer. Christians do not automatically know how to pray just because they have been baptized. We learn to pray by praying. Every Christian needs guidance in learning to pray purposefully and effectively, in moving beyond the "gimme list" to establishing a firm foundation of prayer for Christian living during both adversity and prosperity. It is far more difficult to pray in prosperity than during crisis points in our lives. Clergy and laity need to be reminded frequently to pray...and to pray frequently.

- Learn to listen more and speak less in prayer. One who would be a prayer guide needs to cultivate the prayer of silence. Find a quiet place where you will not be disturbed. Close the door. Take the telephone off the receiver. Release all worries, burdens, fears, anxieties. Give thanks. Ask for help in seeking to silence the clutter of the mind. Learn to listen in silence to God-in-Christ. He will come in the still small spaces of your mind, heart, and soul. When we prepare the place, Jesus will come.

Marianna Frost

Forget My Sins, Remember Me

PSALM 25:7

Rev. Dr. Frank Pollard
First Baptist Church
Jackson, Mississippi

FORGET MY SINS, REMEMBER ME

PSALM 25:7, NIV

I heard a story about a civic club where a graduate of Yale University was called upon to make a speech. He decided to use the letters of his alma mater as the structure for the speech. He talked about Y for fifteen minutes, noting that it stood for youth and a lot of other things. Then he took the A and talked another fifteen minutes about words like action and attitude. After thirty minutes, having finished with Y and A, one of the members of the club punched another and said, "I'm certainly glad he didn't attend the Massachusetts Institute of Technology."

Our Yale friend was trying to use an acrostic. Acrostics are good teaching tools because they give us a simple way to recall information. There are even acrostics in the Bible. For example, there are at least five Old Testament acrostic psalms that use each letter of the Hebrew alphabet for the first letter of each line. This helped people to remember these psalms.

Psalm 25 is written as an acrostic and it is a marvelous prayer. The psalmist prays for a wonderfully strange thing in this psalm. In verse 7 he prays, "Remember not the sins of my youth/and my rebellious ways;/according to your love remember me,/for you are good, O Lord." Is it possible to pray, "Forget my sins but remember me"? Is it possible that God would forget our sins and remember us?

Forget my sins. That's the way of God. It's his way to forget sins. That's what God is like. I have decided that to find the mind of God, you should gather the sharpest people you can find, learn what they think, and then do the opposite. How do you become great? You become a servant. Who is going to be first? The one who is last. How can we work our way to heaven? We cannot. God's way is not our way. Thus God's way is to forget the sins of his people.

In Jeremiah 31:34 the prophet says God will forget our sins and remember them no more. In Hebrews 8:12, God will forget our sins and remember them no more. In Hebrews 10:17, God will forget our sins and remember them no more. God is trying to tell us something. He says that he can forget our sins and remember them no more. That's the way of God. He forgets sins.

The great missionary E. Stanley Jones had another way of saying what our text says. "God buries our sins in the sea of his forgetfulness and puts up a sign, 'No Fishing Here.'" God forgets our sins. He remembers them no more. That's the way of God.

Years ago a friend of mine was learning to use a computer. He is an outstanding preacher and has also written many books. We were together at an encampment in Oklahoma. He had just finished typing two chapters of his next book on his computer. There was a sudden power failure and when he restarted his machine everything was gone, two chapters of his manuscript. I overheard his telephone conversation with the computer salesman. It was interesting.

My friend asked, "Where did it go? I put it in there. It's in there. I know it's in there. I worked fourteen hours putting it in there. Where did it go?"

The man on the other end of the line said, "It's gone."

My friend continued, "You can't tell me it's gone. It has to be some-where. Where is it?" But as many of you know, when you lose something on your computer, it's gone.

Like my friend's two chapters, when God says our sins are gone, they are gone. God has pushed the delete button, and they are no more.

We need to find simple everyday language to describe the faith experience in a new and more profound way than the church language that

Christians use and nobody else understands. I remember the first time I went to church. A woman gave her testimony and said, "I went forward and was washed in the blood." Imagine how that sounds to a ten-year-old who has never been in church before. Washed in the blood. While it is a wonderful thing to be covered in the blood of Jesus Christ for our sins, I did not understand what that woman was talking about at the time.

The New Testament is written in a beautiful secular language. There was no church language when the New Testament was written. When certain topics came up the New Testament writers used everyday words that everyone could understand.

The word "forgive" comes from the word meaning to pay a debt. In those days, of course, they did not have computers, business machines, typewriters, or even paper. They used a slate on a wall. When somebody bought something on credit, the merchant would write down his name and how much he owed on the wall so everyone could see it. This encouraged everyone to pay their bills.

There are two words in the Greek language that are very precise having to do with the paying of a debt. We translate those words as "forgive." One means you draw a line through it, like stamping "paid" on an invoice. The other means that the merchant took a rag and wiped the record clean. There is no more record of that debt. It is wiped clean. Every time, without fail, in the word of God, when we read, "Our sins are forgiven," the New Testament writers used the word that means the record has been wiped clean. There is no more record of it.

It is the way of God to forgive sins, to forget them, and to remember them no more. That's the way God works. That's the way he is. But we have trouble with that. This is not just the way of God, it is the challenge of Christians to live like they believe that.

I heard of a husband who said to his wife, "Why are you always reminding me of my past mistakes? You told me that you would forgive and forget." The wife said, "Well, I don't want you to forget that I have forgiven and forgotten." That's the way we are. We keep those records filed in our memories for years. It's hard for us to forgive and forget.

Do we understand that ours is the glory of a faith we cannot live up to? We cannot be everything God calls us to be in the Bible. Nobody can. No one will ever have that kind of faith until Christ comes again. We are all trying to struggle toward what God has called us to be. We won't be there until he comes and changes us. Be perfect as I am perfect, God says (Matt. 5:48). Has anybody kept that commandment? Is anybody perfect? Our Lord calls us to be something that we can't, but the goal is always there. We must always strive. Ours is the glory of a faith we can't live up to.

"Husbands, love your wives, just as Christ loved the church and gave himself up for her" (Eph. 5:25, NIV). Is there a husband here who loves his wife as much as Christ loves the church? I have been married forty-one years, and I haven't been there, but I would like to be. That goal is always before us.

Wives are to submit to their husbands as the church is submitted to Christ (Eph. 5:22–24, NIV). Any wives here able to say they have done that? Of course not. It's a goal.

Another goal before us is found in the last verses of Ephesians 4: "Be kind to one another, tenderhearted, forgiving one another, even as God in Christ forgave you" (Eph. 4:32, NKJV). What a goal! What a challenge! Yet that is our challenge. These are the commandments God has called us to do. We are to forgive each other just as we have been forgiven by Christ. How have we been forgiven by him? God has forgotten our sins and remembers them no more.

A pastor in Boston was beset by a member of his church. This person lied, slandered, started rumors, and wrote letters to the bishop about him in an effort to have him removed from the pulpit. This person finally moved to another town and there had a genuine experience with Christ and was immediately convicted about this sin. She wrote the pastor a long letter outlining all she had done and told him that she was sorry and asked him to forgive her. The pastor sent a telegram saying, "Forgiven, forgotten forever." That's the challenge of being a Christian.

First Corinthians 13 tells us what love is really like. "It keeps no record of wrongs (v.5, NIV)." Our challenge is to forgive and to forget. We are not to keep records of wrongs done against us. We are not to keep score. God does not keep score in heaven. We are to forgive and forget just as God does. It is our challenge.

Do you think it's possible to remember people without remembering their sins? In Shakespeare's *Julius Caesar,* Mark Antony says, "The evil that men do lives after them;/The good is oft interred with their bones." It's true. When we speak a name, we usually remember their mistakes or evil deeds. What do we remember when we say the name Brutus? Even in his speech, Mark Antony made sure we remembered that Brutus was one who had stabbed Caesar.

What do we remember when we say the name Judas? We remember that he was the one who betrayed Jesus.

What do we remember when we speak of Pilate? We remember that he was the one who washed his hands and said, "I'm going to let you kill him, but I'm not going to have anything to do with it."

What do we remember when we hear the name Herod? We remember that he was the one who tried to trick the wise men into telling him where Jesus was and the one who ordered all the babies under the age of two killed.

Is it possible that God will forget our sins and yet remember us? If so, why should he answer our prayer? When we say, "Lord, forget my sins and remember me," one of the things God may ask us is, "Why should I?" The answer is in our Scripture verse: "According to your love remember me, for you are good, O Lord." Why? Because God loves us. He loves us enough to die for us. He died on the cross to pay for our sins. God paid a tremendous price to forget our sins. The Scriptures describe it as having our sins "covered by the blood of Jesus Christ." The Scriptures tell us that when Christ was nailed to the cross, our sins were nailed to the cross. That is what took our sins away. That is how our sins are forgiven and forgotten.

When they got those nails out of the commissary that morning, they were nails that could have been used to build a boat, a house, or a bridge, but instead they were used to hammer the Son of God to those hideous logs. Hate took those nails and said, "These are my nails and I'll kill you with them." But love received the nails and said, "No. They are my nails and I will save you with them." God does indeed forget our sins and remembers them no more because he loves us and because he paid the price on the cross for us that we might have eternal life.

"According to your love, O Lord, remember me." How do we know that God has forgotten our sins and still remembers us? Psalm 25:1 says, "To you, O Lord, I lift up my soul;/in you I trust, O my God." How do we lift up our soul?

Soul means life. It means each one of us. It means our emotions, our intellect, our will. The soul is us. It is that part of us that is never going to die. It is that part of us that will not return to dust like our bodies will. "To you, O Lord, I lift up myself, my soul, and in you, O Lord, do I trust." If we want to know that God has forgotten our sins and remembers us, then we give the life that we have to him so he can give us back the life that he wants us to have and intends us to have.

What was the psalmist giving to the Lord when he said, "To you, I lift up my soul"? In verses 16–19 we read what he was giving up. "I'm lonely and afflicted. The troubles of my heart have multiplied; free me from my anguish. I have affliction and distress. I have sins. I have multiplied enemies." This is the life the psalmist was giving up, and God said, "I want that life." God wants our sins. He wants our afflictions. He wants everything we are. Some people are so guilty of pride, which is the greatest sin, and God says, "I want your pride." Some people say, "I have done this and I have done that," and God says, "Bring that sin to me, and I'll forget it and I'll make you what you ought to be. I'll help you."

To many people a person is made up of his or her sins. To many people a person is the sum of his or her mistakes. To God you are as spotless as Christ when you become a Christian, and you are what God pictures you to be…what he has in mind for you.

In the story *Alice in Wonderland,* Alice says, "It's a poor memory that only works backwards." God's memory does not just work backwards, it works forward. Remember that Saul of Tarsus was evil, religiously evil. He was the worst kind of mean person in all the world—he was religiously mean and he was trying to get rid of every Christian he could find. Saul was there when Stephen was stoned to death. Saul blasphemed Jesus and was committed to putting women and children in prison. Then he met Jesus. Jesus forgave him. He saw him and remembered him. Do you know what Jesus saw? He saw the greatest missionary who ever lived and the author of half the New Testament. Saul, now Paul, experienced what the psalmist prayed for: "Forget my sins, remember me."

Remember Mary Magdalene? She was so evil the Bible describes her as having seven evil spirits. But when she met Jesus and confessed her sins to him, Jesus remembered her. He made her to be the person that she came to be...a committed follower of Jesus Christ. Her name is in the Word of God because Jesus forgot her sins and remembered her.

Simon Peter was a man who had up-and-down emotional swings all the time—valiant and vacillating, brave and cowardly. One never knew what to expect of Simon Peter. Jesus met him and said, "Your name is Simon Bar-Jona. You are Simon, the son of John. You are going to be called 'the Rock.'" Peter means rock. Jesus saw him and forgave his sins. He remembered him.

The Lord says, "If you will turn to me." If we will say, "To you, O Lord, I lift up my soul. Lord, I give you my sins. I give you my weaknesses. I give you my life, such as it is. I give it to you and trust you. I trust you to remember me, to make me what you intended me to be," then God can begin this process in all of us right now.

COMMENT

PURPOSE

Imagine you are dining in a fine restaurant. You've just enjoyed one of the finest meals you have ever eaten. Every aspect of the dinner was superb. As you sit enjoying the afterglow of satisfaction, there's a good chance you will...

> ...ask the waiter or waitress to convey your compliments to the chef?
>
> ...add this restaurant to your list of favorite dining spots?
>
> ...do a careful analysis of the ingredients you've just ingested, including a breakdown of the percentages of salt, sugar, carbohydrates, protein, and fat?

If you're inclined toward the last item on this list, be aware that you may be accused of overanalysis. Why would you ruin a wonderful feast by picking it apart? The food was delicious. Why not leave it at that?

In our efforts to evaluate the effectiveness of the spoken word, we run a similar risk, walking a fine line between savoring the message and overanalyzing the method. The last thing we want to do is destroy the mystique of the listening experience by dismembering the body of content. However, if a satisfied diner ever wishes to recreate a marvelous meal, he or she will have to acquire the recipe. Whether it's cuisine or sermons, there is usually a formula for success.

STYLE & STRUCTURE

As we sit down to "dine on" Frank Pollard's fine message, "Forget My Sins, Remember Me," let's look at the preacher's recipe. This sermon goes down like a fine meal. In part, this is because there's a direct relationship here between quality and quantity. To see it, let's begin by applying a mathematical measure to Pollard's recipe.

In reviewing the sermon, consider the following numerical observations:

1) Even though the biblical text for the message consists of only one verse—which itself is repeated numerous times—no fewer than seventeen other scriptural passages are quoted, and allusions are made to three or four additional texts.

2) Besides Jesus himself, seven other biblical characters are used as illustrations.

3) At least a dozen anecdotes are brought into the sermon for the sake of illustration, including references to Shakespeare's *Julius Caesar,* first-century usage of the Greek language, *Alice in Wonderland,* and several of the preacher's own experiences.

4) The main theme, "God forgets our sins but remembers us," is repeated twenty times throughout the sermon.

5) On thirty-three occasions, the preacher asks a question (both rhetorically and literally) of his audience.

What do these numbers tell us? Several things. First, Pollard is a biblical preacher, drawing liberally upon the full expanse of the Scriptures. Second, he is a good storyteller; his cumulative life experience provides him (and us!) with a rich library of illustrations. Third, he understands the value of delivering the central point through the effective use of repetition. Fourth, the preacher is well-enough read to integrate his breadth of knowledge into his message without pretentiousness. Fifth, Pollard is directive in his purpose, guiding his listeners toward answers by first posing good questions.

CONTENT

Pollard gives us a clear message of God's astounding grace. Obviously, this is a sermon about forgiveness, but more than that, it takes us beyond the familiar terrain of theological platitudes. (By his own admission, Pollard dislikes "church language.") Not only is God ready and willing to forgive our sins, he is generous enough to forget our many transgressions. More than that, God will remember us in love.

Is this message faithful both to God's Word and orthodox Christianity? Absolutely. In fact, it is a basic teaching in that it covers several of the foundation stones of the faith: humanity's sinfulness, the need for salvation to come from beyond ourselves, and the redemptive work of God in Jesus Christ. If we never heard another sermon, we could do well to hang our faith securely upon the content of this presentation of the gospel. This is not an occasional message, intended to address a specific situation or audience. Rather, it is universal in scope, capable of speaking relevantly to anyone in any place.

In assessing the theological credibility of any sermon, find the preacher's main theme and compare it to the biblical text on which the message is built. Are they in harmony? Is what the preacher is saying consistent with what the scriptural passage says within its own context? In addition, ask yourself if the central theme is consistent with the wider biblical teaching on the subject. Then ask if it stands up well to the scrutiny of historical-doctrinal teaching. Pollard's message passes muster by any and all of these measures.

PROBLEM, TEXT & PROCLAMATION

The problem Pollard addresses in his sermon is that of our sinfulness and our need for release from guilt. Within this predicament, the sermon addresses a secondary problem: our need to live as forgiven individuals and our willingness to forgive others. The problem the sermon addresses is our tendency to break relationships: with God, with ourself, and with others. Every aspect of the message points to the evidence of our predicament and then gives us the scriptural assurance that God has provided the remedy in Christ.

How is the liberating power of this truth proclaimed in the sermon? Pollard uses many methods. First, we see grace fleshed out through the lives of people Pollard has known and through people in the biblical story. Second, through Pollard's discussion of the New Testament usage of the Greek word for forgiveness, we come to understand the linguistic basis for the concept. Third, through the explanation of the word *soul* ("It means your emotion, your intellect, your will"), we discover our need to give our-selves to God totally. And finally, through his closing appeal, Pollard sheds light on our weaknesses and our need to trust in God. Not only are we told we need to be forgiven and to forgive, but we're told how this happens.

How are we to respond to this message? Pollard answers in his con-cluding paragraph:

> The Lord says, "If you will turn to me." If we will say, "To you, O Lord, I lift up my soul. Lord, I give you my sins. I give you my weakness. I give you my life, such as it is. I give it to you and trust you. I trust you to remember me, to make me what you intended me to be," then God can begin this process in all of us right now.

Sounds like the preacher's tossing the ball straight into our court, wouldn't you say?

SUGGESTIONS

- Notice Pollard's skill at using a myriad of illustrations without mud-dling the focus of his message. Every quote, anecdote, and explana-tion points back to the basic theme of forgiving and forgetting. With some preachers there can be a seemingly endless flow of disjointed illustrations—each of interest in its own way but unrelated to the cen-tral point. When this happens, the audience is left shell-shocked and, in the end, wondering what the preacher was saying. This doesn't happen with Pollard. His focus is so clear and consistent that his every breath serves the higher purpose of supporting the central theme. How do you go about structuring a sermon so that your quotes and illustrations are tightly woven into the theme?
- Never underestimate the effectiveness of repetition when it is done well. It's easy to make the mistake of thinking that originality and freshness in a sermon are sacrificed by returning again and again to the same thought. Not so. Listen to the sermons of Martin Luther King Jr., Billy Graham, or any of the well-known preachers of our

day, and you'll find most of them have mastered the art of repetition. By revisiting a catchy phrase or a resonant point repeatedly, the speaker is able to create a rhythm that serves to plant the main point firmly in the consciousness of each listener. As evidenced by our mathematical tally of his sermon, Pollard is no stranger to the innate value of repeating key phrases throughout a sermon. Learn from his example. Look at your last few sermons. How do you use repetition in your preaching?

Richard A. Davis

LESSONS FROM THE NARROW PLACES OF LIFE

NUMBERS 22:21–35; LUKE 24:13–16, 28–32

REV. DR. WILLIAM POWELL TUCK
FIRST BAPTIST CHURCH
LUMBERTON, NORTH CAROLINA

LESSONS FROM THE NARROW PLACES OF LIFE

NUMBERS 22:21–35; LUKE 24:13–16, 28–32, NRSV

T he story found in the Book of Numbers about Balaam and his ass is one of the difficult passages in the Old Testament. For some folks, it is clear evidence that the Scriptures are an ancient relic that has absolutely no meaning for us today. For others, it is a clear sign of the miraculous within the Scriptures. How do we deal with a passage that has an animal talking?

First, let us look at the setting of the story. The children of Israel were moving like a conquering army through what we call today the Holy Land. To acquire that land, they had to conquer each tribe as they moved through it. King Balak, of Moab, became very frightened as he saw this approaching army. He summoned to his court Balaam, who was a seer, visionary, prophet or soothsayer. When Balaam first received the message from the king of Moab, he realized that Balak wanted him to place a curse on Israel to harm them. After he prayed for guidance, God told him not to go, so he refused Balak's summons. Balak, however, felt that all Balaam needed was simply more inducement. He offered Balaam bigger and better possessions if he would come and curse the Israelites. Balaam responded, "Although Balak were to give me his house full of silver and gold, I could not go beyond the command of the Lord my God, to do less or more" (Num.

22:18). However, he said, he would pray about the matter again, even though he had received a message that God was not going to curse Israel but bless them. The second time God directed him to go anyway and talk to the king of Moab.

On his journey Balaam had to travel on a narrow road to get to Moab. The animal on which he was riding saw an angel with a flaming sword standing in the pathway and tried to get off the path. This happened three times, until finally the animal found itself in such a narrow place there was no room either to turn around or to get off the road. So it just lay down! Balaam got up and hit the animal angrily. At this point the animal spoke. The ancient Israelites hearing or reading this story must have found it hilarious, a wonderful piece of narrative folklore. The fact that Balaam did not seem surprised or express any wonder at the animal's ability to speak indicates the nature of this ancient drama. The important thing for the original audience was the message and not the medium of the message.

In several other places in the Scriptures one reads about trees speaking and snakes talking; here an ass talks. To the Israelites, this story would have been filled with humor. Balaam, who was pompous and overly confident, was not an Israelite, yet he was depicted as being used by the God of Israel. His own animal had to tell this pompous religious seer about the presence of God, because he was unable to see God in his path.

Our problem is that often we cannot hear a story because we take it too literally. We seek to make the story historical instead of hearing the ancient message delivered through the medium of humorous folklore to an ancient people. Many of us often miss the truth about the presence of God because we get bogged down in the impossibility of an animal's talking. The important point here is not that the animal spoke but what it had to say.

After the animal spoke, Balaam did see the angel standing in the path, who then told him that he was going against what God wanted him to do. That word seems troublesome to us in itself. Had not God told him to go to Moab and carry a message? We do not know exactly what had happened, but in some way the message was obviously distorted by Balaam.

He was attempting to do something that God did not want him to do. His pompous attitude had left him blind to the warnings of God along the way.

The story we read this morning from the New Testament is the account of Jesus' talking with two of his disciples on the road to Emmaus after the resurrection. These disciples could not believe the reports which they had heard. They were baffled, confused and depressed. Jesus walked along with them on the short journey from Jerusalem to Emmaus—about seven miles. As they walked, he unfolded the Scriptures to them. They did not know who he was until later, when he broke bread with them in their house. Then their eyes were opened and they recognized him.

These two stories have some messages we need to hear today and carry with us.

The first is this: Balaam represents one who felt he could live his life in total independence. He felt that his own self-reliance and his own direction were sufficient. He twisted and distorted the message he got from God, and decided to carry his own word as the word from God about the people of Israel. He felt he could rely upon his own strength, his own understanding, his own methods, and his own ways. He was sufficient. He did not need to rely only on God's word. But God confronted him with his own message and directed that he was to share that message, not his own words.

How many of us are like Balaam today? We go through life thinking that our self-reliance, our self-sufficiency, and our independence can take us through every situation. We believe that we do not need the power and presence of God. Nor do we really need other people.

None of us, however, is really self-made or totally self-sufficient. The story is told of Napoleon planning the battle of Waterloo. As he instructed his soldiers where he wanted the artillery, the cavalry and the infantry placed, one of his aides asked him, "Should we not consider what the Divine might want in this? After all, man proposes and God disposes." Napoleon drew himself up to his full short height and responded arrogantly, "Sir, Napoleon proposes, Napoleon disposes." But that very battle proved his undoing. The one who thought that he could always make his own decisions and set his will against nations soon found that he was defeated.

Too often we attempt to set our own will, purpose, and way against God. To those who do so, it doesn't make any difference what God might want or what guidance other individuals might want to offer. They alone make the decision. When we try to live this way, we may find that life collapses around us, because we are not open to the power and presence of God's direction. We have made ourselves the only source of guidance, and so our path may become blocked by our blind selfishness. Many of us live as though there were no God.

A Scottish shepherd once said that when sheep are caught in a blizzard, they can live seven or eight days protected by their own wool. But if the blizzard continues too long, they will freeze to death. When we attempt to live off our own resources, without drawing on the power and presence of God or the help other people can offer us, we soon find that we lose our stability and we may encounter the presence of God who blocks our way.

Notice also in these stories that these people met God in unexpected places. Balaam thought he already had a message from God. After all, he had his vision; he had his dream, and now he was traveling to deliver that message to the king of Moab. But he met God unexpectedly when he was hemmed in—caught in a narrow place. The disciples thought that everything was over in their dream about the coming Messiah. They were defeated and depressed. While they were going home on the road to Emmaus Christ walked with them and later revealed himself to them.

How often God encounters us in unexpected places. We hadn't anticipated meeting God, we hadn't planned it, yet God appears and is present and touches our lives. Moses was attending sheep on a mountainside when he encountered God in a wilderness place. Isaiah went to the temple grieving because of the loss of his beloved king, and there in that experience of worship, he met God. Jeremiah was on a casual walk when he saw an almond tree blooming, and from that ordinary experience, he had a revelation from God. While Paul was traveling on the road to Damascus to persecute and put to death the first Christians, he met the Christ whom he was seeking to defeat. His life was changed forever. Down through history people have encountered God in all kinds of places.

You and I may meet God in strange places. We may meet God in affliction and illness. We may meet God in our work, on the playground, in the gym or in a school classroom. We may meet God at a ball game, in our living room, on a trip or in church, in a conversation with a friend or in an encounter with a stranger. Sometimes unexpectedly, God comes into our lives. We may be washing dishes, changing a tire, doing our daily work, helping a friend who is ill or recovering from surgery. Suddenly we sense the presence of God. We had not anticipated it nor expected it, but God comes.

I recall standing by the bedside of a fourteen-year-old girl. She was dying and her family had gathered around her. I thought there was going to be only depression and despair. Suddenly in that moment of tragedy, the whole family, including myself, was gripped with an overwhelming sense of God's presence. I have been beside the beds of people when they were in their last hours, and have sensed great peace and strength emanating from them. As they died, they had an awareness of the presence of God. In the narrow places of life we may encounter God unexpectedly when God comes to meet us and assist us.

I also recall some beautiful places in which I have met God. One was the fellowship hall of my home church where I made my profession of faith as a fifteen-year-old. There God's Spirit moved into my life. Later, while working in scout camps in the Blue Ridge Mountains of Virginia, I would get up early and walk over the mountain trails to a small lake and sense the awesome presence of Another. One summer I worked in the Hawaiian Islands, where the beauty and splendor spoke to me again of the presence of God. In later years, as I looked down on my newborn children and beheld the life that I had a small part in creating, I experienced in a new way the presence and power of God. In unexpected, narrow places, and sometimes in beautiful places, we may find God.

In one community a store called The Surprise Shop advertised items for people eight to eighty and urged them to come in and browse. The store continued to attract visitors because people were really surprised at what was sold there.[1] Life, I think, is a surprise shop. I think God meets us again and again in surprising places. In unexpected places and in unexpected ways God speaks to us. It may be in a narrow pass, or it may be on a beautiful, lovely day.

But notice also in these stories that the word of God came in judgment. When Balaam finally saw the angel of God, the angel held a drawn sword. God confronted Balaam as an adversary. Balaam was going to Balak with the wrong message. We are not certain how the message had become distorted. It is uncertain whether Balaam was going there to misrepresent what God had told him to say. Was he going there to curse the people of Israel and not to bless them? Had he assumed that his message was God's message?

That has become the curse of too many preachers. We turn our opinion into God's word. Whatever we think and whatever our opinion is automatically God's opinion. Perhaps that is what happened to Balaam. We do not know for certain, but he is confronted by the angel of God. God told him to go and deliver only what he had told him to say. God confronted him in judgment.

For the disciples walking on the road to Emmaus, Christ came to rebuke their disbelief, perplexity and despair. He judged their lack of faith by opening the Scriptures to them and revealing the power and wisdom of what God had done.

Before we can sense the power of God, he must first come in judgment into our lives. He comes in judgment to change us and direct us to open our lives so we can be transformed by his power, to become the people he has created us to be.

Sometimes in our churches, before miracles are performed, there must be the casting out of demons and devils. God's Spirit must sweep through our lives to purge the sinfulness within us and make us clean and whole. Tragically, we think that we can keep on sinning and still be loyal church members. We refuse to respond or turn to God. God comes to us bringing love, grace and redemption. But if our lives are constantly filled with hatred, self-love, jealousy, and other sins, we are not able to receive God's love and grace. First he must cast out the evil spirits within us so that he can fill us with love, hope and righteousness. When our lives are filled with lies, distrust and hatred, God cannot fill us with his grace, hope, love and mercy. He must first come in judgment. The holiness of God cannot stand in the presence of sin. God must purge us, transform us and cleanse us.

A church youth worker was walking on a beach one day and saw one of his teenagers wearing a T-shirt. When the young man saw his leader, he immediately crossed his arms. The leader walked up to him and said, "Oh, you have on one of those T-shirts with a message. I can't quite read what it says. Does it say, 'University of Virginia'?"

The teenager looked down and said, "No."

"Well, let me see," the man said.

The youth dropped his arms. Written on the shirt were the words, "Stamp out virginity." "If you don't think I ought to wear it," the young man said, "I'll take it off."

"I have a better suggestion," the youth worker said. "Why don't you take it home, have it laundered and put it in a bag. You look like a young man who's going to get married some day and have a family. Save it, and when your daughter goes on her first date, I want you to give it to her then."

The teenager looked back at the youth worker and said, "I get your message. If my father had said that to me, I would never have worn it."

When does the church stand up and pronounce judgment against the sinfulness of today's distortion of sex? It is *not* okay to do anything, anywhere, at any time. There is a sanctity to sex that needs to be recovered. Free sex and free love as depicted on our television sets and movies is not the Christian lifestyle. Free sex is never free. It is always costly. Too often young people are never told what its price tag is.

The word from God may come to us as judgment. God comes as the change agent to transform us by his Spirit. So, God may first come as an adversary to tell us our lives need to be different. As we walk with the God who is the holy God of the universe, we cannot do anything we want to and still think we are being Christian. God has called us to a higher way, a higher lifestyle. We are to follow in his steps.

Finally, notice that in both of these stories, the main characters are met by the presence of God. The Old Testament expression "the angel of the Lord" does not refer to God's helpers but to the presence of God himself. When Balaam is confronted by the angel of the Lord, it means he experienced God himself. God confronted him and challenged him. When the disciples were walking on the road to Emmaus, their eyes were not opened until the invited guest, Jesus, broke bread, blessed it, and handed it to them. Then they saw that this unknown companion had been the Lord himself.

It is in the narrow places of life that we may experience the presence of God, the angel of the Lord who comes and ministers to us. He may come to you in the narrow place of grief, illness, pain or suffering. He may come to you in the narrow place of rejection, ridicule, loneliness, or depression. He may minister to your need and lift you up through a friend's voice, a telephone call, a note, or a letter. God may come to you in many places and ways and communicate his presence to you as power, grace and love. In the narrow places of life God is there. Let him open your eyes.

One of the messages that comes to us from Jesus' Emmaus appearance is that God is not always just at our disposal. After Jesus revealed himself, he disappeared. The two disciples met him in the word and in the fellowship at the table. But God is not somebody we can manipulate with little schemes and systems. We cannot memorize a few things that will automatically produce God for us. God is not on a string for our use. The Lord is not simply available at our whim or our disposal. He may surprise us by the manner of his coming, but we do not control or manipulate him. He is the God who comes at his own will. He is the God who moves in our lives in his own way. We must be open to his coming in unexpected places and in unexpected ways. We need the miracle of the "opened eyes" and the "burning heart."

The great preacher Paul Scherer wrote in one of his books about the misrepresentation of a phrase that he stumbled across. Often, he said, we talk about seeing something through "to the bitter end."[2] In the research he did on that phrase, Scherer discovered that the phrase really implies "the better end." It's a nautical phrase. When a ship was caught in a storm, the anchors were let out full into the water. Then the ship moved out to the end of the cables that reached deep into the hull of the ship and were secured around the bitts far within the hull. They moved to the bitter end. When the storm battered the ship, because the cables were secured, the ship could ride out the storm and endure it.

Too many of us try to live out life to "the bitter end," when the alternative is to let God be with us to "the better end," trusting that God is holding us and will sustain us. God may first come to meet us in judgment. We may sense him in narrow places and in unexpected ways, where we may be surprised by his coming. Come he will. Be assured of that. But we cannot predict how or when. I hope that we will not give way to the bitter end. I hope we will learn to embrace the better end where the presence of God will sustain us and carry us through.

Notes
1. Lloyd John Ogilvie, *A Life Full of Surprises* (Nashville: Abingdon Press, 1969), p. 41.
2. Paul Scherer, *The Word God Sent* (New York: Harper & Row, 1965), pp. 242–43.

COMMENT

The question every conscientious preacher ought to ask is this: How can I faithfully and effectively convey the message of the Scriptures to a generation that appears to be, at best, indifferent and, at worst, resistant to such a message? As today's pulpiteers, we might think ourselves unique in having to face this challenge. But of course, we are not. Every generation of preachers, from Moses onward, has faced the same dilemma. The human condition is such that we never have seen—and likely never will see—people breaking down church doors to get to the gospel. But still, week after week, many faithful listeners fill our pews hoping for inspiration. How do we "preach to the choir" and at the same time address the unchurched, taking an "insider's message" and making it relevant to the uninitiated?

In facing this task, we can benefit from William Tuck's "Lessons from the Narrow Places of Life." His style is biblically faithful without being inaccessible to someone who knows little of the Bible. This sermon is refreshingly free of church talk, preacher jargon, and theological rhetoric. Yet the bulk of its content is straight from the Scriptures. No gimmicks. No compromises. No pretense.

STYLE

From his first utterance, Tuck addresses the lesson of the day. Absent is the obligatory warmup, either a joke or a cute anecdote. So clear is Tuck's speaking style that it isn't necessary here. Right at the beginning, he acknowledges the difficulties of the Balaam story. Some read it and say that it "has absolutely no meaning." Others take just the opposite tack, seeing this narrative as "a clear sign of the miraculous within the Scriptures." Which is it? Is this an off-the-wall myth or a piece of literal history? Tuck already has us hooked. We're curious to see what he'll make of this seemingly ludicrous tale of an Old Testament "Mister Ed."

Once he hooks us, Tuck immediately ushers us into the heart of the narrative by paraphrasing the story. He does so adeptly. Within the first three minutes, we have a firm grip on the story, even if we've never read it before. It isn't easy for a preacher to summarize a long passage without losing the listener. But Tuck does it well, because he's a capable storyteller.

Tuck also acknowledges the problems most skeptics have with Bible passages like this—stories about animated trees and talking animals. We all have wondered about such things. So we listen carefully, curious to hear the preacher's take on biblical credibility, especially as it relates to a talking ass. Other preachers might choose to ignore the credibility factor. But Tuck knows that skepticism has an energy all its own when it's handled carefully. And handle it carefully he does, tiptoeing along the thin ice that covers the turbulent waters of controversy over biblical interpretation.

The controversy over the nature of Scripture isn't the issue here. If we hope to get the right answer, Tuck says we must ask the right question. So he advises us to take more interest in a speaking God than in a speaking ass. Here Tuck lays the foundation of the sermon. It remains to be seen what shape the sermon's subsequent structure will take.

STRUCTURE

If the significance of the Balaam story lies not in the medium (the ass) but in the message, what is that message? Tuck builds his sermon on four main points gleaned from the Balaam story. Then, for emphasis, he adds to it the New Testament account of Jesus and the two disciples on the road to Emmaus. There is both a rhythm and an order to how he does this. Within each of the four points, Tuck follows the same formula:

1) embellish the biblical action and give it meaning;
2) emphasize this meaning with an illustration;
3) establish a connection with the listener's life.

Embellish. Emphasize. Establish. Three easy steps. Let's see how Tuck applies them to his subject matter.

Point 1: Reliance on self vs. reliance on God
Embellish: "Balaam represents one who felt he could live his life in total independence."

Emphasize: "Napoleon planning the battle of Waterloo."

Establish: "Too often we attempt to set our own will, purpose, and way against God."

Point 2: Meeting God in unexpected places

Embellish: "[Balaam] met God unexpectedly when he was hemmed in—caught in a narrow place."

Emphasize: Further examples: the disciples on the road to Emmaus, Moses attending his sheep, Isaiah grieving at the temple, Jeremiah and the almond tree, Paul on his way to Damascus, and Tuck himself in the Blue Ridge Mountains and in Hawaii.

Establish: "You and I may meet God in strange places…in our work or on the playground, in the gym or in a school classroom, at a ball game or in our living room or on a trip or in church."

Point 3: The word of God coming in judgment

Embellish: "God confronted Balaam as an adversary."

Emphasize: Preachers who spout their own opinions, Jesus' rebuking the disciples on the walk to Emmaus, sin in our churches blocking God's Spirit, a church youth worker's encounter with an embarrassed teen.

Establish: "God may first come as an adversary to tell us our lives need to be different."

Point 4: Being confronted with the presence of God

Embellish: "When Balaam is confronted by the angel of the Lord, it means he experienced God himself."

Emphasize: "The two disciples [on the Emmaus road] met [Jesus] in the word and in the fellowship at the table."

Establish: "We must be open to [God's] coming in unexpected places and in unexpected ways."

There we have in a nutshell the entirety of Tuck's sermon. Well-ordered, clearly communicated, and applied to our lives. The preacher's simplicity of method is his artistry.

PROBLEM, TEXT & PROCLAMATION

Having analyzed the sermon in terms of its component parts, we can see more easily how, in developing his four points, Tuck integrates our human problem with the biblical solution. Notice, however that he does not present the problem first and then follow up with the solution. Quite the opposite. In outlining each point, he begins with the biblical story, then identifies the human problem it illustrates, and finally prompts us to make the connection for ourselves. In a sense, the solution precedes the problem. Balaam's problem is also our problem. The blindness of the disciples on their way to Emmaus is also our blindness. Napoleon's pride is our pride. And so it goes.

Tuck discovers our problem within the biblical text and also within the adjacent illustrations. Then he announces the divine remedy, which, not coincidentally, is also found in the text. In preaching as in our individual quests for truth, it's not so much how we get there as it is that we finally arrive at our destination.

RESPONSE

What does this sermon invite from us in the way of response? Besides recognizing our own rebellious tendencies in the biblical narrative, Tuck would have us revisit some dark closets in our own lives. In fact, he's quite specific. He urges me to ask myself who is in control of my life, is it God or me? He beckons me to expect to meet God in even the most unlikely places of my life. He warns me to prepare for a judgment before change comes. He recommends that I evaluate my own church's openness to the movement of the Holy Spirit. And, not to be lost in the mix is one of the preacher's own pet peeves, namely, our generation's sexual confusion (the story of the teenager and the T-shirt). In all of these, Tuck says, "Stop. Look. Think. And if the shoe (or the T-shirt) of sin fits, make the effort to change." This is what every effective sermon does. It gets our attention, asks us to take inventory, and then prompts us to realign ourselves with God's will.

SUGGESTIONS

- Go through the sermon a second time looking for religious jargon. You may be surprised how few Christian catch phrases Tuck uses. For example, when he talks of how we stubbornly cling to our own self-sufficiency, he never slips into doctrinal or dogmatic rhetoric. Rather, he speaks clearly of our illusion of self-reliance and colors it with a couple of vivid illustrations: the plight of the Scottish sheep left out in the cold too long and Napoleon's obstinate vanity on the eve of the battle of Waterloo. The listener is given the opportunity to tune out. Tuck has discovered more pedestrian ways to present God's lofty truths, and he utilizes them to make the gospel more accessible to the common person.

- Observe Tuck's skillful handling of the question of the Bible's credibility (debates over inerrancy, historicity, etc.). To his credit, he doesn't sidestep the issue. Instead, he gracefully moves his audience from wondering about "the facts" of the story to contemplating "the truth" within the story. He says just enough not to trip us up. Had it been handled differently, his listeners might have walked away from the sermon debating the preacher's personal stance on questions regarding the literalness of the Bible. If that had happened, the message of the text might never have been heard. The lesson? Be careful not to let your own personal biases or opinions become barriers to the gospel.

- Try drawing up a brief outline of this sermon. It's so well crafted that it serves as a model for organizing a message. All the essential pieces are in place: introduction, a four-point body with appropriate illustrations, summary, and conclusion. It's wonderfully basic. Let's face it: homiletics isn't rocket science. All it takes is a simple plan and an engaging style of presentation. Tuck's sermon hits the mark because he never diverges from this simple design.

Richard A. Davis

Rich Young Ruler Meets Poor Young Servant

LUKE 18:18–30

REV. DR. DAVID L. WILLIAMSON
FIRST PRESBYTERIAN CHURCH OF HOLLYWOOD
HOLLYWOOD, CALIFORNIA

REV. DR. DAVID L. WILLIAMSON

RICH YOUNG RULER MEETS POOR YOUNG SERVANT

LUKE 18:18–30, NRSV

L et us place ourselves in this scene. Come up close to see and hear what is happening. Notice this attractive, successful, young man who comes to Jesus and asks an important question. Matthew tells us that he was young, all of the Gospel writers say that he was rich, and Luke tells us that he was a ruler. The rich young ruler, the city's prominent yuppie.

For those of you who read this morning's paper, we might refer to this young man as "a rich urban biker"! Apparently, the annual Harley-Davidson roundup in Sturgis, South Dakota, is attracting more and more doctors, lawyers and occasionally a few pastors. These rich urban bikers (RUBs) are making their pilgrimage to Sturgis on their Harley-Davidsons.

Perhaps this prominent young man, this rich young ruler, is curious or anxious or both. At any rate, he took a face-to-face encounter with Jesus as an opportunity to ask a crucial question. It is a question that each of us has asked or wondered about: "What must I do to deserve or have eternal life?" The young man prefaces his question with a compliment, addressing Jesus as "Good Teacher." Jesus immediately responds by reacting to the adjective "good," in a sense questioning the man's motive. Is it flattery, is he patronizing, is this a set-up, or does he really believe that Jesus is divine? "No one is good but God," Jesus says. The adjective is reserved for God.

Jesus goes on to tell the rich young ruler what he already knows. If you want eternal life, keep the commandments, and he lists five of the Ten Commandments as a kind of checklist. Without blinking an eye, without hesitation, our friend, everybody's hero, this young rich CEO says, "I've done all of that, I've obeyed each of them. I have lived a good moral life as long as I can remember." There is no dirt whatsoever in his background. Nothing. (He has not only not inhaled, but he doesn't even know what drugs smell like!) He kept himself clean and did it right all the way. Certainly if anybody deserves eternal life, it is this person.

In fact, in Jesus' day great wealth was understood as the evidence of God's blessing, his endorsement on a person's good and righteous life. If this young man kept the commandments, God would bless him with prosperity. But listen carefully; there is a surprise in this passage. Jesus responded in a way that this impressive young man did not expect, nor did his bystanders, nor the disciples who listened in, nor would we if we were hearing this conversation for the very first time. Jesus is drawn to this attractive young man. The rich young ruler is impressive. Mark says that Jesus looked him hard in the eye and "loved him" (Mark 10:21). But rather than congratulate and affirm him, Jesus tells him there is still one thing lacking. What? How could there be? He has done it all! Done it well! What could be left? If wealth is a sure sign of God's blessing, what is the problem? "Go and sell all that you have and give it to the poor," Jesus told him. "Let go of what you are clutching, give it away. Let go, let God have his way with you. Then you will have your reward. And come, follow me. Come, take up your cross and follow me."

Jaws dropped, eyes opened wide. All his hearers were shocked. Eugene Peterson in *The Message* paraphrases this verse: "This was the last thing the official expected to hear. He became terribly sad. His strategy for salvation was critically ineffective and it had failed. He did the right things, but he missed the point. He missed the humble, simple faith of a child" (Luke 18:28, Message).

Unwilling to let go and let God, the young leader walks away, deeply hurt, utterly hopeless, still clinging tightly to a lot of things, holding on to his old ways, his familiar strategy, holding on to his wealth and good works.

Jesus, too, is sad and disappointed. He uses the occasion to teach a lesson about the subtle dangers of wealth, the tremendous barriers it can build to living a kingdom life. "How difficult it is," Jesus says, "for people who have it all to enter God's kingdom."

The disciples are surprised and perplexed. Their assumptions have been challenged, their perspective has been changed. "Who has any chance at all of making it?" they ask. If this materially blessed young man has missed out, it must be impossible for ordinary humans. Who then can make it into the kingdom? "No chance of making it at all, if you think it is up to you," Jesus responds. "Every chance in the world if you expect God to do it."

The scene closes with good old Peter ready for a confrontation, pressing the issue. Speaking for all the disciples, he says, "Then what about us? We left everything for you—where is our reward?"

"Yes, and you won't regret it," Jesus replies. "You will get back what you left behind and gave away, many times over, and a huge major plus—eternal life."

But let's take a closer look at our up-and-coming star, this baby-buster CEO, this congressman, this prodigious executive producer. He is the person many of us aspire to be. He has it all—wealth, good looks, intelligence, position, power, good name, high profile, comfort, security, accomplishment. And, to top it all off, he's a nice guy, a truly nice guy. Highly religious, he has kept the commandments from his youth. He is the kind of person that at times we resent, but if we are honest with ourselves, we would love to change places with him in a minute.

Yet, something is missing. He is not fully satisfied with his life. He's not fully convinced that things are okay. And so he comes to Jesus, boldly, in the middle of the day with others around, and asks the ultimate question. Perhaps, in spite of his good works, his excellence in performing God's law, there is an emptiness in meaning, there is lack of a satisfying, fulfilling relationship. Perhaps he is anxious regarding his own righteousness and desperately wants reassurance. Matthew tells us that he wished to be perfect (Matt. 19:21). Maybe in his pride or his narcissistic focus he wanted some public affirmation. Whatever the reason, his question reveals a deep hidden insecurity.

Fulfillment of the law, obedience to the commandments, accumulation of wealth—none of these was enough to convince him that he had eternal life. There was a God-shaped vacuum in his life, a longing in his heart. Unfortunately he couldn't let go and let God. He couldn't release his grip on his wealth, let go his trust in financial security to trust the eternal security that comes from abandoned commitment to a relationship with Jesus. In the end, the real god for this man, this young superstar, was financial security, a comfortable lifestyle, economic control, or a trust in his own righteousness.

What is it that makes it so hard for the rich to receive and to enjoy God's grace? Perhaps his wealth blinded this young man and kept him from recognizing his deep-seated needs and anesthetized his hungry heart. Perhaps it was hard for him to shift from self-sufficiency to God-dependency, from achievement to relationship.

So the young man leaves, sad. He missed the parable of the pearl of great price where God invites people to sell everything that they have to go and purchase this greatest treasure, the kingdom of God. In so doing, he missed the kingdom by an inch, so close yet so far. The closing scene is really a pathetic one. He becomes terribly sad, holding on tight to a lot of things and not about to let them go: his wallet, his portfolio, his financial empire, his many possessions, his self-accomplished righteousness. The rich young ruler is a good guy who misses the kingdom of God.

There is a lesson for us in this encounter. We are there in this encounter. We are there in this encounter. Like the rich young ruler, we too wonder what it will take to deserve eternal life. We don't have it all, and often we feel that something is missing in our lives. We are not fully satisfied. Perhaps we are anxious about our own righteousness, the sufficiency of our own devotion. Even if we have a theology of grace and strongly affirm salvation by faith and faith alone, deep down we may be counting on our own goodness, on our keeping the commandments to put us in an acceptable standing with God. So, we come to God looking for reassurance. Or perhaps we too want Jesus to publicly honor us for a job well done: "Fantastic! Look, everyone, this person is a spiritual star!" But is it possible to keep all of the commandments and miss the kingdom of God?

Let me ask you that again: Is it possible to keep all of the commandments and miss the kingdom of God?

We too have strategies for our salvation: fame, fortune, or faith, or a combination. We too have security blankets that we hang on to. Like the Linus character from the Charlie Brown cartoon, we clutch to certain things with a tight fist unwilling to let go and let God. What do you clutch? Perhaps an addiction or perhaps it's a hope and a dream that you have, a dream for a career or success, a dream for a relationship that finally puts all of the pieces together. Perhaps you are clutching a reputation, or your family, your religion, your wealth, your goodness. The rich young ruler kept tight hold on his perfection in keeping the law, and he lost everything. The Apostle Paul, on the other hand, another good leader who had kept the law faithfully, counted all his self-achievements and his righteousness as rubbish, trash; he gained everything.

Jesus is calling the rich young ruler—and each one of us—to a radical commitment to him, a relationship of trust, fellowship and partnership. Christ and Christ alone. "Nothing in my hand I bring, / Simply to Thy cross I cling," we sing. Jesus says in effect, let go of everything that gets in the way and let God's grace embrace you—grace alone!

Yes, there is a word for us in this story about the seductiveness of wealth. But there's also a word about the seductiveness of our own self-righteousness, about trying to achieve salvation by ourselves, about cherishing our own efforts rather than giving ourselves away to Christ. Keeping the commandments is not evil; the evil is trusting in our own success.

I see in myself a rich young ruler "wanna-be," in terms of wealth and lifestyle, all the while maintaining a proper piety. I've never been rich. I grew up in a middle-class home but always longed for wealth, power and fame. I am no longer young and am definitely not rich—yet I still hope that someday I will win the lottery, or the Publishers Clearing House Sweepstakes. My subtle identification with the rich and powerful is made clear to me whenever I look at my shirt. When I was preparing this sermon, I noticed the little emblem on my shirt—a polo player. Now I have never been a polo player, and I never want to be a polo player. But I would love to have the money that would let me be a polo player. We all have our dreams about what it might be like if someday we suddenly became rich. Why, we would tithe ten percent for sure! Since we'd honor God in return, we don't understand why God hasn't done that for us!

Jesus tells us to seek first God's kingdom and his righteousness—*his righteousness*—"and all these things will be given to you as well" (Matt. 6:33, NRSV).

Yet, dear friends, I want us to focus not so much on this interesting, rich young ruler, nor on the lesson about wealth and our attempts at self-righteousness. Rather I want us to take a closer look at the other young man in this encounter. He is a poor man, but he carries the truth, love and authority of God about him. He is the Son of Man, the Savior of the world, the "good teacher" who gave his life as a servant on the cross.

Notice, first, that this Jesus has an incredible interest in and care for people. He is naturally attracted to this rich young ruler. He looks at him with love in his eyes. He is spontaneously attracted to each one of us, and looks on us with love in his eyes. His emotional and relational life is active. He is responsive to little children, to his disciples, to the rich young ruler, to all of us. He knows us. He knows the heart and mind of each of us.

Second, observe how Jesus responds and relates to this young man— with directness, integrity and simplicity. "Why do you call me good?" he asks. "You know the commandments…how hard it is." Jesus is not impressed with wealth or position or external piety. He welcomes little children and sinners whose hearts are right.

Third, note Jesus' commitment to the poor. Throughout the Gospels we continually see Jesus' response to the needy, how he urges compassion on the poor. Wealth insulates from the poor, but Jesus removes that insulation. He enables us to see, to feel, to know and to care as he cares.

Further, Jesus is the divine Son of God. "No one is good, but God alone." In a sense Jesus accepts that label as belonging properly to him. Yet as the Son of God, he "did not cling to his prerogatives as God's equal," Paul says in Philippians (2:6, Phillips), "but emptied himself, taking the form of a servant," and as a servant, he "became obedient unto death" (Phil. 2:7–8, RSV). Paul also writes about Jesus, "that though he was rich, yet for your sake he became poor, so that by his poverty you might become rich" (2 Cor. 8:9, RSV). The eternal Son of God is a poor, young servant. But listen to the question Jesus asks: "For who is greater, the one who is at the table or the one who serves? Is it not the one at the table? But I am among you as one who serves" (Luke 22:27, NRSV).

You see, Jesus turns the world upside down. The rich, eternal Son of God becomes the poor young servant who encounters this rich young ruler and calls him to become poor so that through Christ he might be truly rich. Jesus welcomes sinners and lets a very good man walk away.

Dear friends, I want you to focus this morning on Jesus, a lover of people, who knows our hearts. I want you to come and fall in love with Jesus, the servant, the Son of God, who is the champion of the poor, who turns the world upside down so that it can be right side up!

Luke 18 records the meeting of two men face to face. They are of comparable age: a rich young ruler and a poor young servant. They meet and that encounter makes all the difference in the world to the rich young ruler. As far as we know, it did not have a happy ending. But this first-century meeting points to another meeting, another life-changing encounter with Jesus, one at the end of the twentieth century. It is our story, our encounter, our face-to-face meeting with Jesus. How will our story end? Sadly? With disappointment? Will you walk away clutching your wealth, your spiritual accomplishments, your false securities, whatever it is that gets in the way? Or will it end on a continually joyous note, as we choose to let go and go with Jesus. The poor young servant said to the rich young ruler, "There is still one thing lacking. Sell all that you own." Will you choose to hold nothing back? Seek Jesus first, receive the One who comes to serve you, the poor young servant. Then you can say, "I have decided to follow Jesus, / No turning back, no turning back."

COMMENT

Sermons on narratives from the life of Jesus, such as this one by David Williamson, often invite the listener to identify with a central figure in the story. However, given the democratic society in North America, the story of the rich young ruler appears remote enough from the current social paradigms to allow most of us to remain outside the place of the rich young ruler. We assign to ourselves a lower position on the socio-economic ladder than such an aristocratic character. We consider ourselves neither rich, nor in any sense of old world royalty, ruler of anything. We find it fairly easy to keep ourselves at a safe distance from this story that, in an affluent society such as ours, is potentially highly subversive of the privileged place many of us occupy in the global economy.

Yet the unique approach of Williamson's sermon, which incorporates a charmingly sophisticated sociological and psychological interpretation of a main character, draws us in so that we come to identify with the rich young ruler's outlook. As Williamson explores this man's inner values, we find the ruler to be very much like us. We recognize our faces in the mirror of the rich young ruler for, like him, we value this world's definitions of success. A creative pastoral approach to this sermon allows us to admit that as we stand before Jesus, we are like this rich ruler who could not release his hold on possessions—or the hold his possessions had on him—to follow Jesus.

PROBLEM

Williamson's sermon addresses our natural human tendency to withhold our whole selves from God. We are unable to yield all of ourselves to God, including position, power, and material possessions; therefore, God's fullness does not permeate the whole of our lives and we lack the commitment to which Jesus calls us. We easily see the problem in others, but we find it difficult to admit it in ourselves.

This sermon begins with the rich young ruler as someone "other" than ourselves. Williamson explores the probable motives from which the ruler acts, especially the tendency to hold on to the world's power, position, and wealth. He then highlights these values within our own capitalistic society, a society which values "financial empires" much like the first-century Roman and Jewish world did.

Even though the rich young ruler possesses all the status of title, wealth and righteous behavior, he is obviously not content. The ruler recognizes that Jesus can fulfill his own inconsolable longing which his possessions and position are unable to satisfy. The sermon explores ways the ruler has leaned on his good works and moral behaviors to be saved. These acts have apparently defined him in life. But Jesus' response dismisses the man's moral righteousness and good works; they are of no account to God's kingdom. He needs to let go of them and follow, Jesus says.

Williamson then invites us to share the feelings of envy which bystanders in the scene may have had. He voices our own questions: "One thing lacking? What? How could this be? He has done it all! What is the problem?" We are led to become bystanders who admire this young man's achievements, money and power.

By developing this stream of inner dialogue, Williamson leads us to confess that we are actually quite like the rich young ruler. Yet, at the same time, we do not want to walk away from Jesus and so disappoint ourselves. Thus, the sermon serves as a therapeutic tool that leads us through a process of self-discovery and self-recognition. Probing the inner life and motives of the young ruler, we realize that we, too, find success and wealth to be powerful motives for much that we say and do. By examining the ruler's attitudes and his dependence upon his possessions, the problem of not being able to trust God entirely becomes our issue. Williamson frees us to admit that we too do not yield all to Jesus.

TEXT

By the use of contemporary images and idioms, Williamson updates the Lukan narrative, making it fresh and relevant to today's hearers. Within the opening lines, Williamson forges our connections to the young ruler by calling him "the city's prominent yuppie." We see him holding positions unknown to the first-century: "baby-buster CEO, up-and-coming star, congressman, executive producer." He could even be, Williamson suggests, a "rich urban biker" in Sturgis, South Dakota, at the bike rally with other urban professionals, doctors, lawyers, and even a few pastors! The scene portrays the young ruler as one of us. Williamson humbly admits that he himself is not immune to the comparison; by including himself, the preacher stands "with" us.

Williamson quotes today's language from Eugene Peterson's paraphrase of the Bible, *The Message*. "People who have it all" and "building a financial empire" reflect our own idioms, a technique which updates the New Testament scene for our day. The barrage of contemporary phrases connects the passage to our own experience.

Through the exploration of the rich young ruler's possible motives and values, the sermon helps us become aware of some of our own motivations in life. As we consider the story, Williamson points out that the ruler might be trying to ingratiate himself to Jesus. For instance, addressing Jesus as "Good Teacher" may be flattery rather than straightforward regard, an approach that may be patronizing Jesus. We begin to understand why the ruler could not do what Jesus asks of him.

In this sermon the preacher is a psychologist at work, helping us uncover what is hidden in the text—the values this man holds. At the same time, we examine what is often hidden to us—our assumptions that we really are counting on our own goodness in order to make ourselves acceptable to God, just as the rich young ruler did. We explore with the preacher what may have caused the young ruler's "deep hidden insecurity," and we come to recognize some of our own insecurities and anxieties.

PROCLAMATION

God's grace comes to us as we step into the shoes of those disciples standing by Jesus. Williamson lets us know their emotional reactions to Jesus' reply to the young ruler by describing their faces: "jaws dropped, eyes opened wide." By highlighting their faces, Williamson captures the emotional impact of Jesus' words. These facial expressions clearly demonstrate that "all his hearers were shocked." We experience their surprise and shock.

Williamson does not leave us standing on the sidelines. He deals with the disciples and Peter, who are distraught by Jesus' reply. The sermon restates the questions in their minds and in ours: "Who then can make it into the kingdom?" The grace and freedom which Christ offers is stated in a casual manner: "'No chance of making it at all, if you think it is up to you,' Jesus responds. 'Every chance in the world if you expect God to do it.'" Such paraphrasing effectively captures the straightforward style of Jesus.

Williamson has helped us identify with those who count on doing well in this life to get to the next one. He repeats a central question to emphasize importance; repetition also gives us time to consider it: "Is it possible to keep all the commandments and miss the kingdom of God?" The sermon impresses upon us the irony that, like the young ruler, we may be working to "earn" salvation, not accepting the free grace of God.

The preacher admits that the call to let go of the things we "clutch with a tight fist" is a radical one. "What do you clutch?" opens us to explore our own grasping after our hopes and dreams in this life. Williamson confesses that the polo emblem on his own shirt hints at a desire for wealth and affluence. Again, Williamson is not standing above us, but "with" us. Yielding all to God is difficult even for him. We are freed to admit the problem too.

Williamson then turns to examine the second man, the "other" person who is the central figure in the story. The four observations about Jesus and his relational characteristics appeal to our social consciousness. Numbered observations help the listener. Jesus is seen as 1) a person who cares deeply about people; 2) a man of integrity and directness; 3) a man with compassion for the poor; and 4) the divine Son of God who came to us as a lowly servant. We are given a view of Jesus as a "lover of people, who knows our hearts." We hear the grace proclaimed through this One who meets us and loves us as we are.

RESPONSE

Williamson notes that Jesus let "a very good man walk away." Immediately we are struck, for we might be that "very good man" ourselves. We must now choose to walk away from or toward Jesus. Williamson brings us face to face with Jesus. We can walk away, or follow him with a new understanding of the temptations of this world which lure us away from God. We have been brought to the place where we have the freedom to yield all to God and to depend upon God's grace for everything.

The conclusion calls us to account: "How will our story end? Sadly? With disappointment? Will you walk away clutching your wealth, your spiritual accomplishments, your false securities, whatever it is that gets in the way? Or will it end on a continually joyous note?" Williamson urges us to hold nothing back from God. The young ruler's fate need not be ours. The sermon calls us, as Jesus still does, to "Go, sell your possessions and follow me." We have a real encounter, a meeting with Jesus and, like the young ruler, we must choose. Words of the hymn conclude the sermon with their emotional impact: "No turning back, no turning back."

Throughout this sermon, Williamson's style, and especially his use of contemporary expressions for the young ruler, identify him as a person in a powerful social and economic position today. The sermon leads us through a process to recognize our own "tight clutch" on things and to explore our own anxieties and "inconsolable longing." In a nonthreatening way, the sermon shows us who we are—people who do not easily give our whole selves to God. Like the young ruler, we are often tentative in our faith and weak in our commitment to God. The sermon provides a process of self-discovery. We can quit measuring our value and worth by traditional standards of success, and turn to follow Jesus whose way is one of free grace, a grace we do not earn, a grace God generously offers us.

SUGGESTIONS

- This sermon text can be useful for stewardship. Richard Foster's book, *Sex, Money and Power: The Challenge of the Disciplined Life* (San

Francisco: Harper & Row, 1985) discusses the possessions and power which we value, but which can diminish our spiritual growth. Foster notes our reluctance to yield all to God. Luther said it well: "There are three conversions necessary: conversion of the heart, mind, and the purse" (p. 19). The most difficult, Foster notes, is often the purse.

- Consider developing a sermon about people's attempts to simplify as a way to follow God by actually selling their possessions. Is this the way to eternal life? Vernhard Eller, in *the simple life* (Grand Rapids: Wm. B. Eerdmans, 1973), reviews the rich young ruler's encounter with Jesus in a fascinating discussion on the limiting of one's possessions to make life simple. He notes that the point of Jesus' suggestion to the rich ruler is to set his mind on the kingdom of God before everything else. Ultimately, the defining factor of life is one's relationship to God.

- To make relevant a first-century scene, try some imaginative and playful word-association to develop contemporary images. For example, a word-association exercise to consider who today's "rich and powerful" are, could have given Williamson the images he used to characterize the ruler in today's terms. He supplies images of an urban biker, a CEO, a yuppie, or an executive producer. Transferring such labels to a first-century character brings the text alive for today.

Dixie Brachlow

THE LONG WAY HOME

MATTHEW 2:13–21

REV. DR. GARY A. FURR
VESTAVIA HILLS BAPTIST CHURCH
BIRMINGHAM, ALABAMA

REV. DR. GARY A. FURR

THE LONG WAY HOME

MATTHEW 2:13–21, NRSV

C hristmas is about a lot of things, but it is at least about getting back home. We have all those songs about it: "I'll be home for Christmas, if only in my dreams"—surely a good song for a young man landing in the quagmires of Bosnia this week.

And how about that classic, "Over the river and through the woods"? My father used to sing it whenever we went home to North Carolina—for Christmas or in June. He didn't realize how early we children became inoculated against corniness. It pained us to listen to this grown man singing this ridiculous song. It was embarrassing.

Over the river and through the woods,
To grandmother's house we go;
The horse knows the way to follow the sleigh
Ba-bumm, bumm-bumm-bumm-ba-bumm, hey!

And he would turn around and grin, as though to involve us in the song. The car would swerve, we would scream, and he would move on to the next verse.

My father sang every song that way, because he never knew all the words to a verse.

Dashing through the snow
In a one horse open sleigh,
O'er the hills we go
Laughing all the way;
Ba-bumm, bumm-bumm-bumm-bumm ba-bumm.

In fact, the only one he got the words right to was "The Little Drummer Boy." You know, that part that goes, "A rumpabumm-bumm"!

As a kid I was always embarrassed about this "over the river and through the woods" thing. Really! To be stuffed into a back seat with two brothers whose violations against my comfort would today get them sent to juvenile court! Gifts under the seat, under my feet, a cookie tin up in the back window that would come down and clunk me on the head when Dad stopped suddenly. "Sorry," he would say, then go back to singing. "I'll have a blue Christmas without you, ba-bumm-bumm-bumm-bumm, ba-bumm-bumm."

No sleigh, no snow, no horse, no river, no woods. Just a '63 Impala and five hundred miles, that's all. Not what I had in mind—white Christmases and chestnuts and Frosty the Snowman. It's tough when you're eight and life is already disappointing!

It's not like it won't happen soon enough. Before you know it, the innocence of childhood is stripped away and life gets serious, even harsh.

Which brings us to this first trip of the holy family. Of all the dreams of Christmas, this one is the strangest even if it makes common sense. Joseph goes to bed with his conversations with the Wise Men on his mind. What should he do? And in the night, God speaks through his imagination in the form of an angel. "Get up and flee to Egypt. Herod is going to try to kill your child."

To Egypt? Why such a long way? But lately I have begun to think, "Why not? The long journey is so much more typical of the spiritual life." It's the far country, the place outside the gate, the burning bush in the desert we must turn aside to see, the dream in the night, the sojourn out of the way, that leads us safely home.

Matthew sends Mary and Joseph a long way to make a point: Jesus is the new Moses. "Out of Egypt I have called my son," the Scriptures say (v. 15; Hosea 11:1). And, of course, to get away from Herod.

But something else is involved here, I think. Getting where we want to go, really want to go, often involves going the long way home. Because it is in the journey that we are given the chance to deal with our brokenness, to discover what is missing in our lives, to confront our unanswered questions. I recently came across this wonderful quote by a writer named Harriett Richie: "In the places where we are broken, in the dark holes where something is missing, in the silence of unanswered questions, the wondrous gift is given."[1]

A JOURNEY INTO BROKENNESS

The gift is given, "in places where we are broken," Richie says. We tend to equate brokenness with shabbiness. We toss our spare change into a pot for the entire lot of people who stand on the street corners and mumble to themselves, whom we view from inside our locked cars with their cardboard signs and speculate whether they're scamming us or not. We have words for them like "homeless," "unemployed," "marginalized," and a thousand other subtle ways of saying, "Not like us."

Not so. The journey into wholeness leads us first to our own brokenness, to an inner Egypt. We can drive a Lexus and be the toast of the town but find our souls wandering in the desert wilderness.

Recently, a friend told me of a conversation with Father Keating, a famous writer on prayer. The spiritual journey is into the unknown, Father Keating said. We have to get rid of the need for certitude. When he was asked about what was going on after a person has been doing centering prayer for three or four years, he said that at that point the person is vulnerable to the unconscious and the person's motivations are challenged more and more. The journey into our brokenness is a journey deep into our own being and outward into the unknown, where God is.

To find God we must be willing to undertake the journey to Egypt, into our own questionable motives and hidden wounds. It means leaving behind the familiar and going where only God's love can feed us. Then we learn truly what Jesus means when he tells us, "Blessed are the poor in spirit." For we all are.

A DIFFICULT JOURNEY

The journey is about "the dark holes where something is missing." We don't like to think that anything is missing. We bring one definition of perfection to life while the actual process of life is something else altogether. Most of us wish that life could be without trouble and trial. But as John Sanford has said, we operate under a false view of a perfection that can be reached without darkness, without trouble and without sin and suffering.[2]

Another view of perfection is that it is wholeness. This means the process of discovering the full life God always intended for us to have. It means finding our true selves. "In the long run," Sanford writes, "the search for our true self is a fascinating journey with rich treasures and great rewards. But it is a painful enterprise and one that never ends."[3]

There are stories in early Christian lore about the journey to Egypt. They idealize and try to smooth out the difficulty of the journey. They tell of palm trees that miraculously bent down to feed the holy family, lions and leopards that wagged their tails in worship. One story even tells that in one of the towns they passed through, all the idols in the local temple fell to the ground. It's human to idealize.

But Scripture doesn't. The flight to Egypt is also a reminder, an anticipation, of the costly and painful price of wholeness for us all. If Jesus is the new Moses, come to deliver us into a new kingdom, it is by entering into Egypt where all of us are and bringing us out by a dangerous and difficult way.

It is tempting to sit and wait for life to come to us, to forsake the journey and simply subsist. But doing that, we stop living life and squander it. Life will not come to us on our terms. Joseph's dream was a call to enter the full danger of the spiritual journey.

A JOURNEY WITHOUT ANSWERS

God's wondrous gift is given, says Harriett Richie, "in the silence of unanswered questions." Joseph and Mary knew some of the reasons for their journey. Their preeminent motivation for leaving was to escape the possibility that Herod would come after Jesus. But here we meet the question of suffering head-on. Innocent baby boys are killed for nothing more than political insecurity. The point is not how many died, but why God, who could intervene to save Jesus, did not intervene to save these twenty or thirty little innocent babies.

Never is the idea of life's purpose more at risk than in the face of innocent and undeserved suffering. Many come to Christmas every year with some unbearable sorrow that seems to render life senseless. "Why did this happen?" they ask. And there is no answer.

Matthew makes a subtle grammatical point in the text that we cannot see in the English translation. There are three significant quotations from the Old Testament in Matthew's birth story, one about the birth to a virgin in Bethlehem (2:6), this quotation about the flight to Egypt (2:15), and the third about returning to Nazareth (2:23). All are to show that Jesus' life was a fulfillment of the Old Testament.

But in this one, Matthew leaves out the purpose word, "in order that." He softens his quotation to make the point that God is not the author of evil, even though God knows that this will be Herod's response.

Yet even this does not eliminate the problem. Evil is not God's will, but its occurrence is still God's dark mystery. Jesus did not escape death at the hands of tyranny so much as postpone it. The death of the innocents was not a tragedy Jesus avoided but a tragedy that anticipated the darkest tragedy of all: the saving tragedy of Jesus' cross.

Matthew affirms that God is not the author of evil. But he does assert that God is evil's editor. God has the final word. God reframes, restates and corrects evil until it fits within God's deeper purposes. That is what we want to know in our tragedies and sorrows—that they are not in the end merely empty and sad coincidences, random and broken bits of unfortunate pain.

Did you read recently about Billy Graham's choice of his successor in his organization? It will be his son, Franklin. A few years ago, Franklin could only have been elected "Least Likely to Follow in His Father's Footsteps." By his own admission, Franklin's rebellious ways eliminated him from contention for the place. His three main achievements during college were chain-smoking, whiskey drinking and expulsion. But at twenty-two he was converted to the Christian faith. And he has continued to grow and mature. Said a friend, "[Billy Graham] has been waiting for Franklin to mature, but he's had this in mind for fifteen years."[4]

I like that. And God is like that. God's way is to outwait evil.

We hear from friends all over the United States during the Christmas season. Sometimes in their Christmas letters there are hints of a long journey: a death, an entry into a nursing home, an illness that has changed the course of life forever, a child's accomplishment.

This week we received a card from a friend who has given marriage a second try after a long and disappointing first marriage that ended in divorce. The card simply read, "I will call soon to tell you about things. I am so happy."

There is a long way into and out of Egypt that leads us home. It is not the way we would necessarily choose, given our perfectionist ideals and our reluctance to experience pain as a price for joy. But that way is there.

But it is not only in the struggle with evil and tragedy that our questions come. They come as we ask, "Does my life add up to anything at all? What does my life mean?"

Several years ago I met a man who was in his eighties and still lived in the house where he had been born. Bright in mind, keen with opinions, interested in the larger world he saw on television, his imagination longed to see and know more. But now age prevented that possibility. And one day I was summoned for his funeral. He had died in the same place where he had been born and lived.

Sometimes life seems never to go anywhere. We are stuck. We wish we could go even to Egypt—somewhere! But even if we never physically leave home, there is still a journey we can and must make. "In the endless, sometimes meaningless daily grinds, in the comings and goings of our lives," says Harriett Richie, "our souls are often far from home whether we know it or not."[5] The spiritual journey does not depend upon geography for its drama.

It may seem to us sometimes that our lives are disconnected, or insignificant, or full of pain, with no real or obvious meaning. We see no thread running through our lives, no words to make sense of them. We just mutter and hum something that sounds like the right words, hoping we are close. The danger in mumbling is that we can lose hope that there really are words for me, for my life.

Frederick Buechner once wrote, "If God speaks to us at all in this world, if God speaks anywhere, it is into our personal lives that [God] speaks."[6] It is not that some people get a real song and you just get a sad and tragic little ditty whose words were never completed. Every life is a song penned by an Author who knows every word. Every baby boy in Bethlehem is a song whose words God knows. Every hungry refugee in Bosnia and Mogadishu is a song. Every forgotten prisoner in a faraway tyranny is a song.

But so is every dozing old man in a nursing home hallway. And every unpopular child at the school. And every suburban housewife who drives to carpool with a world of trouble on her mind that no one knows. And every one of us who lives to keep up appearances in this success-worshiping society of ours. There may be no words in the local songs for failure and darkness and suffering. This may cause us to fear that there are no words at all.

But you are a song with all the words. Words that God knows. Start singing it, keep singing it, this holy song that is yours, until one day when you can go look in the old piano bench, and there, under the old Broadman hymnal or the Reader's Digest's *One Hundred Favorite Songs Americans Sing*, you will find your song. And the words will come back to you again. And you will be home.

Notes

1. Harriett Richie, "He'd come here," *The Christian Century* 112 (December 13, 1995), p.1206.
2. John Sanford, *The Kingdom Within: The Inner Meaning of Jesus' Sayings* (San Francisco: Harper & Row, 1987), p. 70.
3. Ibid, p. 71.
4. John W. Kennedy, "The Son Also Rises," *Christianity Today* (December 11, 1995), p. 59.
5. Richie, p. 1206.
6. Frederick Buechner, *The Sacred Journey* (San Francisco: Harper & Row Publishers, 1982), p. 1.

COMMENT

One of the perennial struggles in preaching is how to travel from the ancient world of the Bible to the modern world of our listeners. Another challenge is casting a fresh and creative spin on the well-known stories of our faith. In his sermon, "The Long Way Home," Gary Furr effectively meets both of these challenges. Furr creatively bridges the "then" of Joseph, Mary and Jesus' flight to Egypt to the "now" needs of our day.

Through the continuous interplay between the text and proclamation, Furr weaves together a powerful declaration on one of the major themes of human existence: the purpose and direction of life.

During the Christmas season, one comes to church assuming to hear the story of Jesus. But Furr has captured something most overlook during Advent/Christmas. Christmas is fundamentally about God and his character. Christmas is the celebration of God's salvation plan. How appropriate that in this sermon Furr addresses the real issue of Christmas: life's imperfection and God's answer to it.

OPENING

A good introduction creates interest in the speaker and message, orients the listener to the biblical context, and gives direction on how to listen. While it is easy to create an interesting introduction, it is much more difficult to make the introduction truly apply to the biblical sermon.

In a fun and lighthearted manner Furr fulfills the requirements for an effective introduction. It is brief and to the point. His sentences are simple. His words are well-chosen. The listener is immediately drawn into the story by Furr's vivid word picture and lyrics to several famous Christmas tunes. We see Dad, Mom, the kids and the Christmas presents packed into the '63 Impala speeding along the highway. The listener cannot help but smile, even chuckle, at Furr's childhood memories. And then, Furr sneaks in his point.

Furr directs the listener to an unexpected place: life's disappointments.

He says, "It's tough when you're eight and life is already disappointing." We can readily identify. We all have dreams of what life should be like; unfortunately, life rarely turns out as we envisioned.

Furr tackles a tough and all-too-timely topic during the Christmas season, when depression increases, suicide attempts rise, and the workloads of pastors and therapists dramatically increase. For many, Christmas is a painful, depressing time. Furr's sermon is both timeless and timely in communicating the unchanging word of God to an ever-changing, broken world.

TEXT & PROCLAMATION

This sermon is effective because it is creative in composition, relevant in its application, and biblical in its message.

Creative. There is nothing more discouraging and disheartening than listening to a preacher give a lifeless recounting of a biblical narrative. Furr is a master at moving in and out of the ancient world, allowing the biblical story to speak with new meaning to our world.

The sermon is poetic, filled with imagination. It has a fresh and compelling twist, and breathes new life into the very old Christmas story. Word selection is precise and image-laden: "the first trip of the holy family," "God is evil's editor," and "every life is a song penned by an Author who knows every word." Even the quotations from Harriett Richie and Frederick Buechner give poetic quality to the sermon.

In an image-oriented society where television, movies, and videos rule, preachers must be more conscious than ever of the power of visual imagination. We must ask, "How can this abstract biblical truth become concrete, become alive, in people's minds and souls? Is there a picture to paint? A story to tell?"

Relevant. The sermon addresses a universal theme of human existence. In every culture and generation men and women have questioned and debated the meaning of life and its inherent difficulties. Why is life difficult? What is the point? Where is God in all of this? Who of us hasn't asked these kinds of questions? Who of us would not like to have the answers? It is this

COMMENT

relevancy to life that draws us into the sermon and keeps us there.

Furr refuses to settle for cheap and quick solutions. After all, he is wrestling with a topic that has intrigued and puzzled great thinkers, philosophers, writers and theologians. Furr realizes that simple, easy answers only cheapen God's truth, and leave the dilemma unresolved in most minds. Why do most sorrows and tragedies seem to make no sense at all? Furr says, "There is no answer." On suffering and evil, Furr says that although God is not the author of evil, "its occurrence is still God's dark mystery." We know two things: suffering is inescapable in this life, and God has the final word.

Furr's closing words deal with another universal question. If life is hard, if it seems disconnected from meaning, spinning directionless, then do we have any worth? Yes, says Furr, life has meaning. We have infinite meaning because our life is a unique song composed by God: "Every life is a song penned by an Author who knows every word." Furr invites us to hope, not to despair in the face of life's realities. He wants to help us rejoice in the mystery of God. More importantly, Furr is not content to allow the good news to remain in the intellectual realm. Furr seeks a change of heart—a new hope for us as listeners.

Biblical. Furr rarely quotes Scripture and refers sparingly to the gospel. The sermon is heavy in application and lighter on exegesis. Furr spends most of his time in the present with us and very little in the past with the text. Some might find this disconcerting. But remember, it is the Christmas season, when new faces come into our churches from the cold, or rarely seen faces come back for their annual Christmas-worship pilgrimage. Christmas and the Sundays before it are among the highest of the year in worship attendance. There are a lot of marginal Christians in the pews.

But more than this, a biblical sermon is not determined by the number of verses quoted or a certain language that is used. A biblical sermon is one in which the message flows out of God's truth and is applied to our lives.

Furr acknowledges that life is a difficult journey, and that our spiritual journeys can be even more difficult. He recognizes that we do not have all the answers to life's questions. But notice that his hope, our hope, rests in the knowledge that God is alive. God is working in our world and in our lives. Even when things do not make sense and God seems absent, God is ever-present and always working. The sermon invites us to embrace this truth with confidence and hope.

RESPONSE

Some of us need to be disturbed from our complacency. More importantly, *all of us* need the comfort of God's love. This sermon gives comfort and hope. "You are a song with all the words. Words that God knows. Start singing it, keep singing it...." Furr challenges us to take the high road, the long way into and out of Egypt. He invites us to live. Live with boldness and courage.

SUGGESTIONS

- Be creative. Ask yourself, "How can this abstract biblical truth become concrete, even alive, in people's minds and souls? Is there a picture to paint? An image to describe?"
- Be real. Don't give into the temptation to give simplistic answers to the problems of life and faith. Teach your congregation how to live with life's ambiguities.
- Develop new and creative angles on frequently preached biblical texts. Occasionally, use a neglected text to cast a fresh spin on yearly events like Christmas and Easter.
- Be timely with the timeless truth of Scripture. Answer the "how" question. How does the biblical idea apply to the lives of people in your congregation?
- Know your audience. How biblically literate are they? How committed to the truth are they? Preach to the problems and issues of your people.

Karen Fisher Younger

TIME:
THE BEST
OR WORST?

MATTHEW 9:10–13, 35–38; 15:1–12

REV. DR. EDWARD A. SAUCIER
GRAND AVENUE BAPTIST CHURCH
FORT SMITH, ARKANSAS

TIME: THE BEST OR WORST?

MATTHEW 9:10–13, 35–38; 15:1–12, NIV

I t was the best of times. It was the worst of times." So begins Dickens'
classic, *A Tale of Two Cities*. Which of those two statements would you
suppose is most true today in regard to the state of things in our
churches?

In terms of sheer numbers, the Christian community in America represents a formidable society—the best of times. There are fewer than eight
million Jews in America. The Mormons are topped out at about five million. Muslims, to the chagrin of Louis Farrakhan, number less than two
million. Scientologists—such stars as Tom Cruise and John Travolta—are
also less than two million. The largest group of non-Christians in America
are the atheists, at about twenty-five million. Compare those figures to the
sixty-five million adults who attend an evangelical church every week, the
thirty million American adults who attend a small group Bible study per
week, the forty million American adults who read their Bibles outside of
church services, and seventy-five million American adults who classify
themselves as evangelical Christians. Things don't look so bad, do they?

On the other hand, these figures hide the far less encouraging realities
that represent the worst of times in the church world. Church attendance
has been declining for four decades in America, and is presently at its all
time lowest level. The most dramatic period of decline has been the past

five years, 1991 to 1996, and the trend continues. Among U. S. adults in their 30s and 40s, church attendance has declined by more than fifteen million in the last five years. In spite of the positive effects of ministries such as Promise Keepers, only 28 percent of adult men attend church compared to 46 percent of women; and men are far less likely to read the Bible, pray or become involved in a church. In 1991, of those who attended church services, 53 percent of them were non-Christians; today that figure is 38 percent. This statistic doesn't reflect evangelism among those people either—it means they've simply stopped coming to our churches. Sunday school continues its slow but steady decline with less than one out of every six adults attending.

While the proportion of adults volunteering their time and services has increased for every major nonprofit organization, in the church the number of volunteers has declined significantly. The proportion of adults who donate money to churches has declined by more than 20 percent in the 90s. Among evangelical Christians only 8 percent are involved in personal evangelism. In past generations, Bible reading, church attendance and giving have increased as people moved from their midforties to their midsixties. That trend no longer holds true.

Is it the best of times or the worst of times? Does it really matter? I do know, now is the only time we have. And if we want to stop the erosion of church attendance, we haven't any time to waste.

C. B. Hogue, one of the foremost missiologists in the world, recently said, "The center for world evangelism is moving away from America. We expect the next Great Awakening to occur in Africa or perhaps South America. Without some sweeping changes it will not happen in America."[1]

According to the Barna Research Group, there are some identifiable reasons that may help explain these alarming trends.[2] You've heard some of this before but I think I need to at least mention some of it again. Please don't tune this out. All is not well. The church in America is dying! Why?

For one thing, the church is perceived as being irrelevant to the lives of Americans. The church seems to be living in the past and refusing to wake up to the present, a present in which American families are fatigued and stressed out from longer work weeks than any previous generation and family tensions, as well as financial difficulties, are therefore on the rise. Men are distancing themselves from Christian practice. Teenagers, whose tastes in music and manner of communication are far different from previous cultures, find difficulty relating to the traditional church which they perceive to be hypercritical and intolerant of those whose opinions differ. Among those who have been divorced there's a feeling that, since the position of the church is "anti-divorce," they're second-class people in the church. Additionally, among the younger "boomers" and "busters" there are two problems. First, the worship atmosphere in most churches is staid and bland. Second, the monotonous worship experience comprised of boring music and irrelevant preaching isn't something they value. It's not reaching them; therefore they have very little incentive to come.

It doesn't have to be that way. It's not supposed to be that way.

While Jesus was having dinner at Matthew's house, many tax collectors and "sinners" came and ate with him and his disciples. When the Pharisees saw this, they asked his disciples, "Why does your teacher eat with tax collectors and sinners?"

On hearing this, Jesus said, "It is not the healthy who need a doctor, but the sick. But go and learn what this means: 'I desire mercy, not sacrifice.' For I have not come to call the righteous, but sinners" (Matt. 9:10–13).

"Go and learn what that means," Jesus says. Well, what does this lack of interest in attending church really mean? I'd like to suggest to you at least four things we can learn from it through this story.

First, it means that it's possible for the church to become its own god, worshiping its own ways, refusing to make any changes, or to admit that it might be wrong. That's why the Pharisees, who were the equivalent of today's church leaders, always had trouble with Jesus. Because he wouldn't do things the way they wanted him to, he challenged their authority. He didn't have much use for their crusty customs or religious traditions, pointing out how they were ignoring God. Jesus refused to honor their stilted worship, and he wouldn't let them influence his actions. "Why do you break the command of God for the sake of your tradition?" Jesus once asked the Pharisees and teachers of the law (Matt. 15:3).

Second, the dwindling interest in the church means that Christ's redeeming work exists for those outside the church (Matt. 9:10–12). Imagine walking into Calico County for lunch today after church, being shown to your table and seeing Billy Graham sitting there, having lunch with a known drug dealer, a prostitute, a crooked politician, a local member of the police force who was on the take, and a pickpocket. There they sit, having a good time, relaxing, talking, laughing, eating those great cinnamon rolls and drinking tall, frosty mugs of ice cold root beer.

That's the kind of scandalous atmosphere that got under the skin of the Pharisees. They didn't much like the idea that someone representing God and a righteous lifestyle would spend his time, or should I say, waste his time, on those obviously nonrighteous types of people. Just exactly how far off these ancient preachers and church leaders were in their assessment of God and his way of doing things is apparent: "These sinners are why I'm here," Jesus says. Here's a message for those who are involved in God's work—it exists for the sake of the outsiders.

Third, the decline of church interest means that God loves the outsiders. That God loves sinners isn't even an arguable point from the perspective of the New Testament. "For God so loved the world that he gave his one and only Son, that whoever believes in him shall not perish but have eternal life" (John 3:16, NIV). "But God demonstrates his own love for us in this: While we were still sinners, Christ died for us" (Rom. 5:8, NIV).

Fourth, the erosion of church support means that God wants us to love the outsiders too. These Pharisees were committed "churchgoers." That didn't impress the Lord. They had worship down to a fine art. But Jesus said he wasn't so interested in that either. "Until you can look at those others with mercy and compassion, your church attendance and worship are meaningless to me" (see Matt. 9:13). It's very difficult for those who are on the outside of the church to believe God loves them when we who are on the inside of the church don't even like them.

There were people all around Jesus who weren't believers. The Jewish clerics in Jesus' day didn't care. But Jesus had compassion on the crowds

(Matt. 9:36). He prayed for them and asked his disciples to pray (v. 38). Things haven't changed so much since then. Maybe we need to pray about "the crowds" around us as well.

When Jesus took a walk in his world, he noticed it was a world filled with people who were so totally lost in relation to God that they reminded him of sheep without a shepherd (v. 36). Most of us don't have a lot of sheep, but it seems to be the general consensus of those who know about sheep that they're incapable of making it on their own. They've got to have a shepherd.

Can you see the sheep in our society today? They're still out there. They're everywhere. And they're different from us, aren't they? Society today is very different from how things were when so many of us were growing up and raising our families. But the world is still just as Christless as it's always been.

Naturally, those who are lost don't share Christian values. Things that bother us don't bother them, and what consumes their interest doesn't touch ours. So many of us grew up in churches where we learned Judeo-Christian values. We didn't question them either. It's just how it was. But not any more.

They're different, those who are out there. Do you see them? They're everywhere. You're going to run into them before you get home most likely. They're going to be driving cars, buying groceries, taking walks, eating out—just like you and me.

How do you see them? When you see them—those different people, those others, those "lost sheep," those who don't share your values, tastes and opinions—what emotion arises inside you?

Do you see them and become irritated at them? So often our first response is irritation. "They ought to know better and do better," we feel. Since they don't, it just irritates the daylights out of us.

Do you see them and get mad? I guess that's a step past irritation. Irritation can become anger and then it can tempt us to say or do things that are completely disobedient to our code of ethics and conduct as Christians.

Do you see them and condemn them? Christian people too often view non-Christian people as though they were our enemies. They aren't. That was not the case in the life of Jesus at all. The sinners loved Jesus—it was the preacher types who hated his guts and put a price on his head. It was self-righteous religious bigotry that Jesus hated and that led people to reject Jesus. And it was the love of religion that incited his farce of a trial and his execution.

Or are you "moved with compassion"? None of us—not you, not me—are honestly in tune with God and the things that are important to him unless we're able to look at the multitudes of lost others with eyes of love and be moved with compassion on their behalf.

Do you ever pray for them? I know we pray about them. Sometimes we even pray against them. But do you ever pray *for them?* Do you pray for opportunities to get to know them? Do you pray for an occasion to do a good deed on their behalf? Do you pray for a chance to lead them to Christ? I've discovered that I pray about things that matter to me. I pray when I care about someone or something.

Will you become a missionary and reach them? I really don't believe in the legitimacy of any prayer when the person praying isn't willing to be a part of the answer. I take Jesus' prayer request here as reason enough to pray—and I take that prayer as reason enough to become personally involved.

Now, let's get personal for just a few minutes. I know some aren't comfortable with change and especially with the nature of my pastoral leadership. I understand that too. I think change for the sake of change is a nuisance. However, the world at this moment is waiting on change. When the needs of the world demand change, we must move ahead for the sake of the gospel.

I'm asking of you today a huge commitment—to be as genuinely willing right here in your home city to see the lost multitudes and view them as your very own mission field as those who move to another country, learn another language, live in another culture and willingly surrender their own preference for life as it used to be for the sake of leading those lost others to Christ. I'm asking you if you're willing, for the sake of those who are without Christ all around our church, to become a missionary who's willing to give up in God's way things that are valuable to you?

I'm dreaming of a day when people can come to church here without being concerned about what they are wearing. Some people wear suits all week long and they really don't want to have to wear one on Sunday. One church growth guru says that only 40 percent of America's men ever own a sport coat and only 10 percent ever own a suit. For the sake of those outside the church, are you willing to forget about the T-shirts and shorts and just be thankful to God that they're here?

If you can concede that outsiders can dress as they do and still have your love, how much are you willing to bend in worship? Many of you grew up in a day when the church service was a more solemn affair. Times have changed haven't they? The way people like to worship is changing. I just wonder if we're willing to move into a new sphere as God works in new ways.

Every generation defines itself by its music at least to some degree. How long has it been since you bought a long-playing record? I don't know anyone, other than me, who has a working 8-track tape player and still listens to it. We still buy a lot of cassette tapes, but the in thing now is the compact disc, which sounds as good after a thousand plays as it did on the first one.

The kinds of things they manage to put music on isn't the only difference though. Music sounds different. It used to be that things were so simple. Now you can't keep up with all the gadgetry—and it's never loud enough!

It used to be just the organ in church. Then came the piano. Next some long-haired kid brought in a guitar, then another. Now we have an organ, a piano, guitars, drums, an orchestra, and a synthesizer making music for us every week.

I'm dreaming of the day when we worship in freedom, singing praises to God with as much music as we can put together. A few weeks back, when our choir sang, "I've Got Joy," I was so moved I wanted to come forward, join the church and rededicate my life. But after the service some-one said something to me that broke my heart—and I'm not over it yet. They offered sympathy, saying they hoped I didn't catch any flak or take any heat over that piece of music. *God, what's wrong with us?* I thought as I went to my office. When we fear that there's going to be trouble in church for singing joyful praise to our God, something's wrong.

Are we willing to respond to what I believe is a new movement from God? I know what I have to do in order to be obedient to what I believe is God's leading. And I'm going to do it. But we can't do it together unless you lend your blessing and support. It's your call. The future is in your hands.

Notes
1. C. B. Hogue; the quotation used in this sermon was a statement made during a person-al conversation.
2. The Barna Report, Summer 1996.

COMMENT

A prophet is one who both "tells forth" and "forth tells." In this respect, preaching in a very real sense is prophetic. The preacher is a prophet. He or she is called to "tell forth" God's will for today *and* to "forth tell" what God has in store for the world and his people in the future.

The prophetic role of the preacher can be difficult. Listeners can be both challenged and offended. The pew can become a place of discomfort and an invitation to change. Edward A. Saucier in his sermon "Time: The Best or Worst?" has fulfilled his prophetic calling as preacher with distinction.

The premise of this sermon is that all is not well in today's church and God is calling his people to redeem the sickness by being his arm of proclamation and compassion. The strength of the sermon is that it names the problem and offers a solution in which the listener can participate. Saucier challenges the listener to action. His concluding words are: "The future is in your hands." These words would be even more powerful if they read: "The future is in our hands." The church is always a community of "us," clergy and laity together.

PROBLEM

Saucier does an excellent job presenting the problem. He uses firm statistics to make his case. Initially, he begins by appealing to the listener's comfort zone. He presents the good news statistics that can lead one to believe that all is well in the church. But then he reveals the bad news. Saucier effectively presents a case that today could be the worst of times in the life of the church. The 1990s have been a period of decline in church attendance and in individual participation in church activities and programs.

After his statistical introduction, Saucier names the problem that confronts the church today: "Is it the best of times or the worst of times? Does it really matter? I do know, now is the only time we have. [We] haven't any [time] to waste." These are urgent prophetic words. They challenge any serious listener. Saucier then expands on his observation that all is not well. He points out why and offers the listener both hope and challenge.

TEXT

One of the problems in prophetic preaching is identifying and utilizing a text. The preacher is moved by a particular situation or circumstance that he or she feels compelled to address. Given the situation or circumstance, at this point the preacher often searches for an appropriate text. Once the text is identified, it is vital that the Scriptures serve as the focal point of the sermon development. The authority of the sermon should flow from the living Word of God.

In this sermon, it appears to me that Saucier began with a topic of grave importance and then went in search of an appropriate text. This method does not necessarily present inherent problems as long as the sermon holds the biblical text as its primary focus. It seems to me, however, that the flow of this sermon is directed more by the topic than the Scripture text. This raises some important questions regarding "topical" preaching. What is the proper relationship between topic and text? How can we allow the biblical text to be *primary* in a topical sermon?

Three texts were chosen: Matthew 9:10–13, 35–38, and 15:1–12. One of these three texts would have been sufficient. Saucier uses the first two. Both texts speak with relevance and direction to the situation being considered in the sermon. The third text is not brought into play significantly.

Saucier introduces the first text with a striking and intriguing point: "It doesn't have to be that way. It's not supposed to be that way." He continues by reading the first Matthew passage: "While Jesus was having dinner at Matthew's home, many tax collectors and 'sinners' came and ate with him." The Pharisees questioned Jesus' action of associating with sinners. Jesus replied: "It is not the healthy who need a doctor, but the sick. But go and learn what this means, 'I desire mercy, not sacrifice.'" The sermon moves forward with a powerful, thought-provoking transition: "Go and learn what this means" (the words of Jesus from the text). Then Saucier continues, "Well, what does this lack of interest to attend church really mean?"

Saucier has prepared the listener for this question from the first words of the sermon. The church of today is in trouble; now go and learn what it means that God desires mercy, not sacrifice. These words offer the cure for the soul sickness in today's church.

Saucier identifies four lessons from this text. The thrust of the text is that God loves the outsiders (sinners) and calls upon his people to love them (to show mercy). The point of the text is summed up by these paraphrased words of Jesus: "Until you can look at others with mercy and compassion, your church attendance and worship are meaningless to me."

PROCLAMATION

Saucier strengthens the premise and direction of the sermon by moving to the second text: Matthew 9:35–38. Here are the words of great hope. They center on the compassion of Jesus: "When Jesus saw the crowds, he had compassion for them, because they were...like sheep without a shepherd." They were lost. They were sick and in need of a physician. The problem, we might assume, is that Saucier is preaching to the choir, to those who are found and healed. Or are they? Could it just be that they are sick and lost in their exclusive and smug outlooks? And that they will not be found and cured until they reach out to outsiders with mercy and compassion?

Theologically, the real issue is that insiders in the church require a cleansing of the heart so that as redeemed and loved people of God, they will spontaneously reach out to the outsider with genuine love and understanding.

RESPONSE

A real strength of this sermon lies in the masterful way Saucier leads the listener to see the need for loving outreach to outsiders. He does this by asking a number of questions: "Do you see them? They're everywhere.... When you see them...what emotion arises inside you? Do you see them and get mad? Do you see them and condemn them? Or are you moved with compassion? Do you every pray for them? Will you become a missionary and reach them?"

Saucier uses these provoking questions to set the stage for a genuine commitment from his listeners. "I'm asking of you today a huge commitment—to be as willing right here in your home city to see the lost multitudes and view them as your very own mission field.... I'm asking you if you're willing, for the sake of those who are without Christ all around our church, to become a missionary?"

Saucier continues to narrow the world of his listeners down to the very pews in which they are sitting. His approach in this regard is moving. He continues: "I'm dreaming of a day when people can come to church here without being concerned with their clothes.... And if you can concede that the outsiders can dress as they do and still have your love, how much are you willing to bend in worship?...I'm dreaming of a day when we worship with freedom, singing praises to God with as much music as we can put together." Saucier has done a masterful job of moving from the global perspective to the specific climate of the congregation. Perhaps he could have made an even more specific statement that being inclusive and understanding of outsiders and visitors is a concrete way of showing mercy and compassion. He might have even stated that the current congregation climate of exclusiveness is more "sacrifice than showing mercy."

The sermon concludes with a final call to respond to "a new movement from God." The listener is asked to bless and support this movement, to be the arms and hands of Christ in showing compassion, hospitality, and openness to change. "It's your call. The future is in your hands."

SUGGESTIONS

- Develop your own sermon on Matthew 9:10–13. How does this text speak to your local situation and congregation?
- In Matthew 9:13 Jesus quotes Hosea 6:6, "I desire steadfast love and not sacrifice, the knowledge of God rather than burnt offerings." Develop a series of sermons or teachings on the book of Hosea focusing on the theme of the book in Hosea 6:1–6.
- Study the theme of "insiders" and "outsiders" throughout the biblical tradition. What Old Testament and New Testament texts and sto-

ries can be brought together for a thorough exploration of this biblical theme. List them and begin developing sermons or studies on these texts for presentation in your congregation.

Donald K. Adickes

BETWEEN THE GARDEN AND THE CROSS

MARK 14:32–42

VICKI COVINGTON
NOVELIST
BIRMINGHAM, ALABAMA

VICKI COVINGTON

BETWEEN THE GARDEN AND THE CROSS

MARK 14:32–42

L isten to the words of the American novelist James Agee:

On the wet grass of the back yard my father and mother have spread quilts. We all lie there, my mother, my father, my uncle, my aunt, and I too am lying there. First we were sitting up, then one of us lay down, and then we all lay down, on our stomachs, or on our sides, or on our backs, and they have kept on talking. They are not talking much, and the talk is quiet, of nothing in particular, of nothing at all in particular, of nothing at all. The stars are wide and alive, they seem each like a smile of great sweetness, and they seem very near. All my people are larger bodies than mine, quiet, with voices gentle and meaningless like the voices of sleeping birds. One is my mother who is good to me. One is my father who is good to me. By some chance, here they are, all on this earth; and who shall ever tell the sorrow of being on this earth, lying, on quilts, on the grass, in a summer evening, among the sounds of night.[1]

Tonight we are here to celebrate sorrow. The resurrection is three days away. We are not there yet. We are in the garden. I want to tell you where I am right now. I want to tell you a story.

This is a story about my mother. It began a year ago on a spring day. I had asked my mother to go with me to the Civil Rights Institute. I had already been several times because I had worked on a novel set in Birmingham, Alabama, in 1961. I wanted to take my mother because she had been a quiet revolutionary of sorts. During the 1950s she had defied the city bus ordinance. Every time we went to town we rode in the back of the bus where we were not supposed to ride. Because I had been to the institute I knew that there was a book at the end of the tour. It was a book for people who had been active in the movement. It was a place for them to sign their names. I was so happy, so proud, so eager to get to this place where Mother could sign her name and in the space provided note that she had defied the bus ordinance.

But when it came time to sign the book, something awful happened that reverberates within me to this day. My mother, whose name is Katherine, picked up the pen and turned to me and said, "I've forgotten how to make a K." I made the K for her. She picked up the pen again and said, "I've forgotten how to write my name."

I knew in that moment that something was terribly wrong. My very educated mother suddenly could not write her name. Over the next several months I noticed other things. She would stumble over words—a woman who had always been articulate. She would stop in midsentence, like someone learning a foreign language and unable to remember a word. Her hands would not do what her brain told them to do—simple things like peeling potatoes or buttoning buttons.

A month ago, after weeks of neurological tests, we received the diagnosis of Alzheimer's disease, and as I speak to you tonight I am still grappling, still trying to understand the depth of this. My father, I might add, has Parkinson's disease.

The day after I received the news of mother's illness I left on a book tour. I cried in hotel rooms throughout the Southeast. I could not even pray. I came to understand that there was no way out of this. The only way out was through it. I had spent forty-three years dodging pain, and there was nowhere to hide anymore.

This is Gethsemane. Like the disciples, I try to sleep or pretend to be asleep. I know many of you are in this same place. I know you are struggling with some kind of spiritual pain. If you are past thirty-five, you surely grieve something. If nothing else, you simply grieve for the passing of time, for the swiftness with which your children are growing and changing, for your own mortality, for the helplessness of knowing that tragedy can occur instantly and without warning. This creates a kind of low-lying, gnawing anxiety peculiar to people at midlife.

Writer Anne Lamott tells the story of a mother whose two-year-old child accidentally locked himself in a room one night. She heard him calling for her. "Mommy! Mommy!" She could not open the door from the outside, so she kept saying, "Just jiggle the doorknob, honey." But he did not understand because he was afraid and sobbing. The woman did not know what else to do and finally fell to her knees and simply slid her fingers beneath the door in the space between the bottom of the door and the floor. She told him to bend down and find her fingers. Finally he did, and they stayed like that for a long time, on the floor with him holding her fingers in the dark. He stopped crying. Once he was calm, she gently said, "Now stand up and jiggle the doorknob." He did, and after a while the door popped open.

It is the image of the fingertips under the door that the writer of this story could not forget. It was the way that we are like the two-year-old in the dark and God is the mother and we do not quite understand what she is telling us.[2] Why doesn't she just break the door down and rescue us? Why are we here anyway? Why must we be, as the writer of the Book of Hebrews says, "strangers and pilgrims on the earth"? Who are we? Why must we have to see through the glass darkly? Why can't this cup be passed? "Abba, Father, all things are possible for you. Take away this cup from me."

That was where Jesus was, and that is where we are. That is where I am every time I get in my car to go visit my mother and father. That is where you are every time you walk into the room, into the life of someone who is suffering—especially if that someone is a person you love.

When you get to this point, there is nothing to do but what good writers have always done: step back. Step back from the story so that you can remember this is a story. Life is a story. The gospel comes to us as a story. The characters of this story will suffer if they are going to be real people. It is the suffering that makes the story worth telling.

Tonight we are at the place in the story where Jesus said, "I go to prepare a place for you" (John 14:2, KJV). My friend Bill O'Brien tells me that maybe Christ did not just mean a place in heaven. Maybe he meant places on earth, too. Maybe he meant this sanctuary. Maybe he came here at five or six this afternoon to prepare this place for us. Maybe he means that he will enter a room where you have a friend or family member suffering or dying. When you have worked up the nerve to visit this person, when you walk in, you will discover that you are suddenly no longer afraid or depressed and that the room is full of light and so are you. Maybe that is because the Holy Spirit is there, in that room, and has been there preparing the place for you. You are suddenly appointed and anointed and ordained to minister to this person, and you know it. You know it like you know the back of your hand.

This is the place in the story where we stop being the child in the dark, frantic to touch his mother's fingers under the door. This is the place where we become the fingers, where we become the mother as we become more like the Father.

This is the place in the story where Jesus said, "I will not leave you comfortless: I will come to you" (John 14:18, KJV). This is the place in the story where I tell my mother and father, "I will never forsake you. I will always love you. If your body becomes crippled, I will love you more. If your mind becomes crippled, I will love you more."

This is the place where we learn to love one another. Where we wake up in the garden and begin to survey the cross. Where we do things we never dreamed we could do. Where we learn to bear all things, believe all things, hope all things, and endure all things for the sake of the story, for the sake of the family, for the sake of Jesus.

In this moment we stand together between the garden and the cross and listen to him, and for the first time we truly believe him when he tells us, "If you ask anything in my name, I will do it. You know where I am going, and you know how to get there, too. If you believe in the work I have done, you can do it, too. It will be even better because I am going to my Father. Abide in me and I in you. I am the vine. You are the branches. Love one another. Lay down your life for your friends. If I do not go away, the Comforter cannot come to you. But if I depart, I will send him to you. I will not leave you comfortless. I will come to you."

Come quickly, Lord, for you are the root and the offspring of David, the bright and morning star. Come quickly.

Notes

1. James Agee, *A Death in the Family* (New York: Bantam Books, 1985), p. 15.

2. Anne Lamott, *Operating Instructions: A Journal of My Son's First Year* (New York: Fawcett Columbine, 1993), pp. 220–21.

COMMENT

Pain alters life. Cancer, AIDS, a drunken driver, a sudden heart failure, a tragic accident. When our world is shattered by pain's searing reality, questions haunt our thoughts, fear overshadows faith, and answers are nonexistent. When we wake in the morning and the nightmare we experienced the day before is still with us—not just a dream as we hoped in those first fleeting moments of waking—we know Gethsemane.

Vicki Covington knows what it is to be in Gethsemane. In her sermon, "Between the Garden and the Cross," she takes us with her into the questions; she allows us inside the confusion and pain of an unwanted diagnosis; she invites us to walk with her on her journey from the garden to the cross.

This is a sermon for everyone. Covington speaks simply, directly, poignantly, when she says, "If you are past thirty-five, you surely grieve something." The recent diagnosis of her mother's Alzheimer's coupled with her father's Parkinson's disease, forms the backdrop for a sermon with a universal message: Bad things, tragic things happen. No one is immune. Traveling the journey of "why" is a journey we all unwillingly travel, sooner or later. The issue for people of faith is "How do we pick up the pieces of our lives even though the pieces don't seem to fit? How do we cling to faith in the midst of life's assaults and obscenities?" Every minister who walks hospital corridors, visits the grieving, or stands in the pulpit week after week faces the difficulty of proclaiming the gospel to those whose lives have no good news, those who cannot be comforted.

I, too, have known Gethsemane. Only a few months ago our son was killed when a gun accidentally discharged. Rather than standing in the pulpit as pastor, as the proclaimer of good news, I sat in the pew weeping, knowing the reality of Covington's words: "I couldn't even pray. I came to understand that there is no way out of this." I, too, echo Covington's words, "Why must we have to see through the glass darkly? Why, oh why, can't this cup be passed.... Take away this cup from me." At the memorial service for my son, a good friend, Gardner Taylor, said, "The Bible is short on 'whys' but strong on 'hows.'"

Covington reminds us that the faithful throughout history have come into the presence of God, crying out in their pain and helplessness. She asks the inevitable "why," but takes her listeners beyond the "why" to the essential "how"—how do we find comfort when there is no comfort? Covington does, indeed, address a universal reality.

TEXT & PROCLAMATION

Covington invites us into her story, allowing us to see one of the grimmer realities of life breaking through the exuberance and success. It is in the midst of her pain that we realize we have joined her face to face before God with questions, complaints, agonies and anxieties. We hear our own story as we listen to her fight for footing in the terrible roar and swelling of the overwhelming fear she is facing when someone she loves is suffering.

Covington chooses the method of "story" rather than a traditional three-point sermon structure to remind us that life is a journey, an uneven journey. And through the unevenness, there are directions and choices. Our own stories join with Covington's as we are drawn to the biblical story to find strength and hope. Covington is brave enough to let us peek through her questioning pain and wounded heart, so God can reveal himself to us.

Covington begins the sermon with a quotation from James Agee that does not go immediately to the important thoughts she is about to communicate. She chooses to lead us along with a number of stories and rhetorical questions before bringing us to the heart of the sermon. It is there that she makes the connection for us that there is a way through the darkness that builds strength to move on. Covington leaves the hopes, assurances and promises of Scripture reverberating within our hurting lives. We are left with the refreshing assurance that God identifies with us in our suffering and enables us to turn tragedy into triumph. God is not a disinterested spectator. God is an active participant with us in the stuff of life.

A high mark of the sermon comes when she tells Anne Lamott's story of a frightened two-year-old locked in a dark room. The story serves as the axis on which listeners can give a knowing nod as they too have faced the tough times which trouble and terrorize their souls. Like Covington, we want to believe so badly that it seems that our lives depend on it, but our faith falters, and we still have those nagging fears and unanswered questions. It is there that hope must come to life. We must cling to it, slender as it may seem. Covington bids us to hold on for dear life with both hands because it is all we have to help us keep our head above the waters of despair. While holding on, we come to know that we are not alone in the doubts and hopes, the longings and fears, the strengths and weaknesses of the human heart. She echoes the illustration in the conclusion when she says that this is the place we stop being the child and become the fingers of the mother and then become like the Father.

Covington builds her personal story into the introduction of this sermon. Although this is a growing practice in today's preaching, it should be used carefully and never be motivated by ego. Covington's story serves this sermon well. Through her story, the hearer is able to see the application of the good news of Christ to the various particularities of human experience. We can and do identify with her struggle.

Another strong element of this sermon is its open-ended conclusion. Covington's litany of "maybes" leaves room for an individualistic response from her hearers and is well suited for the flow of her story. What first appears obscure becomes concrete and particular. The gospel offers hope. Covington demonstrates this by peppering her conclusion with a number of Scriptures as responses to some of the questions and doubts we face.

RESPONSE

When life is painful, too painful to fit our souls into the ten correct steps of grieving, when all the self-help books no longer help, our only hope is to march ourselves into the presence of God and cry out the doubts, the pains, the broken dreams in our souls. Through Covington's sojourn in her stretch of darkness, her Gethsemane, where all souls need some assurance, she surrenders her burden to God's care.

BETWEEN THE GARDEN AND THE CROSS 187

Covington confirms the adage that preaching, at its best, is not a solo undertaking. She involves us as listeners. She invites us to overhear her story. Her story gives direction, clearly and vaguely, to the way of Christ and the kingdom. Her simple, honest story-telling helps listeners remember that the preacher is one of them; weakness to weakness—the two in the darkness together—no longer alone or without hope. This gives the gospel a new attractiveness. She holds up her own pain, questions, and struggles not as a model of righteous behavior but as a mystery. She joins with us to see God through this mystery. She moves through her pain and brings the unutterable to voice. Covington makes us acutely aware of the presence of God as well as the dark mysteries surrounding life. We hear echoes from the deep chambers of our souls where the fragile creations of our hope begin to shatter, at the bottom of our darkness. In the words, "Come quickly, Lord," the preacher calls us to affirm that Christ is our sustaining strength.

SUGGESTIONS

- Preach a sermon on the characters in the Bible who seem to be confronting life and a God who seems to have his eyes shut, and his ears closed. Stories where God does not answer the prayer the way the character wanted. Deal with how the character reacted. Consider: 2 Samuel 12:15–23; Psalms of lament; Matthew 26:36–48; 2 Corinthians 12:7–9.
- Develop a sermon to non-Christian people on the question of a good and loving God who allows a bleeding world. Be specific. Be sure to deal with the paradox of why one and not another—fatalism, luck, favored by God, etc.
- Develop a sermon using a strong descriptive story that drives a biblical text home (e.g., Anne Lamott) or a story of a personal struggle. Be sure that your story is not shared for egotistical purposes but to uplift the congregation to a God who loves and cares for them.

K. Thomas Greene

BETWEEN "ONCE UPON A TIME" AND "HAPPILY EVER AFTER"

2 KINGS 4:8–37; MARK 1:29–39

REV. DR. J. BARRY VAUGHN
ST. STEPHEN'S EPISCOPAL CHURCH
EUTAW, ALABAMA

Between "Once Upon a Time" and "Happily Ever After"

2 Kings 4:8–37; Mark 1:29–39, RSV

Today's Old Testament and Gospel readings have to do with healing. Healing is a persistent, important, perhaps even central theme in the Bible.

The first story is especially poignant. Shunem was a town in northern Israel, located in the Jezreel Valley, not too far from Galilee. A wealthy woman of that village generously showed hospitality to the prophet Elisha, who often traveled through the town. Although wealthy, she was barren, a condition that bore a severe stigma in a time and place where women were valued for their ability to bear many healthy children. But the prophet interceded on her behalf with God, and told her that in a year's time she would "embrace a son." The news was too good to be true: "Do not lie to your maidservant," the incredulous woman responded. But it was true, and she conceived and bore a son.

The text tells us of only the one child, a son. Imagine the love lavished on that child, her only child, her only son! She must have watched his every move, recorded his first steps, memorized his first words. One day the beloved son went out to be with his father and the field hands in the hottest part of the day. The sun beats down fiercely on the Jezreel Valley, and the climate is such that it is unwise to go out in summer without a hat and plenty of water. Dehydration and heat stroke are ever-present possibilities. Suddenly the boy cried out, "Oh, my head, my head!" Before anything could be done for him, the boy was unconscious and seemed to his parents to be dead.

The wealthy woman of Shunem summoned one of her husband's servants and took him with her to fetch Elisha. The text underlines her urgency: "Urge the beast on," she said to the servant. "Do not slacken the pace for me unless I tell you." When she found Elisha at Mount Carmel, contrary to rigid social custom she herself approached the holy prophet and spoke to him. She even touched him, catching hold of his feet. Her plea is a bitter indictment: "Did I ask my lord for a son? Did I not say, Do not deceive me?" At once Elisha realized that something was gravely wrong and went with her to see the child. The story, of course, has a happy ending; by Elisha's prayers and ministrations, the child was restored to life.

The reading from Mark's Gospel also speaks of healing. Simon took Jesus to his house, where his mother-in-law lay sick with a fever. Jesus "took her by the hand and lifted her up, and the fever left her; and she served them."

To speak of healing is to raise many questions: Why is there sickness and suffering and death at all? And if God is able to heal, why does God not heal all who call upon him?

I do not have the answer. Some modern theologians argue that God is self-limiting, that somehow God is developing and unfolding along with the universe God has created. I cannot reconcile that solution with the God revealed in holy Scripture. For better or worse, the God of the Bible is revealed to us as both all-powerful and all-loving.

Well, then, if that is true, how can this all-powerful God allow suffering and death at all? What kind of God is revealed in the story of the wealthy woman of Shunem? A child is given; a child is taken away; a child is restored. Is this God a cosmic sadist? Is the universe a cruel joke?

I hope you have had the opportunity to see the film *Shadowlands*, the story of C. S. Lewis and his wife Joy Davidman. It's based on a BBC television production and a subsequent play that ran in London and New York.

Although a very fine film, miles ahead of anything else on in the theaters at the moment, it does not bring out Lewis' dilemma as sharply as the TV production or the stage play.

As you may know, late in life Lewis became acquainted with Joy Davidman, an American poet. First, they became friends, then they became romantically involved. He first married her in a Registry Office (the equivalent of our Justice of the Peace), and then, after she had been struck with bone cancer, they were married by a priest of the Church of England in her hospital room. Her cancer went into remission, and Lewis regarded it as a miracle. Then the cancer returned, and she died. Lewis came close to losing his faith, and wrote of it in his powerful book, *A Grief Observed.* Lewis wrote:

> What reason have we, except our own desperate wishes, to believe that God is, by any standard we can conceive, "good"? Doesn't all the *prima facie* evidence suggest exactly the opposite? What have we to set against it?[1]

The TV production and the stage play open with Lewis expounding confidently about "the problem of pain" to a packed house. Full of certainty, he proclaims, "Pain is God's megaphone to awaken a sleeping world." Then, the lecture over, the play commences, and we watch the unfolding relationship between Lewis and Joy and her sickness and death. Finally, at the end, Lewis once again gives the lecture. With an uncertain voice, he begins, "Pain is God's megaphone." And with that he dissolves into tears.

The problem of pain is no longer something he has considered in the abstract; it is something he has encountered existentially, and he is no longer able to speak about it in easy clichés.

I do not have any easy answers to give you about why there is pain and sickness, about why the good suffer and the wicked prosper. But I want to suggest a way of looking at things that might be helpful.

Recently Birmingham novelist Vicki Covington wrote an article in *The Birmingham News* about her grandmother's death. She offered these thoughts which help me to understand suffering and pain a little better:

> The ultimate reason for depression and suicide is that a person
> reaches a point where not only is life meaningless but also there is
> no mystery about that fact; not only have we failed to be the hero
> of this story, but in fact there is no story. And it is the task of
> Christianity to re-establish belief that there's a story. Not that the
> characters won't have pain, accident, or calamity; that the story
> won't be sad. Just simply that there is a story.[2]

We read our children fairytales that begin, "Once upon a time," and
that end "and they lived happily ever after." But between the "once upon a
time" and the "happily ever after," anything can happen. The heroine may
be called upon to slay a dragon. She may have to cross tall mountains and
forge raging rivers. She may have to rescue the handsome but incompetent
prince from the wiles of an evil sorceress. She may be injured or even die.
But we know that somehow it will come out all right in the end.

That is the Christian faith. Our faith is not that life will be pleasant and
easy. We do not hold that if you have enough faith you will not experience
pain and suffering. What the Christian faith teaches us is that there is a *story*
and a *Storyteller.* The Christian faith proclaims that although there will be
suffering and pain in life, it has a purpose, that the God who was in Christ
reconciling the world to himself, is still with us, redeeming our pain and
bringing meaning to our suffering.

After all, the central symbol of Christianity is the cross, the sign that
God is present in suffering, the sign that Resurrection will swallow up
death, that "happily ever after" will follow "once upon a time," some day,
somehow, in God's time. Amen.

Notes
1. C. S. Lewis, *A Grief Observed* (New York: Bantam Books, 1961), pp. 33–34.
2. Vicki Covington, *The Birmingham News,* (January 23, 1994), p. 2C.

COMMENT

PROBLEM

Why Do Good People Suffer?

Sickness and death are ever-present realities of our lives. Good people do suffer. Why? How can a good God allow good people to suffer? There was a time when suffering was considered evidence of sin, even if one did not recognize the sin. This, however, is not the Christian answer to suffering.

In the Old Testament, Job, a most righteous man, suffered far more than anyone. He lost it all. His great wealth was stripped from him; all his children died; his health was destroyed; his friends turned against him. In the anguish of his righteousness, Job dared to challenge God. Why do good people suffer while wicked people prosper? Job didn't learn the answer to his questions. He did learn that God is sufficient. The power and the presence of God are in evidence in the world. Job came away from his confrontation with God without knowing the answers to his questions, but he was satisfied. We still ask the same questions. We may or may not be satisfied with the answers we receive.

TEXT

Dramatize the Story and Relate It to Contemporary Life

The Old Testament and Gospel lessons have been read before the sermon commences. They are repeated in the text of the sermon. In essence, the preacher is following here the approach: "I tell 'em what I'm gonna tell 'em. Then I tell 'em. Then I tell 'em what I told 'em." It most often takes more than one hearing for remembrance to sink in, for learning to occur. The wise preacher will use every opportunity for reaffirming the gospel lesson in the text of the sermon. Make it memorable. Confirm the importance of the lessons from the Scriptures for contemporary living. Repetition is one way of accomplishing the desired result. Another way is to relate it to contemporary life.

Vaughn uses both methods most effectively. He dramatizes the story by giving additional information not contained within the readings. Shunem was a town not far from Galilee. Now there's a place the Christian can relate to. The person in the pew may not know much about the geography of the Holy Land, but most Christians will recognize Galilee.

Vaughn tells us women were valued for their ability to bear many healthy children. He brings to mind our own children. "Imagine," he says, "the love lavished on that child." He draws word pictures. Parents in the congregation can relate to their own children. This is a good method of developing the sermon and helping the congregation embrace the text.

Vaughn relates to the text to contemporary life by sharing two illustrations drawn from his reading. The first is from the life of C. S. Lewis. Every preacher needs to read C. S. Lewis. The extraordinary life and writings of this man should be a part of every minister's preparation for work as a servant of the Lord. The sickness and death of the wife of C. S. Lewis presented a major challenge to the faith of this great Christian writer. Sickness and death challenge the faith of every Christian at some time during life. This is a story most listeners over thirty will relate to immediately through their experience of loss at the death of parents, grandparents, sometimes even children or other significant people in their lives. Death happens. How does the Christian reconcile feelings of loss and loneliness with the faith proclaimed as good news?

The second illustration is from Vicki Covington, an Alabama novelist. Her thoughts regarding suffering and pain following the death of her grandmother are worth sharing. The preacher draws inspiration from the daily news and shares it. It is no longer sufficient for the preacher simply to repeat biblical stories and quotations without relating them to contemporary life by bringing them into the present with good illustrations. Vaughn does this exceedingly well. Others who proclaim the Word made flesh and dwelling among us would do well to follow his example.

PROCLAMATION

Vaughn confesses he does not have the answers to suffering and death. We who have been called to proclaim the gospel of Jesus Christ do not always have the answers. When we don't know, we should not hesitate to confess our ignorance. The gospel will survive the ignorance of the preacher! God-in-Christ is present and active in our world, in our lives. That is the good news. That is the gospel. God is present in our pain and suffering. Christ is strength for our weakness; light for our darkness, joy for our sorrow.

The Christian faith is not proclaimed as an easy journey without heartaches and obstacles along the way. To do so is false proclamation, the prostitution of the gospel. Good people will suffer too much. Good Christians will die too young. But we do not suffer alone. The cross of Christ reminds us of the glory of resurrection. We are called to endure the suffering of the present moment knowing One who has suffered for us understands and guides us through the darkness to the glorious light beyond our comprehension.

RESPONSE

The sermon calls for reflection from the Christian in the pew. Although we may not have answers to tough theological questions, we are called to examine our faith in light from the Scripture, from Christian tradition and experience, and from our own lives. If our faith is so fragile it cannot endure examination, it's not worth much anyway.

The lessons to be learned: the active Presence we call God is sufficient to our every need. We do not have to understand the reasons for suffering to benefit from the Holy Presence in our lives. Suffering calls forth an active response to the availability of the presence of a good and holy God who loves us and cares about our every need. Jesus, the Christ of God, does not abandon us in our sickness, pain and death. He is a present reality who helps us to endure and overcome the tough times in our lives.

COMMENT

SUGGESTIONS

- Read widely. Good preachers must be prolific readers. Read for education. Read for enlightenment. Read for entertainment. Read the daily newspapers and the local weeklies. Read the classics. Read biographies. And it goes without saying, Read the Bible, both Old and New Testaments, regularly. Preferably every day.

- Copy or clip and save notes and articles that grab attention. Organize articles either on computer or in filing cabinets under useful headings where they can be found quickly when preparing sermons, writing speeches or articles for the church newsletter or other publications.

- Write in your books. Be in dialogue with the great thinkers of the past. Highlight sentences and paragraphs you want to remember. When reading something worth remembering, write the page number on the cover page with a few words to describe the reference or text.

- Be highly selective in choosing sermon illustrations. A good story in the wrong sermon loses impact. Always start with the gospel and illustrate the text chosen for the sermon. Try to avoid writing a sermon around a good illustration, then trying to find a biblical text that fits the subject.

Marianna Frost

THE
MOST DIFFICULT
PRAYER

LUKE 6:27–31; ROMANS 12:14–21

REV. DR. MARTIN B. COPENHAVER
THE WELLESLEY CONGREGATIONAL CHURCH
WELLESLEY, MASSACHUSETTS

REV. DR. MARTIN B. COPENHAVER

THE MOST DIFFICULT PRAYER

LUKE 6:27–31; ROMANS 12:14–21, NRSV

E very once in a while the headlines come home. There are times when news that is followed on an international scale can take on a personal dimension. That is what many of us have experienced in this past month during the harrowing days of David Rohde's captivity in Bosnia. Many Americans have tried to keep this horrifying conflict at some distance from their thoughts. But because David's family are members of this church, for us it has hit home and hit hard. On this Thanksgiving weekend, we are particularly thankful for his release, even as the broader dimensions of that war and fragile peace continue to haunt us.

Another international conflict took on a personal dimension for me about a dozen years ago when Tom Cullins, a member of my church in Vermont, was on the TWA airliner that was hijacked in Beirut and held for several seemingly endless days. All of a sudden, in that event, the reality of international terrorism was no longer an abstraction but terrifyingly real and close.

For me, there was yet another time, the time I want to tell you about this morning, when Lloyd Van Vactor was kidnapped. At the time it happened I was associate minister of Saugatuck Congregational Church in Westport, Connecticut, a position Van Vactor had once held. Though at the time he was halfway around the world in the Philippines, many in

Westport remembered him well, regularly exchanged letters with Lloyd and his wife, and never failed to see them when they made their yearly trip to New York. Lloyd had gone to the Philippines as a missionary of the United Church of Christ, and he was adopted as a special kind of missionary from our church. Each year we held a large fund-raising event to support his ministry there.

Lloyd had gone to that troubled and distant land of the Philippines to assume the presidency of Dansalan College. The primary goal of the college is to educate the people of that country. But a strong and explicitly stated secondary goal of Dansalan College is to improve the relationship between Christians and Moslems in the Philippines by bringing together as classmates the future leaders of both groups. This was, and remains, an ambitious goal because, like the Protestants and Catholics in Northern Ireland, and the Hindus and Moslems in India, there has long been great enmity between Christians and Moslems in the Philippines. Violence was, and still is, common. Although Lloyd had achieved great success in improving interreligious understanding within the college, the hostilities in the surrounding communities remained stubborn and intense. When violence erupted, Dansalan was a frequent target.

It was only hours after Lloyd had been kidnapped by members of a Moslem sect that word reached the staff of our church. The senior minister of our church immediately wrote a letter to tell the members of the congregation. He passed along what little hard information he had, and then he added something like this: "Pray for Lloyd in his captivity. Pray for his wife Maisie as she anxiously awaits word. Pray for both the Christian and Moslem communities in the Philippines, that the violence might stop. And pray for Lloyd's captors that they might know the peace of God."

Word of Lloyd's captivity, of course, affected our entire church. But the last request in the letter, the request for prayers for Lloyd's captors and persecutors, sent a strong and immediate jolt through the congregation.

We did not need to be told to pray for Lloyd and Maisie. Our prayers turn easily to the people we love. We have great concern for them. We want good things for them.

And it may not be too difficult to pray for Christians and Moslems generally, because such words as *Christian* and *Moslem* can seem comfortably vague. They can lack a human face. The easiest prayers are always the most general. It is when our prayers gain in specificity that they can gain in discomfort. As one of the *Peanuts* characters puts it: "I love humanity. It's people I can't stand."

So perhaps it is not surprising that it was the last request in the letter that seemed so difficult. There we were being asked to pray, not for humanity or even a slice of humanity, but for people, for individuals who now held and threatened to kill our friend and minister.

Many confessed that they experienced great difficulty following that final request to pray for Lloyd's captors and persecutors. In one of our church gatherings we recalled together those passages of Scripture that, like the headlines, were also coming home to us and taking on a personal dimension: "Bless those who persecute you; bless and do not curse them," wrote Paul (Rom. 12:14). And these words from Jesus: "Love your enemies, do good to those who hate you, bless those who curse you, pray for those who abuse you" (Luke 6:27–28). But those words did not make the prayers any easier and may have even contributed to our discomfort. The words which once sounded wise and benign enough to stitch on a sampler and hang in the living room now sounded too radical to allow in the house.

That is when I learned that a prayer for an enemy—a specific enemy—is the most difficult kind of prayer there is. Our reaction toward an enemy is more likely to be unrestrained bitterness, or the desire for revenge or, at the very least, the desire to have nothing more to do with the person. Prayer for an enemy allows none of those things.

Nevertheless, Jesus told us to love our enemies, to pray for them: the one who has made it hard for us to go to work in the morning, the one who left scars that have not yet begun to heal, the one who betrayed our trust. We are to love our mortal enemies, too: the one who killed an innocent person just a few blocks from where we work, and in the process took something precious from each one of us. Love him, pray for him? And the terrorists who make us feel like we live in a war zone without battle lines? Do good to them, pray for them?

During the Gulf War I was asked to offer a prayer at the meeting of a local service club. It's not a religious organization, but for some reason they like to have clergy around. I remember how difficult it was to fashion that prayer. I was aware that there was one prayer that I wanted to pray, and another very different prayer that Jesus told us to pray. It is a prayer for our enemies. Jesus said that anyone can pray for a friend. There is nothing special in that. Why, even a heathen can do that. It comes naturally. But something else is required from those of us who bear the name of Christ, something more and much more difficult. We are to pray for our enemies in the same way we might pray for a friend. I would not claim that this is easy. I know it is not easy for me, but I also know that Jesus will not let us forget that that is part of our charge.

So, in my prayer that day I prayed for our fellow countrymen and women who were under the threat of death in a distant and hostile land. That was the easy part. But I also prayed for Saddam Hussein and our other enemies, the very people who threatened our loved ones, and I attempted to pray for them with the same loving concern with which one might pray for a friend. It was not an easy prayer to offer, and it obviously was not an easy one for people to hear. After the meeting I had to face the anger that my prayer had engendered in many, some of them the same people who had greeted me warmly before the meeting began.

As I say, it was not an easy prayer to offer, and it did not go down easily with those who attended the meeting. But we should be suspect of any prayer for an enemy that *does* seem easy, for then, more often than not, such a prayer is really a self-serving prayer in disguise. I am thinking of those prayers for an enemy that provide an opportunity to review and summarize for God's benefit—and our own—all the wrongs inflicted by the enemy. Those prayers are merely a disguise for our bitterness. And I am thinking of those prayers in which we ask that our enemies be given full knowledge of the wrongs they have inflicted. Those are a disguise for our desire to punish. And, with all due respect to Paul, I am also thinking of his advice to the Romans that they aid their enemies for in so doing they will, in his words, "heap burning coals on their [enemy's] heads" (Rom. 12:20). That sounds to me like another variation on the age-old advice, "Love your enemies. It will drive them nuts"!

To pray for an enemy in the same way we might pray for a friend—that is, not because we want to do anything to them, but because we want to ask for good things for them—that remains extremely difficult.

Notice, however, that both Paul and Jesus assume that we will have enemies. They assume that no one escapes life without ever confronting or creating an enemy. There are enemies we have never met, who are part of some larger conflict, like the Moslems who kidnapped Lloyd Van Vactor or those who held David Rohde. And then there are enemies that we know quite well. They may work in our office, or even live in our homes. As G. K. Chesterton put it: "The Bible tells us to love our neighbors and to love our enemies—probably because they are generally the same people."

Notice also that Jesus does not suggest that we pray for our enemies because we have affection for them. Nor does he suggest that we pray for our enemies so that we will learn to have affection for them. We are asked to pray for our enemies as an expression of love, but that love has precious little to do with affection or approval. Rather, we are to love our enemies and our neighbors as we love ourselves. How do we love ourselves? Walter Russell Bowie gives this answer: "We do not look at ourselves in the mirror and think how amiable we are....It means to want for ourselves the best that life can give and to reach out and try to get it....That, then, is what the love of one's neighbor should mean. It is regarding him [or her] as worthy of all the best in life that God can help us make available for him [or her]."[1]

Now the prayer for an enemy begins to sound even more difficult. We might imagine that we should learn to like the enemy, learn to better understand the enemy, so that our prayers will spring unforced from the heart. But Jesus does not ask this. He does not let us wait until we "feel" something. This is a command, and one cannot "feel" on command. Rather, Jesus asks us to pray for our enemies no matter what we feel. We are to love them as we love ourselves, which means to ask that good things happen to them, that they receive the best that life can give, that they might find God's blessing and God's peace.

You see, to pray is to share God's point of view for a moment, which includes having higher and urgent hopes for everyone, even those we consider our enemies, even the persecutors, even those who have their missiles pointed at us, even those who hold us captive, or hold a friend captive. We pray that our enemies might experience the grace of God, not because this is our point of view, but because it is God's point of view, a point of view we can assume in a moment of prayer.

Prayer is not offered as an easy solution to our hostile feelings toward those we consider our enemies. Nor do we offer such prayers for an enemy simply to help ourselves recover from the wounds they may have inflicted on us. Rather, we pray that our enemy might receive the best that life has to offer because that is God's intention. We pray that our enemy might receive the peace of God because that, too, is God's hope.

And yet, if we offer such prayers for our enemies persistently and hopefully, something else can happen, a kind of blessed bonus. Having assumed God's point of view in prayer, we can come to share a bit of God's point of view, even about our enemies. That does *not* mean that we must approve of our enemies or their actions. By assuming God's point of view, however, we can come to understand our enemies just a bit better, what motivates them, what they are seeking, why they behave as they do. And because sharing God's point of view can do some almost miraculous things, we should not be too surprised if even our former feelings of hostility toward our enemies are transformed into something resembling compassion.

Yet, even as I say these things, I am aware that they may sound too much like a preacher's glib sentiments, out of touch with the hard realities of the world, either too simple or too difficult to be true. So let me complete the story of Lloyd Van Vactor. While he was being held captive, we received word that his wife Maisie had died, news that, in his captivity, Lloyd himself had not yet heard. Naturally, news of Maisie's death only increased the anger and resentment that Lloyd's friends in our church felt toward his captors. But the people of the church turned their anger into something constructive. We started a memorial scholarship fund in Maisie's name for American women who might want to go into the ministry or social work, as she had done.

After several weeks Lloyd was released, as quickly and inexplicably as he had been abducted. He was released without the benefit of any of the ransom money that had been collected for his release. In the ensuing weeks after his release, a question arose about how the money that was intended for his ransom should be spent. Lloyd was given the choice as to how to use the funds. And do you know what he decided to do? It still astonishes me. He, too, decided to give the money for a scholarship fund, but the fund was not to be used for American students. Rather, the fund he established was very specifically earmarked for Dansalan College students who are part of the very Moslem sect that kidnapped him and threatened his life for those tormenting weeks of his captivity. You see, all during his captivity he had prayed for his enemies and persecutors, and now his prayers were finding fitting expression in this gift of love.

A prayer for an enemy. It is the most difficult prayer of all. And the most beautiful.

Note
1. Walter Russell Bowie, "The Gospel According to St. Luke," *The Interpreter's Bible*, Vol. 8 (Nashville: Abingdon Press, 1980), p.121.

COMMENT

Have you ever walked out of a movie theater deeply moved but unsure what to say or think? Not wanting to talk to anyone for a while? In some mysterious way you were "caught" by the moment, captured by the movie's proclamation.

I imagine that those in the congregation listening to Martin Copenhaver's sermon, "The Most Difficult Prayer," experienced that "caughtness." The sermon reaches out, grabs us, and shakes us up and down. This is because Copenhaver challenges us to rethink the implications of an idea that we accept intellectually but rarely practice—the idea of praying for our enemies. So many of our accepted Christian beliefs are like ghosts in the basement of our souls: hidden away, relegated to the back of our thoughts and wills. Good preaching, like that of Copenhaver, brings these buried beliefs to the surface. Through the power of story and the strength of his interplay between text and proclamation, Copenhaver unleashes one of our ghosts.

OPENING

What happens when other people's problems become ours? What are the implications of news headlines taking on a personal dimension? These are the opening questions Copenhaver poses to prepare us for the biblical text and proclamation. To drive the point home, he alludes to the congregation's current situation, a time when the headlines are hitting home. The congregation is "hooked."

Copenhaver alludes to another personal example of headline news taking a personal dimension and then begins a lengthy story that will become the framework for his homiletical idea. Almost a third of this sermon is devoted to retelling this story. The story is not merely an opening, it is part of the sermon plot, an integral part of the message. Through an intriguing and entertaining story the listener is brought in, captured. It is not just any fantastic tale of kidnapping and international espionage. This is a real story that touches close to home because it involves Copenhaver himself. Yet there is more to the story's usefulness. There is a mystery behind its purpose. The listener is left wondering where the story is going. Why is he retelling it? What is the point, the biblical idea?

Finally, Copenhaver provides the missing link, the biblical idea: prayer. Not just any prayer, but prayer for an enemy. "It is when our prayers gain in specificity that they can gain discomfort." Like the headline news, Copenhaver asks what happens when Scripture takes on a personal dimension, when a command or precept takes on a new, more personal nature? What occurs when the words of Scripture "that once sounded wise and benign enough to stitch on a sampler and hang in the living room now sound too radical to allow in the house?" The main idea of the sermon is laid out. Copenhaver will spend the rest of the sermon fleshing out the nature of prayer for an enemy.

This illustration—introduction is effective because Copenhaver is not just any player in the story. He is the foil. He is the one who finds prayer so difficult. He places himself on the side of the congregation. He says, in effect, that even though he has been to seminary, is a trained pastor, teacher, and spiritual leader, he knows that praying for an enemy is difficult for everyone, even ministers. Later, he will use this identification with the congregation to his advantage. "These things...may sound too much like a preacher's glib sentiment...out of touch with the hard realities of the world...too simple or too difficult." Yet as soon as these words are out of his mouth, the listener recalls Copenhaver's earlier self-identification with the difficulty of prayer. These *are not* a preacher's glib sentiments.

TEXT & PROCLAMATION

The sermon is guided by an "us" rather than "you" perspective. One gets the feeling that the congregation is on a journey of discovery *with* the preacher. Copenhaver chooses a personal example of his struggle with prayer to frame the message and adds another in the middle to bolster this idea. His inclusive attitude helps his listeners accept and more readily embrace the discomforting, sometimes hard words. Moreover, his personal illustrations help his listeners know him better. We see Copenhaver's humanity, his struggles. Perhaps most importantly, the congregation gets a glimpse of Copenhaver the person. This is important for all ministers in every church. Appropriate, modest self-revelation enables a congregation to identify with us as human beings and to build bridges of trust and truthfulness with us.

What makes this topic a difficult one is that most of us tend to brush off or ignore Jesus' words to love our enemy and pray for those who persecute us. It is not that we don't believe we should, but that we find it either too far removed from our everyday experience—"I don't have any enemies"—or so impossible we simply choose to ignore it. Loving our enemies is a ghost we have confined to the basement of our souls, giving it little effect on our everyday lives. Copenhaver sets out to unlock the door and loose this ghost. He develops the implications of Jesus' command and Paul's admonition to love our enemies and to pray for those who persecute us.

In this sermon Copenhaver is taking us down a road that becomes more steep and difficult with each step. It's a journey into the depths of our soul where the ghost of love is hidden. It's a scary journey, but because he is walking alongside us, we are willing to stay with him. We want to follow him.

For Copenhaver our first step is accepting the fact that prayer for an enemy is difficult. In fact, the nature of the prayer requires that it be difficult. The preacher uses a story and his personal experience to help us identify with the difficulty. We have passed through our first step of difficulty.

We take another step downward: Prayer for our enemy must be real prayer, not self-serving or full of disguised diatribe, but the kind of prayer we say for our friends. At this point in the journey, Copenhaver gives us as listeners time to catch our breath and relax by outlining the things Jesus and Paul did *not* mean. He even lets us laugh with G. K. Chesterton. We are allowed to have enemies. In fact, we have no other choice. What is more, Jesus does not expect us to like our enemies or learn to like them. For a moment, we feel free and relieved.

But just as we are getting comfortable, Copenhaver resumes the journey. Our enemies may be people we never meet, but more likely, they are those with whom we interact all the time. Here Copenhaver allows us to make our own discovery. If our enemies are those around us, our neighbors and coworkers, then the necessary implication is that prayer for an enemy cannot be occasional. Instead, it must be frequent. We are "caught" in our neglect.

Copenhaver is not finished leading us down into the depth of our souls. We must take another big step. The prayer for an enemy is driven by love. We feel pulled. How can we love our enemies if Copenhaver is correct in saying that Jesus does not require us to like our enemies? The tension between life and the mystery of the gospel is in full force.

In response, Copenhaver resolves the tension with the power of the gospel. The final step: Prayer is sharing God's viewpoint. We pray for good things to happen to those who persecute us, ignore us, and mock us, "not because this is our point of view, but because it is God's point of view." We pray for our enemies not out of affection, not because we understand them better or have learned to like them, but because we pray out of love—a love that is possible only because God is working in and for us.

Copenhaver has brought his listeners down a difficult road, but like all prophets who call for repentance and disrupt our comfort zones, he gives us hope. There is good news awaiting us at the end of the journey. There is the God of all love waiting to receive us. There is resolution. The good news is that when we pray like this we become changed people. When we share God's point of view, Copenhaver concludes, our hearts are transformed. To drive this final point home, he concludes the unfinished story with which he began the sermon. The story that so effectively frames the sermon and restates his main idea: A prayer for an enemy is the most difficult prayer of all and the most beautiful. The problem stated at the beginning, "I learned that a prayer for an enemy is the most difficult kind of prayer there is," is resolved. Yes, it is difficult, but it is also life changing.

COMMENT

RESPONSE

There is a timeliness to this sermon that gives it special power and significance. The congregation had been struggling for months with the issues addressed in the sermon. A member of the congregation had been held captive in Bosnia. But its power to encourage listeners to embody God's truth in their lives is not confined to its original context. One reason for the success is the message's universal application. Everyone has enemies and everyone sees the inadequacies of their own love for these people. The message challenges our comfort zone.

The sermon also works because it gives us hope. We live in a world full of discrepancies and ambiguity, sin and uncertainty. Copenhaver does a good job of joining the tensions of life with the mystery of the gospel. In the end we come out on the other side in resolution.

Copenhaver begins and ends his sermon with a story, a story that combines with the sermon content and leaves the listener "caught." We know we are guilty. We know we don't pray like this. We have nothing to say. The ghost has been unleashed.

SUGGESTIONS

- Use your own experiences of struggle to help your congregation identify with faith's difficulties.
- Be timely. Preach on issues that are facing your congregation. Catch your congregation in life's moments and challenge them to grow and mature.
- What can you learn from this sermon about building tension and heightening discomfort so that in the end your congregation is in a different spiritual location? Do you give your congregation hope to be something more than what they are?
- What are those issues that remain "ghosts" in your congregation's life? In your life? How can you preach in such a way as to unleash them?

Karen Fisher Younger

WITH ME

1 KINGS 19:1–4, 8–15a

REV. CASEY ALEXANDER
CHAPLAIN
WACONIA GOOD SAMARITAN CENTER
WACONIA, MINNESOTA

REV. CASEY ALEXANDER

WITH ME

1 KINGS 19:1–4, 8–15a, NRSV

T he text for this morning is both a fascinating and a troubling one from our Old Testament, the Hebrew Scriptures. I want to look very closely at the story, to discover all it has to say to us, and all the challenges it brings to us.

Our reading begins with Elijah's flight into the desert from the very angry queen, Jezebel. We're helped in understanding this part of Elijah's story if we back up one chapter to see how he got into this terrible jam. Elijah was a prophet who zealously fought for the exclusive worship of Yahweh among the Israelites. He was alarmed to see that the Israelites had begun worshiping other gods of the region—especially the god Baal. King Ahab's wife, Queen Jezebel, was promoting the worship of Baal. Therefore, Elijah devised a clever way to put an end to the lure of Baal worship among the Israelites once and for all. He challenged the prophets of Baal to a competition. He also invited all the Israelites to come out and watch the spectacle. Elijah directed the prophets of Baal to prepare a sacrifice as an offering, but not to set fire to the offering themselves. Rather, they were to call upon their god Baal to rain down fire and consume the offering. The story tells us that they danced and whooped and shouted around the altar for half the day, as Elijah taunted them with sarcastic comments—all without result.

Now it was Elijah's turn. He too prepared an offering. Then, apparently for dramatic effect, he had jars of water poured all over the offering, once, then twice, then a third time—just to make sure everything was really wet. Finally, he called upon Yahweh, the God of Israel. Fire fell and consumed the offering and even licked up all the water. Taking this as an obvious sign of God's favor, Elijah ordered all the impressed Israelites who were standing and watching to seize the four hundred and fifty prophets of Baal and kill them. Which they did (1 Kings 18:40).

Now we see why Queen Jezebel was angry with Elijah. He had killed all her prophets and advisors. He had attacked her religion. Hearing how angry the queen was, Elijah fled for his life to a desert cave. That's where our reading begins this morning—with Elijah fleeing for his life because of what he had done.

Don't you find the whole story just a little troubling? Even if we interpret it as metaphorically as possible, even if we contextualize it and remember its origin in an ancient society which observed customs and practices other than our own, still it doesn't sit well with modern sensibilities. We so easily celebrate the victory of Yahwism that day on Mount Carmel. But we rarely think of the four hundred and fifty prophets of Baal. "Elijah...killed them there."

Recently I toured the Holocaust Memorial in Washington, D.C. *Holocaust* means literally "burned whole," or burnt offering. I couldn't help making a connection between the heart-wrenching tragedy I saw portrayed in the photos and artifacts in that museum and our text. Entirely too much horror has been perpetrated on one group by another through history. Sometimes, as in Elijah's case, the acts may be defended as noble, perhaps even as a defense of God. I'm persuadable on many points, but even for me, that's a hard sell. People can be wrong for the right reasons. Elijah seemed to have wrapped himself in a cloak of independence sure of his own vision of truth and his own way of implementing it. Elijah says repeatedly, in effect, "I'm the only prophet of the Lord." Feeling disconnected from others or isolated, as Elijah did, can lead to distortion, as this troubling introduction to our story shows. It wasn't until Queen Jezebel said, in effect, "You are wrong, Elijah!" that he seemed to have stopped long enough to wonder.

The purpose for my trip to Washington, D.C. was to attend an intensive bioethics seminar. As a group of some one hundred people, we stopped for a while to ponder what we were doing with troubling medical ethical issues, to talk things over and to learn from one another what distortions our individual viewpoints gave us. The issues of bioethics are many, and all of us at that seminar, even those who might have felt we had some grasp of the great moral order of the universe and how we are to act in compliance with it, found the whole experience more than a little humbling. We disagreed a great deal. Finally, though, we came to a point of real mutual respect because we saw that each of us sought desperately in our own ways to do the right thing. With that understanding, even the strongest resolve in one's own private, exclusive claim to truth eventually weakened. A little doubt surfaced.

To go back to our story, do you suppose any such doubts surfaced for Elijah? I, for one, hope they did. Maybe he had expected the queen to recant her idolatry and turn to Yahweh. Instead he heard in no uncertain terms from her that she thought what he did was wrong. His vision of truth was not convincing or compelling to her.

So Elijah fled to the desert cave, in one sense victorious, but also very much alone and unsupported. Try to imagine how he might have felt. He's experienced apparently the greatest triumph of his life, yet finds himself utterly alone. It must have been disorienting. Can he keep on in the same line of thinking and acting in light of this complete lack of support? Doubt must have surfaced here.

The Talmud says that the three words "I don't know" are sacred. Perhaps they are sacred because a little humility, a little doubt, actually brings us closer to the sacred, to God. Maybe if we're less sure of ourselves, less isolated, less wrapped up in our own certainty, we will have room to be a little surer of God.

Elijah's doubt rapidly collapsed into despair, and he fled to a cave in the desert. He just didn't know anymore—didn't know where to go, didn't know who to be, didn't know what to do. He didn't know. Here in the desert, in his despair of not knowing, we're told he wanted to die.

Frederick Buechner, a wonderful, creative commentator on biblical stories says about despair that "God reserves his deepest silence for his saints.... Maybe only the saints can survive such doubt as that."[1] Doubt, despair, and sainthood are an interesting linkage. Buechner doesn't link sainthood with certainty. He links sainthood with not knowing. Elijah does survive his doubt and despair. Through the despair, the not knowing, he reencounters the sacred. He rediscovers God.

Elijah hears God's voice asking, "What are you doing here, Elijah?" (1 Kings 19:9, 13). We can take the question at face value and suppose the question means, "How come you're hiding in this cave?" or perhaps, "Why did you come to this desert?" But surely the meaning runs deeper. "What are you doing here, Elijah? Take stock of yourself, your life. What brought you to this point?" This is an accounting before God of the most serious proportions.

The prospect of answering such a question is daunting, isn't it? How would any of us respond? "What are you doing here?" Not just, "What are you doing, sitting here in a pew this morning?" but, "What is at the core of your being? How is it known by your acts? What are you doing here?" Not only now, but at the important points in your life, how would you answer the question? It demands serious reckoning from every one of us.

Note Elijah's response. In our story he doesn't answer this penetrating question from God directly. Instead he just shouts out his despair and says, "I alone am left." "I am alone." I wonder if that isn't the very essence of his despair—or ours—feeling utterly alone.

When he was young, one of our sons was subject to night terrors, that odd experience of sleeping wakefulness or wakeful sleeping, where people may dream horribly frightening episodes and yet not be reachable, not able to awaken from the terror. I distinctly remember an occasion when he called out in the middle of the night and I found him, eyes open, sitting up in bed, but in the grip of this night terror. I could not break through to him, I could not connect. Even though he was calling for me, and I was there to answer, he felt totally alone. I tried calling him, talking to him—anything to awaken him, but he could not perceive my presence there. He felt totally alone in his terror. I'm sure I will never forget his fright. It's almost intolerable to be in such isolation—to be so alone.

God asks Elijah, "What are you doing here?" and receives the despairing lament, "I am alone." Then God puts on a remarkable display. Strong winds split rocks, an earthquake rumbles, a fire rages by. I think God was trying to awaken Elijah out of his own kind of night terror, a terror of aloneness. But Elijah won't even peek out of the cave. He's not able to awaken.

Finally the world falls utterly silent. Now Elijah ventures out of the cave. God asks him a second time, "What are you doing here?" Maybe Elijah's first answer wasn't to God's liking. Maybe God asked a second time, hoping that after the natural displays, Elijah would come up with a different answer. But Elijah is nothing if not consistent. He answers in just the same despairing way: "I alone am left."

"What are you doing here?" Perhaps such a highly significant question bears repeating in any life, including ours, until we are forced to reconsider our answer. Perhaps such reconsideration will prompt a change of purpose for us, or jar us awake. And then I hope our answers will not embody despair, as Elijah's did, but rather hope.

There's a little sign posted strategically near the top of a very long stairway in one of the healthcare facilities in which I work, just about at the point where people are likely to pause for breath. The sign reads, "There are defining moments in life when one is faced with the choice of giving up or going on." Well, the desert experience was surely such a defining moment for Elijah. Would he, in fact, give up and die, or would he go on? Many of us who have felt utterly alone, or defeated, or abandoned have also faced this choice. What moves us past it? What keeps us going on? What gives us hope?

Recently I read an interesting linguistic observation about the word *hope*. In Hebrew, the word for hope is *tikva*. Within the word *tikva*, it may be argued, is a second Hebrew word, *kav,* meaning "line." *Line,* then, is framed with extra letters, to form the longer word, *hope*. The writer posed the possibility that in Hebrew thought there may be a connection between the two words, that the word *hope* grew up around the word *line.* It's an interesting idea, don't you think, hope as a kind of a line, a connecting line, a link? If we are in trouble, or in despair, maybe we can search out lines of connection to things and people around us which are outside our despair. Drawing on lines of connection could be a means of arousing hope.[2]

God asks Elijah a second time what he is doing. A second time he receives the answer, "I am alone." So God stops asking. But he gives Elijah a new commission. God sends Elijah out, saying, "Go, return on your way...you shall anoint Hazael...you shall anoint Jehu...and you shall anoint Elisha..." (1 Kings 19:15–16). In a sense God was saying, "Come out of your set-apartness, your certainty, your self-sufficient aloneness and distorting isolation. Come out and meet the world, where there's uncertainty...but where there is hope, too, comprised of all your messy, blessed lines of connectedness."

Consider for a moment all your lines of connectedness, all the relationships that are framed by hope and so sustain you. I hope your closest relationships with family and friends do that for you. Nurture them. I hope this community does that for you. We need to provide those lines of connectedness for each other. Add your voice to the community. Connect with it as fully as you can, and let the connection be one of hope. I hope, too, that your faith is a connecting line of hope for you. As God nurtured Elijah and beckoned to him out of his despair and aloneness, so God calls us from our aloneness as well. And in ways we don't fully appreciate, God supports us in our times of being alone.

Perhaps Elijah's most serious error was in not recognizing that even though he had no visible supporters, even though Jezebel wanted his head, even though he'd had to hole up in a desert cave, he was not alone. All the while Elijah sat despairingly saying "I am alone!"—he was not.

I worked for some time with a woman with Huntington's disease, an inherited, degenerative brain disease that slowly isolates its sufferers by loss of speech, inability to control movements, and eventually dementia. This woman, whom I'll call Mary, had been an extremely active woman, parenting a family of ten children, and traveling for her work. She told me stories of the years when she had loved to dance the polka and drink beer—especially green beer on St. Patrick's Day. Always an appreciative audience, she laughed uproariously at all my jokes, and I'm rarely that funny. Life and people were a joy to be shared and savored to the fullest for Mary. But her disease was robbing her of most of the connections that had meant so much to her. It was slowly but surely isolating her.

When I first met Mary, she was able to tell me quite a bit about herself, but as the disease progressed, we resorted to trial and error in our communication. Mostly she'd try and I'd make errors, trying to decipher the few sounds she was still able to make. I knew Mary loved the Twenty-third Psalm, preferably the King James Version, and we'd recite it together as best we could. She'd shout words out with gusto as I got to them in our recitation. So Mary's version of the psalm, condensed to its critical component features, became: "My shepherd! Green pastures! No evil! With me! Anoint! Cup! Mercy!"

As the months passed, and the disease worsened, the psalm was eventually reduced by Mary to just two words: "With me!" Those words say it all: "With me!" If the Talmud claims that "I don't know" are sacred words, words that help us know the presence of God, surely so are these. "With me" meant something very sacred, very precious to her.

As Christians we assert this same precious and comforting insight about the Incarnation—that God finds astounding ways to be *with us*. We are not alone. That is a basis of faith, a comfort in time of isolation or distortion or doubt, a connecting line in a framework of hope.

Notes

1. Frederick Buechner in *The Living Pulpit* 1 (April-June, 1992), p. 6.
2. Rabbi Stephen D. Franklin, "Quotations on the Many Views of Hope," in *The Living Pulpit* 1 (January-March, 1992), p. 29.

COMMENT

Lectionary texts often present the conscientious interpreter with an abundance of hermeneutical difficulties and ethical dilemmas. For example, what is a modern congregation to make of ancient animal sacrifice? How does a preacher who is open to truth in other traditions deal with the Old Testament's reveling in the triumph of God over other deities? What happens when a compassionate and pastoral spirit encounters one of the many slaughters that seem to vindicate God's sovereignty? Can one extrapolate from political texts like this to develop and strengthen personal faith in stressful times?

The joy and genius of lectionary preaching lie precisely in these dilemmas. One can imagine the likes of Jesse Jackson or Pat Robertson gleefully choosing this text. Its heavy confrontational stance, its overlay of self-righteousness and its simplistic division of people into followers of God or Baal fit well with their self-understood "prophetic" sensibilities. But in lectionary-based preaching, the text chooses you. Ms. Alexander is more pastoral counselor than political activist. She brings to her preaching a highly trained intellect, a compassionate sensitivity to human suffering, and a deeply respectful attitude toward individual spiritual direction. One is curious about how she will interpret this lesson.

By situating her reading within her visit to the Holocaust Memorial, Alexander effectively puts the question so many of us are asking. How could our God—the Good Shepherd, the intimate Friend, revealed to us in the Crucified One—how could this God sanction such a slaughter? Does not this text lend credibility to all the horrors perpetrated by one group against another in the name of the Holy One? Indeed, it is a very "hard sell." We are grateful that she recognizes this dilemma and implicitly promises to address it.

But it is not so much God's stunning victory over Baal's prophets that attracts her attention. It is Elijah's treatment of those prophets. She is not impressed by Elijah's demonstration of power. She is impressed by how power has distorted his soul. This distortion and its antidote form the central themes of her sermon.

Elijah's performance in this ancient religious superbowl reveals the epitome of a machismo spirituality. In today's comprehensive and often power-driven world, Alexander's challenge is at least as "prophetic" as many that are more overtly political. Through her gentle questioning, I see the church's tradition correcting itself. I hear in her voice the time-honored Hebraic regard for strangers, aliens and even enemies. In this sermon, the pastor critiques the prophet. The spiritual director engages the political activist. Where other interpreters may see only "representatives" of God or Baal locked in a struggle for mastery, mere characters in an ancient story, Alexander sees real people with real lives. She sees real tragedy unfold, and real harm done. Finally, she allows a very real person (Mary), who suffers from a very real disease (Huntington's Chorea), to offer the needed corrective for both Elijah and the modern listener.

STRUCTURE

I once encountered a public speaker who advocated replacing the traditional speaker's outline or manuscript with a "story board." A good speech progresses, he believed, more like a story unfolding than a case being argued. A story board is not a story but a device used by today's media-savvy masters of persuasion. It has a starting point and a destination. The speech itself becomes a journey through various situations until it arrives at its destination. Sometimes it circles back upon itself. But just like the pilgrim's progress, every situation through which it passes modifies the journey and contributes to its inevitable conclusion.

Alexander's sermon, "With Me," reminds me of this advice. It is linear rather than impressionistic, but it does not follow a typical sermonic outline. Rather, it is linear in the sense of having a "story line" that refines through juxtaposition. It also is linear (*kav*) in the sense of conveying (by its very nature) a message of hope. The structure itself leads from dissonance to resolution. It respects our discomfort. It honors our questions. It promises insight. It teaches faith. In a real sense, Alexander's method is her message; the way she structures her presentation communicates the content of her sermon.

The listener is invited to join Alexander on a journey of exploration and discovery. We begin with a problematic text, react to it, turn it over and around for more understanding. There is something deeply troubling here, and we don't see immediately what it is. The narrated competition which results in such staggering bloodshed, and Elijah's certainty that his God is being served, clash with our knowledge that God belongs to no single tribe, our belief that God's nature is authentic love, and our experience of God as an intimate and caring companion.

We carry the text, and our questions of it, into the Holocaust Memorial. What could be more appropriate? "Entirely too much horror has been perpetrated on one group by another," proclaims Alexander. In today's world, all of us must construct our theologies on this side of the Holocaust. She reminds us that people (even us) can do wrong for the right reasons.

What is particularly poignant here is our awareness that Elijah once had been God's spokesperson for the downtrodden and oppressed. Now he himself orders the slaughter that will guarantee "our" God's ascendancy in the land. "Evil" Jezebel becomes the instrument who convicts him of his wrong. Paradox runs riot here, creating a troubling moral confusion for the listener. Is there no way out?

It is the confusion of an alienated mind and a distorted spirit that we encounter—Elijah's and our own. In the bioethics seminar we find that we are not alone. Some of our country's most highly trained specialists in moral thinking get together—people with good minds and good intentions—and even they are humbled by their lack of certainty. Here, already, the sermon's final destination is foreshadowed. A little self-doubt enters the story, not as a curse but as an antidote to the cures of isolated, private judgment. The ethicists are humbled, but they gain in mutual respect.

The Talmud and Frederick Buechner next appear on our path. Gaining insights from them, we begin to experience our confusion as confession, and our self-doubt as a God-given corrective to our penchant to idolize the self. A softer, wiser and warmer spirituality is emerging, one that is profoundly relational. Alexander is saying that, left to our own devises, we deceive ourselves and harm others. But there is more: to be alone, to be profoundly, utterly and spiritually alone—this is the essence and definition of despair.

Our journey continues into physical and spiritual darkness—the night of a son's terror and a parent's helplessness. This modern parallel with Elijah's isolation becomes a turning point for our exploration. In these night terrors we recognize that what we *feel*—alone—and what is true are not necessarily the same. Indeed, like a distraught mother, God pours out evidence to the contrary (winds, earthquakes, fires or even, according to Alice Walker, the color purple), but we remain convinced that we are alone. Whether in our fear or in our righteousness, in our despair or in our terror, we have an uncanny ability to hold on to our illusion of isolation.

Such despair need only be penultimate, however. It represents a "defining moment" of choice. It is a concealed opportunity. It invites us to take stock, account for ourselves, repent of our self-sufficiency, and connect "to things and people around us which are outside of our despair." Our real choice lies between the ways of death and life, despair and hope, isolation and community. Alexander's Hebrew word study of *tikvah* and *kav* gives us this "life-line" of connection. It has brought us through darkness to the threshold of hope. It is capable of leading us through whatever spiritual desert we experience into a flourishing garden of faith.

By now we are persuaded. Our journey has reached its destination. Our intellects have been satisfied and convinced. Our story has reached its conclusion—almost. One thing remains: to touch and heal our hearts and bring the story "home." This Alexander does with a deftness that is breathtaking.

The rancor and self-righteousness of the early Elijah has dissipated. He who was so powerful, so impressive to the biblical narrator, he who once commanded fire from heaven and mayhem on earth, this man has become one of us: vulnerable, afraid, alone, despairing. We have seen into his soul.

Now we meet Mary, in so many ways his opposite. A modern person like us, she has been "marginalized" by a relentless, progressive disease. She knows a growing helplessness. Her isolation is real. A profound powerlessness over the simplest functions limits severely the quality of her physical life. But with determination and hope she stays connected. Unlike Elijah, Mary looks despair in the eye. She doesn't blink in the presence of growing disability. What is the source of her strength? She is convinced of a truth that escaped Elijah altogether: she is not—not now, never was and never will be—alone. The essential truth is out: God is "with me." In our enemies' presence, God is with us. In the valley of the shadow of death, God is with us. And where God is: "No evil! Green pastures! Anoint! Cup! Mercy!" In the terrors of the night, God is with us. In the midst of ethical ambiguity, God is with us. Even in the Holocaust—dare we say it? We are not alone.

This is a stunning conclusion, more significant than any mere retelling of an ancient story of one god's victory over another. Pastorally, it speaks volumes to anxious parishioners, allowing faith to be deepened through honest questions and living role models. Although it is not a political sermon, activists will find much here that feeds them. Alexander offers a real cure for burnout (connectedness) even as she cautions against easily dividing the world into "us" and "them."

RESPONSE

The sermon requires of us what God requires of Elijah: to respond to the question, "What are you doing here?" It invites us to take stock of our lives, to ponder how we got to where we are. It suggests an accounting before God of "the most serious proportions." We will be missing the point of the sermon altogether, however, if we think we can do this alone. Ancient disciplines of "spiritual direction" or "spiritual friendship" are being revived in earnest to help us meet this need. Imagine how differently the biblical story might have ended had Elijah found and consulted a sensitive, discerning spiritual director! Imagine how differently our own lives might unfold (and our preaching improve!) if each of us were to enter into an intimate and honest relationship with a trusted spiritual friend.

A second response to the sermon is to pay attention to what our ene-mies are saying about us! They probably see us with distinctly unsympa-thetic eyes. They may not be right, nor have they the right to dictate the course of our lives. But we often have more to learn from them than from our more adoring and less critical friends.

A third response, especially for the more dogmatically included among us, is to entertain a little self-doubt. We shouldn't wallow in it, but accept that none of us has all the answers. We need to allow for ambiguity or uncertainty and beware of dogmatism. As much as we can, we should stay in touch with people who are caring and discerning. We should ponder what Howard Thurman used to say: "That which is true in any religion is in the religion because it is true. It is not true because it is in that religion."

A fourth response, and the one most clearly the point of the sermon, is to stay connected! We should stay connected to people, our faith com-munity, nature, art, and faith-nurturing traditions. We should stay con-nected to all the ways that God is trying to connect to us. Especially, if depression is a problem, or fear, or loneliness, or cynicism, or a judgmen-tal nature, we should make a practice of valuing others and discerning through them what God may be saying to us.

SUGGESTIONS

- Select a text that is difficult for you, and live with it for a while. Carry it with you in the back of your mind as you go about your business. Put aside conventional interpretations, orthodox conclusions or "right answers" to the questions it poses, and allow the questions to penetrate or even deconstruct the text. Look for paradoxes. Ponder the point or points of difficulty. Imagine the text speaking to the var-ious situations or people you encounter. Apply a "hermeneutics of suspicion"; how would your view change if the principal characters were really less good or less evil than depicted?
- Consider using a story board to construct your sermon rather than the more traditional outline. Consider your sermon as flow, move-ment, dance or journey rather than argument or instruction. Try

drawing rather than writing your sermon notes. How would they look if they consisted of pictures rather than words? What is the destination of your sermon?

- In your preparation, juxtapose and relate situations, texts and concepts that may have no obvious connections. Look for hidden threads of continuity and meaning. Look for the discontinuities, the dissonance, the gaps through which new insight might emerge.

Gilbert R. Friend-Jones

MEETING GOD WHERE YOU ARE

GENESIS 21:8–21; MATTHEW 10:24–31

REV. DR. GARY D. STRATMAN
FIRST AND CALVARY PRESBYTERIAN CHURCH
SPRINGFIELD, MISSOURI

REV. DR. GARY D. STRATMAN

MEETING GOD WHERE YOU ARE

GENESIS 21:8–21; MATTHEW 10:24–31, NRSV

As we have listened together this morning to that ancient story from Genesis, the impression that we have at the beginning, and that stays with us through much of the story, is that it is all about Isaac. Last week we looked at how Abraham and Sarah were given one of the greatest promises ever. They would be blessed with a son, and through that son all the nations of the earth would be blessed. Can you imagine their delight as they held on to that promise and believed, even through the hardships and difficult times? God would make God's purpose known. The son would come, and the seed that would be the sign of the blessing to all the world would be theirs.

But now the rest of the story.... They became older and older. No promised son came. They got to the point where it was literally laughable to think that they could parent any child. Indeed, when God finally said to them, "You will bear a son next year and his name will be Isaac," they laughed. It is the laughter of incredulity: "How could that be?" It is perhaps even the laugh of derision: "Don't be mocking us at this time." Then, the promise is fulfilled. The laughter turns into the laughter of joy at the unbelievable graciousness and goodness of God. That which had been promised, and seemed hopeless, is now a reality. Can you imagine how much Isaac was loved? Can you imagine how this love that surrounded him was coupled with faith? Every time they expressed their love to him, they also spoke of the faithfulness of God that had brought him into the world.

Duke Ellington, the jazz great, once answered a question about how his life had been so positive with all that was going against him. He said that when he was growing up, he was always being carried by some member of his family. "My feet didn't touch the ground until I was seven years old." Isn't that a wonderful image? If that was said of Duke Ellington, can't you imagine how it was with Isaac? This child whose coming into the world they had despaired of was now a miracle child. He was celebrated every day of his young life and given unbelievable love, acceptance, joy and laughter. I can imagine the first words he spoke were greeted with a party. The first time he took steps, there was a celebration. If you think that's not true, look at the story that we read this morning. When he was weaned from his mother's breast, they had a feast. A "weaning feast." That may seem like an oxymoron. But with the tremendous infant mortality rate of those times, for a child just to make it through to age two or three was a miracle.

There is more in the story. You don't find anywhere else in the Scriptures a weaning feast for anybody. Isaac was a special child. As I have read the story of Isaac through all the passages that talk of him, it seems as though he doesn't have the highs or the lows that you find in Abraham or Sarah or Jacob or Esau. Somehow he imbibes that spirit of trust, love, and God's faithfulness without all the highs and lows. If that happens to us, as it does sometimes, we should not question it or worry about it, but give thanks.

That's only the very beginning of the story. It is not even the greatest portion of the story we read this morning. The story speaks not only of those who are blessed with an almost easy faith in God, it also is about those who wander in the wilderness and wonder if God will ever meet them, or appear in their lives again. This story is for those who have gone through desert times, when everything seems arid. We wonder if all of those things we said we believed were really true: Is there a personal God who cares about us? Has God missed what has happened to us? Those of us who live in the desert and want to know if God can meet us where we are—this story is for us.

In the story Ishmael, Abraham's son by Sarah's servant girl, and Isaac are playing together. They must have been friends. They must have enjoyed each other's company. Yet did you notice the response to this seemingly harmless scene? Sarah goes to Abraham and says, "We have to get rid of Hagar and her son, Ishmael. We must ban them from the camp. Send them out into the wilderness."

If we understand the context of those words, we know Sarah was afraid. Life was difficult in those times. The best chance for survival was your children: in old age they would care for you, sustain you. Even more than that, this child was the sign of God's promise of future greatness. Sarah was afraid of any rival that would take anything away from Isaac. We can, begrudgingly perhaps, understand her motives. What troubles us is why God allowed it. Why did God allow Sarah to convince Abraham to send these two out into the wilderness? I wish Hagar and Ishmael could have heard the promise that was spoken to Abraham. "They'll be all right. He'll be a great person. Out of him will come a great nation. I will take care of them." When they are banned from the camp, they know that their doom is sealed.

The reason some of us can hear this story, when so many other biblical stories fly past us, is that we have been in the wilderness. One of the questions that keeps gnawing at us is "How did I get here?" Because the story is not about deserving the wilderness, it is about being in the wilderness. There are those this morning who have known the pain of losing a job in the full blush of your powers. You have gifts to give and people to help, and the question comes, "Why?" Sometimes circumstances include an unfairness that we cannot make right, and we wonder why.

There are others who have known the wilderness of seeing a child suffer. When that happens we wonder why. We want to grab hold of some great pillar of heaven and shake it and say, "Yes, God, but why the little ones? Why the innocent ones?" There are others who have committed themselves to those they counted both faithful and filled with faith but have encountered faithless betrayal. We want to know how could God allow this? These are our desert places. The desert is the place where we begin to despair, to doubt that God will ever meet us again in a way that really makes a difference.

Look again at our story. Hagar and Ishmael are in the wilderness. We don't know how long they have been there, but their provisions have run out. The bread is no more. There is no more water. For us, too, our provisions for coping, for being able to make sense of the world, are depleted. The assurance that keeps us going, the sense that "all will be well, it will be all right," begins to fade and there seems to be no life-giving vision anymore.

Hagar and Ismael wander in the desert of Beersheba without hope. Their fate seems to be sealed.

What is described next makes every parent shudder. Hagar puts Ishmael under some bushes and moves a distance away, because she cannot bear to watch the death of her child. *God, where are you in the desert?* Then something happens. The child cried out under the bushes where he was. Through a child's instinct, he cried out and the mother wept. The messenger of God, for that's what an angel is, said to Hagar, "God has heard the voice of the boy where he is" (Gen. 21:17).

I want you to write those words down, but not on a piece of paper. My prayer is that the Spirit of God will write them on your heart: "God has heard [his] voice...where he is." Listen to those words. Ishmael didn't have to go back to the camp for God to hear him. Those words mean that we don't have to go back and get our faith in line first. It doesn't mean we quell all the doubts that storm through our souls. It doesn't mean that everything is as it was in the past. God hears us where we are, with all our questions, our doubts, our inconsistencies. God hears us in all the unfairness of events that take place. God hears our cry! The message is that God hears, cares and delivers. This deliverance does not take us back, but moves us forward to a fresh beginning with new vision and new provision.

I don't get too excited about the phrase "back to God." I don't think we go back. I think God is always out in front of us, always ready to do a new thing. That was the God Hagar and Ishmael met in the wilderness. Hear the story: After her tears and the boy's cry, Hagar was able to see a well. There was new provision for them, not back in the camp but in the desert. She was able to take the water, a provision of help and wholeness, to her son. Notice what it says about Ishmael. New provisions are given for his future as well, not back in the camp, not with Abraham and Sarah. He is given a wife out of Egypt. The provision of God comes from a new place. Ishmael also sees himself in a new way, as a capable person, expert with a bow, a person fitted for the wilderness. Ishmael is able, by God's grace, to turn the wilderness into a place of life. Do you hear the word of God? We will not always be taken back to the place that was, but God is going before us to provide new provision and a new vision.

A few seconds before this service, one of the choir members mentioned something I didn't know about the wonderful anthem we heard this morning. It was written at the time of the bombing of Poland during World War II. When the writer should have been devoid of all hope, he went to his writing table and penned this anthem as a way of saying, "Even in this wilderness of destruction, God will carry us through. The Lord gives, the Lord takes away. Blessed be the name of the Lord."

In reading the story of Hagar and Ishmael, I was reminded of a point made by Claus Westermann, a German scholar who has written a three-volume work on the book of Genesis. One idea, in particular, stuck with me. He says that "in this story we have the truth, that in the cry of the outcast, we find Jesus Christ as Savior."[1] Until we know we are in a desert or a "bombed-out land," we have no need of a deliverer. It is when we are in the wilderness that we know we can only be saved by the one who cried out on the cross, *"Eloi, Eloi, lema sabachthani?"* —the cry of dereliction, the cry of the outcast. That outcast became a Savior, and so we who dwell in the desert have hope. Amen.

Note

1. Claus Westermann, *Genesis: A Practical Commentary,* translated by David E. Green, (Wm. Eerdmans, 1987), p. 156.

COMMENT

Towering personalities dominate many of the stories in the Bible. Figures such as Abraham, Moses, David, Jesus, Peter and Paul loom large in the biblical narratives. The writers of Scripture devote chapter after chapter to them. When we read of their exploits, we cannot help but sense that these were special people. God blessed them tremendously and used them to accomplish extraordinary things. They are epic figures, and the accounts of their struggles teach us much about the ways of God.

Fortunately, the Bible also recounts the stories of many lesser, more ordinary figures. Many of these appear briefly and we never read of them again. Despite their lesser roles, these minor characters also have much to teach us about the ways of God.

In his sermon, Gary Stratman draws on the story of Ishmael in just this way. He appeals to Ishmael to remind all of us that God can indeed meet us where we are.

PROBLEM

Ishmael exemplifies the predicament of all who find themselves wandering outside the boundaries of blessing and wonder if God can reach them there. Banished by Abraham, Hagar and Ishmael wander through the desert with few provisions. Their hope dries up with the last of their water. They are forsaken and alone.

Stratman contends that Ishmael's story "is for those who have gone through the desert times, when everything seems arid.... Those of us who live in the desert and want to know if God can meet us where we are—this story is for us." Ishmael's story is for every person who feels unblessed, unchosen, second-best and beyond the reach of God.

Certainly, this accounts for the story's appeal. Most of us struggle day in and day out to keep our meager faith alive. Where our heroes in the faith seem to possess immediate access to God, we often wonder where God is. Where our heroes seem abundantly blessed in every aspect, we often see ourselves as unblessed. We wonder if God can have anything to do with our lives.

TEXT

To present his message, Stratman does not limit himself to the text. He places the story of Ishmael in context by retelling the story of Abraham and Sarah and the birth of Isaac. This strategy is very effective. By recounting the story of Isaac, he sets up a powerful contrast. Isaac is "a special child." He is loved and celebrated at every turn. For him, there seems never to be a moment when he does not recognize that he is blessed.

Isaac's blessedness points up Ishmael's predicament. Isaac is loved and cherished; Ishmael is told he is unwanted and banished from the camp. Ishmael is not the chosen child of the promise. Celebration and joy attend every moment of Isaac's life. He has everything he needs and more. Ishmael's survival is in doubt. He lives hand-to-mouth.

By utilizing the context as well as the text itself, Stratman calls attention to the way life is. Just as Isaac and Ishmael played together, so the chosen and the not-chosen live and play alongside one another in the world as we experience it. The more-blessed and the less-blessed rub shoulders. By setting forth the context of Ishmael's story, Stratman implicitly reminds us of the scandal of God's ways. God chooses! God chooses to work out his purpose through certain human beings, and none of us can say for sure why. But by focusing on Ishmael's story, he affirms a signal truth: God cares for all, the chosen and the ones not chosen. The story of God's ways is not "all about Isaac"; it is also about Ishmael.

STRUCTURE

As noted, Stratman begins this sermon by placing the text in context. He sets up the story of Ishmael by retelling the story of Isaac. Once that is done, however, he focuses exclusively on the text at hand, and the sermon essentially follows the outline of the text. Events in the story propel the development of the sermon. Each new element in the story allows Stratman to comment both on the situation in the story and our own situation in life. This progression leads to the main point of the sermon, which comes near the conclusion of the story itself: "God has heard the voice of the boy where he is."

Not every sermon can be developed in this way, but here it works since the text tells a story. Obviously, the story suggests other themes and ideas that could have served as sermon material. Stratman, however, has remained faithful to the story itself and its basic thrust.

PROCLAMATION

The good news announced by this sermon is that God can hear you wherever you are. No matter how "unspecial" your life seems, no matter how hopeless your life appears, God can meet you. God cares for the outcast, for the person who lives on the edge. Although it is never incorporated into the sermon itself, the message highlights the concluding word of the New Testament lesson: "So do not be afraid; you are of more value than many sparrows" (Matt. 10:31). God values all of us and can meet us anywhere, even when we find ourselves in the most inhospitable and threatening wilderness. Because of God's inescapable care, we never run out of possibilities. Because God hears us wherever we are, we always have a future.

RESPONSE

In this message, Stratman primarily seeks to encourage his listeners. He makes his purpose clear when he says, "I want you to write those words down, but not on a piece of paper. My prayer is that the Spirit of God will write them on your heart." He wants his congregation to take this one word home with them, the word that God hears wherever you are.

Both the style and content of Stratman's appeal here reveal genuine concern for his parishioners. He cares about his people. I have the impression that he preached this text, not just because it was prescribed in the lectionary, but also because he was aware of those who needed to hear its message.

SUGGESTIONS

- This sermon illustrates the value of preaching on the "minor characters" of the Bible. For the biblically literate, familiarity with the big names often breeds contempt. We think we've heard it all before and have nothing new to learn. Then again, sometimes the epic heroes of the Bible just seem too big. There are no obvious points of contact between their lives and ours. Sermons on the lesser characters remove these hindrances. Because we don't know these figures well, they invite our attention. Because they are not larger than life, they appeal to folks rooted in the ordinary. Messages drawn from the experiences of these figures remind us they have something to say to us about God's ways in this world.

- The best preaching touches people where they live. Take some time to think about the members of your congregation. What is the shape of their wilderness experience? Identify their wilderness situations and then preach to them there. Nothing is more gratifying than to hear someone comment after a sermon, "I think you were talking to me."

- Find a biblical story and allow the development of the story to control the development of your sermon. Unfortunately, we often develop artificial structures to convey our message. We boil a story down into a number of "points," sometimes completely unrelated. Sometimes our best preaching occurs when we retell the story and allow it to convey the message it articulates on its own.

William J. Ireland, Jr.

COMMENT

CONSEQUENCES OF FORGIVEN SIN

2 SAMUEL 12:5–14; PSALM 51

BEN HADEN
FIRST PRESBYTERIAN CHURCH
CHATTANOOGA, TENNESSEE

CONSEQUENCES OF FORGIVEN SIN

2 SAMUEL 12:5–14; PSALM 51, NAS

W hen a sin is forgiven—is that all there is to it, as though it never happened?

The woman has been married six times. She has had more affairs than she can enumerate. She has been a gangster's moll, an actress, a model, and quite an accomplished artist. She has also spent twenty-seven months in a federal prison. Yet if you study her face at the age of forty-five, you will not find a line there.

The title of her book is *My Face for the World to See.* Her name is Liz Renay. An interview with her was nationally syndicated. A metropolitan newspaper gave the story an eight-column headline: "If Liz Renay Sinned—It Left No Mark."

How we would like to believe that! Yet the editor who wrote the headline apparently did not read the story too carefully. Following her first marriage at the age of fifteen and a series of escapades with various soldiers, Liz said she was overcome with a sense of guilt. So she went to a psychiatrist. She said he assured her: "You have done nothing wrong. You have no reason to feel guilty. You have simply loved and received love in return. You have done no one harm. You have given only joy."

"For the first time," Liz says, "I was relieved of guilt."

Today no one dwells on how many times Liz has had her face lifted—or whether it has ever been lifted. We simply dwell on the fact that her face is unchanged after forty-five years of all types of experiences that violate the living Lord.

If Liz Renay sinned, it left no mark on her face. Did it leave a mark on her soul?

Perhaps you read in *Nation's Business*[2] the result of a poll conducted among the readers of this widely circulated magazine. Readers selected the ten outstanding men in American business history. They named the following in this order:

1. Henry Ford
2. Alexander Graham Bell
3. Thomas Edison
4. Andrew Carnegie
5. Walt Disney
6. John D. Rockefeller
7. Benjamin Franklin
8. Bernard Baruch
9. Thomas Watson
10. George Eastman

An outstanding group? Unquestionably. Would you agree with the selections? Perhaps so…perhaps not. But the article tells nothing about the effect of their personal lives on the lives of others. It tells nothing about the sins of these men, and the fallout of those sins. But it is about sin and its results that we study today.

I think every one of us would like to know whether, when we are forgiven by the Lord, we then have a certain immunity from the consequences of the confessed sin. The answer is that we do not. Would to God we did, but we do not!

Now then, come with me. Follow the man. He is rich, handsome, a national hero, just about forty years old. He is David, king of Israel. Literally—as far as David is concerned—there are no worlds left to conquer. David is God's man. God says David is a man after God's own heart. If you were to seek the most humble and godly man in all Israel, you would not likely choose a priest. You would probably choose the king—David.

Let's return for a moment to the beginning of the story—to David's youth. The prophet Samuel is grieving over the failure of Saul, Israel's first king, and the Lord's rejection of Saul. The Lord orders Samuel to go to Jesse of Bethlehem. There, he informs Samuel, he has selected a king from among the sons of Jesse. Samuel fears for his life if he anoints another man king while Saul is still on the throne. So God instructs Samuel to take a heifer to sacrifice and to invite Jesse and his sons to the sacrifice. Samuel is to anoint the one whom the Lord designates.

When Samuel sees Eliab, the eldest son of Jesse, he quickly assumes that this is the Lord's anointed. But the Lord reminds Samuel not to look at the appearance or the height of the man. "God sees not as a man sees," God tells him, merely the outward appearance, "but the Lord looks at the heart" (1 Sam. 16:7).

Samuel must have remembered then that Saul was the most handsome man in all the nation when he had been chosen king by the elders. But he had failed.

Seven sons are presented to Samuel by Jesse. Samuel tells Jesse the Lord has not chosen any of them. Does he have other children? he asks Jesse. Jesse says his eighth child, the youngest son, is tending sheep. Samuel asks Jesse to send that son to him. The son is David. When David comes, the Lord tells Samuel to anoint David as his choice.

Scripture tells us that the Spirit of the Lord came mightily upon David from that day forward. And apparently simultaneously, the Spirit of the Lord departed from Saul, and he was terrorized by an evil spirit from the Lord. Saul's advisers urged him to obtain a harpist to calm his mind. It is a young man who suggests David as the harpist. David comes and not only calms Saul but later wins a victory over Goliath the giant. When jealous Saul seeks to kill David, the Lord helps him escape. The Lord gives David the integrity to honor Saul as long as he is on the throne and not to harm him. The Lord gives an awesome patience to David though he has already been anointed as Saul's replacement.

Now all that waiting period is past. Saul is dead. David sits on the throne still very much the hero of the nation Israel. As king he is naturally the commander-in-chief of his army. For reasons not explained, David sends the army into battle but remains at home. He neglects the duty of his office to lead.

One day David looks out on the city of Jerusalem from his rooftop. He sees a woman—Bathsheba—taking a bath. She is the wife of a soldier fighting for his king. He lusts after her, sends for her, seduces her. You know the story. She conceives a child.

What begins as lust ends in adultery, conspiracy and murder.

Now the prophet Nathan comes to the court of King David, who is sitting as judge of Israel. Nathan presents, in an anonymous fashion, the sin of David. David is incensed when he hears his story presented as though it were about a third party. He doesn't recognize it.

Sitting in the seat of judgment, David concludes: "This man, whoever he is, shall surely die. This man, whoever he is, shall repay fourfold what he has taken."

Then very quietly Nathan announces, "King David, you are the man!"

David does not banish Nathan from the court. He does not deny the accusation. He simply confesses his guilt and throws himself on the mercy of God: "I have sinned against God."

Then Nathan spells out the consequences that will follow the sins of adultery, conspiracy and murder that have occurred in the life of God's number one advertisement—the king of the Lord's own nation Israel.

"The son Bathsheba will bear you will die," Nathan tells David. "The sword will never leave your house and there will be evil within your house from this day forward. But the Lord has put away your sin, and you shall not die."

There is a tremendous difference between the forgiveness of sin and the consequence of sin. All of us would like to unite forgiveness and consequence. We want to believe that if the Lord puts our sin behind us, then no consequences lie ahead for us.

Not so. The sin that is behind us, in the sense that God does not hold it against us in judgment, is all too often the sin that is before us as long as we live. Let us look at David's own judgment. "He will repay fourfold, whoever this man is."

First, David loses his infant son after praying with a contrite heart: "Lord, if it be your will, be gracious to me and spare the child, despite what you have told me through Nathan." But the child is not spared.

Second, David's daughter is raped by his son Amnon, and Amnon is slain by his son Absalom. Third, Absalom seeks to overthrow David and he, too, is slain.

Fourth, at the end of David's life his son Adonijah seeks to overthrow and replace David as king. But David anoints Solomon and declares him king. In time, the fourth son, Adonijah, is executed by Solomon.

And what about the effect on David himself? Does he die as God's man? Yes. Does he remain the symbol of faithfulness to the Lord? Yes. Does he turn against the Lord and withdraw into inactivity? No. But the indications are that David was never quite the same, never quite as useable, and never quite as joyful.

This was the king who was so joyful with the return of the Lord's Ark and danced with such total abandon that he offended his wife. She thought David made a spectacle of himself in his abandon. Now there is the consequence of sin. The sword does not leave David's house and evil seems to encompass it.

I am sure that at times David cried out again and again: "If I just had not looked at that woman. If I had just stopped at the point of lust. If I had just stopped at the point of lying. If I had just stopped at the point of adultery. But no. I went further. I actually murdered a soldier who was as faithful to me, his king, as I was faithless to the Lord, my king."

There is a difference between paying for sin permanently in this life and paying for it eternally. No believer will ever pay for a sin eternally. But there is no assurance from Scripture that, as long as we live, we will not have to endure the inevitable consequences of the evil that we have set in motion. There is no such thing as sin in isolation. There is no way that we can sin without affecting another life. And try as we will, sin is not private. Oh, how we wish it were!

We may find our sins affecting the innocent sometimes twenty years later, sometimes in subsequent generations, in what the Greeks call full circle. We may endure a misery and hurt we cannot at first understand. Then it occurs to us: "This is really the inevitable result of what was set in motion when I sinned against the Lord so many years ago."

Well, what is the joy of it? The joy of it is that having committed a sin this serious—a sin as serious as any of us has ever committed—David was forgiven. When David said to Nathan, "I have sinned against the Lord," Nathan replied: "The Lord also has taken away your sin; you shall not die" (2 Sam. 12:13). The spirit of David's confession and cry for forgiveness is captured in the famous psalm:

> Be gracious to me, O God, according to Thy lovingkindness;
> According to the greatness of Thy compassion blot out my
>   transgressions.
> Wash me thoroughly from my iniquity,
> And cleanse me from my sin....
> Against Thee, Thee only, I have sinned,
> And done what is evil in Thy sight,...
> Behold, Thou dost desire truth in the innermost being....
> Purify me with hyssop, and I shall be clean;
> Wash me, and I shall be whiter than snow....
> Create in me a clean heart, O God,
> And renew a steadfast spirit within me (Psalm 51:1–10).

That is the famous prayer traditionally associated with David the sinner. It may have been written by him. It is a prayer for God's help by one who is deeply aware of sin and guilt and needs God's forgiveness.

Do you know the glory and the incentive for remaining faithful day by day? It is so we can avoid the natural consequences of sin as long as we are on this earth.

Back in 1945 I knew a young man who had a new car. And at the time I didn't know anyone else with a new car, right at the end of World War II. One night he went out with friends. He and everyone with him that night got drunk. They did argue about whether he should drive, but he insisted on driving because, as he noted, "It's my car." He drove them at seventy miles an hour—straight into a tree, not even making an effort to make the turn. In the back seat was an only child, an eighteen-year-old girl. She was killed instantly. There were three others who are, in some fashion maimed to this day. One boy lost his leg. One girl never got to pursue her modeling career. All as a consequence of one man who after all, did own the car, was drunk, knew he was drunk and insisted on driving.

Let's assume the driver was a Christian and was forgiven. Did the boy's leg grow back? Was that single child resurrected and returned to her parents? Unless you have lost a child, it's impossible to understand the void, anguish and emptiness her death produced in her parents. So long as that driver lives, he will never forget the tree he hit at seventy miles an hour. The accident was the natural consequence of driving drunk. That is what happened. It cannot be undone.

Was David ever as useable again? I don't think so. I doubt if he ever had the same degree of joy. A lot more wisdom, but not the same degree of joy. Show me a person who is very, very wise and who is a believer. They have probably lost the naïveté of their joy.

Yet we know that the anguish for our sin we endure is just for a while, because we are cleansed, washed thoroughly and completely, and the sins we have confessed in the name and in the blood of Christ are simply not held against us. But being very practical, we have to anticipate that as long as we are here, at any point, at any turn along the road, we may see another side effect of our sin committed long ago.

That is why the private sins of businessmen are so important. That is why the private sin of David was so important. We cannot be king and sin, and not affect the whole kingdom. We cannot be president of the United States and sin, and not affect the nation, and possibly the world. We cannot be in any executive position and sin, and not affect the office, not affect our families and not affect those we love.

That is why the Lord—who intends us good—begs, pleads and urges us, "Do not sin, simply because you know I will forgive you. By all means, remain faithful. Refrain from sinning so you may enjoy me to the fullest. Do not become wise by finding out that I told the truth when I said, 'Your sin will surely find you out'" (Num. 32:23; Rom. 6:1–4).

The world may not know our sin. Our family may not know it. Our closest friend, our spouse, may not know it. But we know it; and in the knowing, we are found out. It doesn't matter how unlined the face is. It doesn't matter whether there is apparent happiness. Each of us is fully aware: "This happened because of what I once did. What else may happen because of what I once did?"

The closer you grow to the Lord, the more serious the consequence of any sin. That is why it behooves a church that declares the Bible to be God's word to honor it, to live our lives as though we were on TV, to be fully aware that our lives are not our business alone. What we do or what we think or what we say is God's business and the consequences may produce fallout from one generation to another.

But how wonderful to have a Lord who says, "I will put away the sin. I will not judge you, David, as you would have judged yourself. I will not take your life. As a matter of fact, I will spend eternity face to face with you. Through the wisdom that has come with sinning and being forgiven, I will make you very wise as to what it means to have a contrite heart and as to what Christ will mean when he comes and dies for you."

It is well to remember that if, today, you have a warm and wonderful relation with Christ, you can jeopardize it. You can remove the joy by deliberately going out and sinning against him. And the greater the believer, the more serious the dimension of sin. That is why Christ calls us "his people." That is why we have the responsibility to live as his people.

"If Liz Renay Sinned—It Left Mark" the headline said. Don't you believe it! It surely did—unless God is a liar.

Notes
1. Source unknown.
2. *Nation's Business:* issue and article unknown.

COMMENT

In the movie *Broadcast News* there is an angry confrontation between the characters played by Albert Brooks and William Hurt. Brooks's character says, "We're talking about crossing the line between right and wrong, here!" to which the slyly sophisticated character played by Hurt replies, "That's the problem. They keep moving the little fellow, don't they!"

There's a popular and growing preconception that morality is a relative concept. Some within Christendom have even tried to incorporate such an attitude into their world-view. Others have stuck to the biblical concept of moral absolutes only to be branded spoilsports and sticks-in-the-mud by others who see no reason for their perceived prudishness.

But moral choices have existential consequences, as Ben Haden's sermon powerfully points out. Haden identifies his intended audience as those Christians who don't see what all the fuss over righteous living is about, since our sins have been forgiven. Building on this premise, he presents the situation of a woman who appears to have beaten the moral system and escaped from a life of "experiences that violate the living Lord" without scarring her appearance in any way. But is that appearance in fact the reality? Are there in fact "consequences for forgiven sin"?

Haden pursues his question with the skilled use of well-turned phrases. Consider some examples: "*Greatness* in business does not necessarily equal *greatness* in their personal lives." "What *begins* as lust *ends* in adultery, conspiracy, and murder." "The sin that is be*hind* us, in terms of judgment, is the sin that is be*fore* us as long as we live." "I actually murdered a soldier who was as faith*ful* to me, *his* king, as I was faith*less* to the Lord, *my* king." (In each case I've added the emphasis to shed light on his style.)

PROBLEM

Haden presents the problem very quickly: "If Liz Renay sinned, it left no mark on her face. Did it leave a mark on her soul?" "Do we have a certain immunity from the consequences of confessed sin? No." "There is no such thing as sin in isolation. There is no way that we can sin without affecting another life. And try as we will, sin is not private."

Any working pastor will find his or her heart assaulted by the physical, emotional, and relational pain in the lives of a congregation and community. Some of this pain is caused by others or by unidentifiable sources, but a substantial amount is caused by our own doing as human beings. The popularity of situational ethics, the sexual revolution, and the "Me Generation," however, will often lead people to deny their own culpability.

This is not an easy message to preach. The good news of God's forgiveness—as well as of the Holy Spirit's power to lead us in paths of righteousness—is not likely to be recognized unless listeners first hear the bad news of their own predicament, including the consequences of sin, even when it is forgiven.

TEXT

There is a skilled variety to the uses of Scripture in this sermon. First, with a simple, "Now then, come with me," Haden invites his congregation to experience the living power of the word of God by sketching the story of David and demonstrating that, long before our own time, someone whom the public thought had it all together fell into a serious series of sins. The drama of David's meteoric rise under the blessing of God is played against what appears to be the beginning of a tragic turn as David moves on from lust to adultery, conspiracy and murder.

One effective way Haden communicates the reality of sin's consequences is his exposition of 2 Samuel 12:6, where David says the unnamed villain (not realizing it is himself) will repay fourfold for his crime. I expect the preacher's demonstration of the ways David had to pay fourfold with the violent deaths of his sons made many listeners sit up and take note. At the same time, Haden further demonstrates the power of the Scriptures by showing with those same examples how the sword—which had been treated idolatrously—would "never depart from [his] house." Such detailing of the moral power of the narrative compels the listener to hear the story in its ethical depth and goes a long way toward getting one's congregation interested in reading the Bible for themselves.

But the crux of the sermon centers on 2 Samuel 12:13–14: "Now the Lord has put away your sin; you shall not die. Nevertheless...the child that is born to you shall die." Haden maintains the biblical and moral tension between forgiveness—"the Lord has put away your sin"—and consequences—"the child...shall die." He knows that the forgiveness of sin is real and important, but he stresses the often-neglected point of the biblical text: the problems sin causes in the sinner's life.

Proclamation

Too often, forgiveness is understood as a whitewashing of past misdeeds. But this sermon stands as a pastoral warning so that the good news can do its work. The core of the gospel comes through as the orientation through which this message is to be understood. When Haden says, "You can jeopardize a warm and wonderful relationship with Christ by deliberately going out and sinning against him," he is declaring the core truth that a living relationship with God's anointed Servant is the Christian's opportunity and privilege. Similarly, the statement, "Christ calls us his people...we have the responsibility to live as his people," bears within it the good news that we, who once were not a people, have now become the people of God.

Response

Haden wants his audience to guard their moral life. He is concerned that his congregation may think that because their sins—past, present, and future—are forgiven, they cannot cause them damage. This sermon cautions us about the serious pain and problems that run in the wake of all sin, forgiven or not. Having reminded us of the inevitable aftermath of sin, the preacher is eager for us to avoid distress by living in righteousness. In theological terms, this is a sermon against antinomianism.

For those who are accustomed to the theological framework of "law and grace" being applied to every sermon, some may think that this sermon has too much "law" and not enough "grace." Some may go so far as to say that this is not a Christian sermon, because the emphasis is clearly on doing works of righteousness, not on the forgiveness Christ has accomplished for the believer by his death on the cross.

One may argue, however, that such a response only proves how important Haden's topic is. The mass-media developments in Christendom—and the disclosures of sin among Christian leaders in all traditions and denominations—suggest that insufficient emphasis is placed on what it means to live in Christian righteousness. Talk of grace easily becomes "cheap grace." *Sanctification* is a word less often heard. The challenges of living in a post-Christian society call for the integrity of the Christian lifestyle perhaps more than ever before.

SUGGESTIONS

- Every age has its fads and passions. Search the *New York Times* non-fiction bestseller list for an indication of what attitudes predominate in current society. Evaluate what popular books say about important ethical topics: materialism, family life, the balance among concerns for the local community, and the world. Develop a series of sermons on these topics. You might consider using a "Devilish-Dialogue" format in these sermons. The devil character's job is to present seductively the subtle heresy—here, the idea that since sin is forgiven it is inconsequential. The voice of the Lord has the task of shooting that snake out of the water!

- After rediscovering the historic Christian emphasis on holy living, most honest Christians will admit struggles with overcoming ingrained or habitual sins. Neil T. Anderson, in *The Bondage Breaker* (Harvest House, 1993) and other books, offers powerful insight into the Holy Spirit's work of sanctification in the life of a Christian. He uses a strong understanding of the saving work of Christ to draw a middle line between psychotherapy and what has often been called "deliverance ministries."

- Help the people you serve keep each other accountable to holy living through small groups. Howard Snyder, in *The Radical Wesley* (Intervarsity Press, 1980), provides some insight into how the

Methodist class meeting model for a cell group might be imported into our time and culture. Richard Lovelace's *The Dynamics of the Spiritual Life* (also IVP, 1979) marks how small groups—meeting frequently for fellowship, personal spiritual growth, and accountability—have been at the core of virtually every major move of the Spirit in the history of the church.

- Help your congregation learn to think Christianly. Determining the will of God has been called "praying over the right information," or in more historic terms, "The Discipline of Contemplation" (Richard Foster, *Celebration of Discipline,* Harper & Row, 1978). Reflect on two very different issues—one global and one personal—and consider what common processes you go through to make sure you have all the information you need to reflect on these matters effectively and prayerfully. Help your congregation adapt the process for issues and concerns that come up in their own lives.

Peter J. Smith

COMMENT

HOW TO SURVIVE THE STORMS OF LIFE

MARK 4:35–41

REV. DENNIS KIZZIAR
CASCADE COMMUNITY CHURCH
SISTERS, OREGON

HOW TO SURVIVE
THE STORMS OF LIFE

MARK 4:35–41, NIV

I t had been a long week. I was just finishing week three of a full-time job to help put our oldest daughter, Jennifer, through her first year of college. With her goal of wanting to be a doctor and another daughter, Amy, beginning college in two years, it was time for me to dust off my teaching credentials and add to the family income. It was January 31, 1992, 6:00 P.M., when the telephone rang.

"Hi, Mom! Guess what? I met two other guys who want to be doctors, too. We studied for our Chem. midterm together and I did really well. Maybe I can end up with an A this term. And I saw a whale down at the beach this week! It was great! I couldn't believe it!"

We continued a twenty-minute conversation, ending with our plans for the following weekend to see her play in a Lacrosse tournament one and a half hours from our home. We missed seeing Jen, being six hours away, but managed to talk by phone a couple of times a week. As we hung up she said, "Love you, Mom. Tell Dad and Amy I'm sorry I missed them, and I love them, too. See you next weekend."

At midnight the same night the phone rang again. "May I

speak with Van or Nancy Switzer?" "This is Nancy." "This is Francisco Torres Dorm. There's been an accident. Jennifer fell from a balcony, and the ambulance has taken her to the hospital. You may call this number to see how she is doing." I broke the pencil trying to write down the number, etching it deeply into the pad so it would be readable. My hand was shaking but I knew Jen would be okay…they had taken her by ambulance, she was being cared for…("Be with her Lord, be real to her right now, may she feel your comfort and presence").

As I hung up to go to a better phone in the kitchen, I spoke to my husband. "Van, it's Jenny. She fell from a balcony." As he immediately jumped out of bed and raced with me to the kitchen phone, I began to panic because of his reaction. He knew she lived on the tenth floor, and if she had fallen from there it would be very grave. I am the family optimist and hoped she had been with some of her friends on the second floor. The emergency room put the doctor on the phone to Van right away. As Van described our beautiful daughter to him for identification, I could hear the doctor's words come through the receiver "…and she did not survive."

The terrible truth set in as we held each other and cried for a long time. Six hours earlier she had been so happy, vibrant, excited about life, and anxious to see us next weekend. We would not see her now until our lifetime was over. She was gone…this child who had grown up into a young lady…had enjoyed life so much, and we had enjoyed life through her as most parents do. She had loved sports, and we loved watching whatever she did. In her short eighteen years she had become an excellent water skier, had biked from Seattle to San Francisco with the church youth, had gone to the USSR with Josh McDowell, and now was beginning to fulfill her goal of being a doctor. As she sat on the balcony railing, as she often did to watch the sunset over the ocean or just to sit and talk with her friends, all her life goals and our dreams for her were shattered in a split second.[1]

This is how an incredible storm came into the life of the Switzer family. They are surviving because of their faith in the living God and their unshakable confidence in his word.

I don't know what storm you are facing or will face in the future, but ⌐ I do know there are some very instructive principles in Mark 4:35–41 that, if applied in the power of the Holy Spirit, will enable you to survive whatever storms you encounter in life.

> That day when evening came, he said to his disciples, "Let us go over to the other side." Leaving the crowd behind, they took him along, just as he was, in the boat. There were also other boats with him. A furious squall came up, and the waves broke over the boat, so that it was nearly swamped. Jesus was in the stern, sleeping on a cushion. The disciples woke him and said to him, "Teacher, don't you care if we drown?"
>
> He got up, rebuked the wind and said to the waves, "Quiet! Be still!" Then the wind died down and it was completely calm. He said to his disciples, "Why are you so afraid? Do you still have no faith?"
>
> They were terrified and asked each other, "Who is this? Even the wind and the waves obey him!"

I. BE INFORMED ABOUT STORMS (VV. 35–37)

Jesus was physically and emotionally exhausted from an intensive, satisfying day of teaching. He fell asleep in the boat on a placid lake while his disciples headed to the other shore. Then the storm began.

There are two key things you need to know about storms.

First, *storms come unexpectedly* (vv. 35–36). The Sea of Galilee is six hundred and twenty feet below sea level and is surrounded by mountains with deep ravines. The ravines serve as gigantic funnels to focus the whirling winds down onto the sea. A severe storm can arise without notice, coming with shattering and terrifying suddenness.

In the same way, storms often come into our lives without any warning whatever. When everything seems to be going well and we think we can kick back and enjoy life, out of nowhere a storm of devastating proportions comes that takes us by total surprise, quickly turning life upside down.

Second, *storms come furiously* (v. 37). It wasn't just a little roughness out there on the Sea of Galilee, it was an incredible, furious squall that threatened to sink the boat.

The furious squall that comes so suddenly and threatens to sink us may be the word *cancer,* it may be divorce, the sudden death of a loved one, a tragic accident, the loss of a job. Any number of things can leave us wondering how we will ever survive such a storm.

Storms come unexpectedly and furiously. The key to survival is to be prepared. It is very difficult to get prepared during the storm; there needs to be prior preparation.

II. BE PREPARED FOR STORMS (VV. 38–41)

Preparation is a continuous process. The more we are prepared, the better we will be able to survive the storms of life. Preparation comes through knowing certain truths that are revealed to us in Scripture. We need to know those truths both intellectually and experientially, letting them become convictions that will grip, change and shape our lives.

First, we need to know that *Jesus cares* (v. 38). The storm did not waken Jesus, but the cries of the men did. Their question was, "Don't you care?" How tempted we are to ask the same question. Sometimes it appears that God is either indifferent to the furious storm that has hit us, or he is ignorant of what we are going through. But even when it seems he may be indifferent and doesn't care, we can know and trust the truth of 1 Peter 5:7: He cares for us.

Frank S. Graeff expressed it well in his beautiful song, "Does Jesus Care?"

Does Jesus care when my heart is pained
  Too deeply for mirth or song,
    As the burdens press,
    And the cares distress,
  And the way grows weary and long?

Refrain:
O yes, He cares; I know He cares,
  His heart is touched with my grief;
    When the days are weary,
    The long nights dreary,
  I know my Savior cares.

Does Jesus care when my way is dark
  With a nameless dread and fear?
    As the daylight fades
    Into deep night shades,
  Does He care enough to be near?

Does Jesus care when I've tried and failed
  To resist some temptation strong;
    When for my deep grief
    There is no relief,
  Though my tears flow all the night long?

Does Jesus care when I've said "goodbye"
  To the dearest on earth to me,
    And my sad heart aches
    Till it nearly breaks,
  Is it aught to Him? Does He see?

Yes, Jesus cares. He loved and cared so much for us that he died upon the cross. He maintains that care and vital interest in every detail of our lives. Be convinced that he cares deeply and intensely about everything that affects you now or ever will affect your life.

That prince of preachers, Charles Spurgeon, expressed it eloquently when he wrote:

> Omnipotence may build a thousand worlds, and fill them with bounties; Omnipotence may powder mountains into dust, and burn the sea, and consume the sky, but Omnipotence cannot do an unloving thing toward a believer. Oh! rest quite sure, Christian, a hard thing from God toward one of His own people is quite impossible. He is as kind to you when he casts you into prison as when He takes you into a palace; He is as good when He sends famine into your house as when He fills your barns with plenty. The only question is, Art thou His child? If so, He hath rebuked thee in affection, and there is love in His chastisement.[2]

Second, we need to know that *Jesus isn't surprised* (v. 39). He wasn't taken aback by the storm, nor was he surprised by it at all. He simply got up and spoke to the waves. In fact, Jesus knew the storm was coming for his disciples. It was part of that day's curriculum. It's a great truth to grasp: God is aware of everything that is going to happen to you. Psalm 139 makes it very clear that God orchestrates all the events of our lives. He is not shocked at all or surprised by what happens. It is part of his sovereign plan and purpose for your life. Know that he anticipates the storm and has it under control.

Third, we need to know that *Jesus will act* (v. 39). In the case of the disciples, Jesus acted immediately and decisively. "He got up, rebuked the wind and said to the waves, 'Quiet! Be still!' Then the wind died down and it was completely calm." He stilled their storm and brought immediate calm to their lives. He is still able to act that way for us, and sometimes he does—but not always. In fact, more times than not, he doesn't work immediately in the storms of our lives. We do not know when or how God is going to act. We cannot write the script for God or dictate the timetable. But we can be assured that God *will* act, in his perfect way and in his perfect timing. We always want him to act on our timetable. We want to tell the Lord, "If you would only do it at this time and do it in this way, everything would be fine." God's ways are higher than our ways. But God will act.

In the meantime, we also need to know that *Jesus is with us* (vv. 35–36). Jesus never left the disciples. He was in the boat with them. We need to be aware of the fact that he is with us. To be aware of his presence is to experience his peace, no matter what particular storm we are going through. It's when we lose the awareness of his presence that we begin to sink in despair. Isaiah 41:10 and 43:1–2 make it very clear that whatever the trials we go through, God is with us and will go through them with us. Therefore it is safer to be in the midst of the storm with his presence than to have no storms and be without his presence. What a great comfort to know that he will never leave us nor forsake us but will take us safely through the storm.

Fifth, we need to know that *Jesus is purposeful* (v. 35). Jesus made it very clear to his disciples where they were going—to the other side of the lake. He didn't promise them an easy trip, but he did promise a guaranteed arrival at their destination. By faith they should have claimed that. And so should we. Jesus is taking us safely to the other side, to heaven, to spend eternity with him. Nothing can thwart that purpose. Job 42:1–2 affirms that, as do Romans 8:28–29 and Philippians 1:6. God will not be denied. Storms are a part of the process of our spiritual growth and maturation (1 Pet. 5:10). Jesus was going to the other side, and the disciples were going with him. Their fate would be his fate. Once you understand that Jesus is purposeful, you can also count on two other great facts: The boat will not sink and the storm will not last forever.

Sixth, we need to know that *Jesus is sovereign* (vv. 39, 41). The disciples had already seen that Jesus was the master of every situation. Now their knowledge was put to the test. Did they believe that? Could he handle their situation?

Is God sovereign? Can God handle your situation? We know God can handle world affairs, but can he handle our own storms, right now? Scripture testifies again and again to the fact that he is sovereign. There is nothing too hard for God. Jeremiah 32:17, 26–27 says it in such a powerful way:

"Ah, Sovereign Lord, you have made the heavens and the earth by your great power and outstretched arm. Nothing is too hard for you...."

Then the word of the Lord came to Jeremiah: "I am the Lord, the God of all mankind. Is anything too hard for me?"

We should be asking ourselves, "How big is our God?" "Is heaven really his throne?" "Is earth his footstool?" If you believe Colossians 1:16–17, you can survive any storms.

For by him all things were created: things in heaven and on earth, visible and invisible, whether thrones or powers or rulers or authorities; all things were created by him and for him. He is before all things, and in him all things hold together. There is not a storm that can ever wreck the program and plan of God. God will accomplish all of his good purposes in your life and in the universe.

Finally, we need to *know our greatest need* (v. 40). Our biggest problem is not the storms that come into our lives—it is our unbelief. The only thing the Lord ever rebuked his disciples for was their lack of faith. Our greatest problems come from within us, because we do not have that deep, solid conviction that our God can do anything. We lack faith not only to believe that God *can,* but faith to believe that God *will.* The disciples had heard Jesus teach the word. They had seen him perform miracles. But, when it came right down to it, they still had no faith that he could work in their situation. "Without faith it is impossible to please God," Hebrews says. Those who come to God "must believe that he exists and that he rewards those who earnestly seek him" (Hebrews 11:6, NIV).

Fear and faith are mutually exclusive. We become afraid and worried when we lose our faith (Matt. 6:25–33). Sometimes a harder work for God than stilling the storm on the outside is stilling the storm of fear and panic and lack of faith within us. As we understand and act upon these things in the power of the Spirit of God, we can survive any storm triumphantly and allow that storm to be used in a powerful way for God's own sovereign purposes and for his glory.

III. BE TRANSFORMED BY THE STORM (V. 41)

The disciples were terrified—literally, "they feared with great fear." Going through the storm and surviving it had a powerful impact upon their lives.

One thing about storms we can be sure of: storms never leave us where they find us. Some people go through storms and come out the other side bitter, cynical, angry with God and negative about life.

Some who are very weak in their faith or have no faith break down when a storm comes. They lose control, they lose hope, they fall apart and are totally devastated. Others, more strong willed, may break out in anger toward God and become hard, defensive and almost untouchable. And then there are those who go through the storm and don't break down, don't break out, but break through to a new dimension of their spiritual life. They come through the storm with their faith deepened and refined, their priorities rearranged. They become more the persons Christ would have them be. They become more peaceful and more assured of God's power and of God's sovereignty. They are more useable servants of God.

I recently talked with Nancy Switzer about the terrible storm in her life. "I can never be complacent again," she told me. She has been transformed and is being transformed by the storm. Storms will do one of two things, they will *deform* you or they will *transform* you. The difference will be your faith and your cooperation with God.

We are always in imminent danger of being swamped by a storm, but panic is unnecessary and unworthy of our God. If we understand the truth of God's word, storms do come unexpectedly and ferociously, and they come into everyone's life. Some people seem to have more than their share of storms, while some seem to get by relatively easy. Storms come in the life of the just and the unjust. "Deep calls to deep/in the roar of your waterfalls;/ all your waves and breakers/have swept over me" the psalmist wrote in Psalm 42:7.

What happens when a storm takes place will be determined by how you are prepared. The way to get prepared is to know these truths, to dwell on them, and to allow them to become settled convictions in your life. Then whatever storm comes your way will transform you, and you will become more like Christ as a result of having experienced your particular storm. Purpose in your heart to cooperate with God as storms come into your life. Be informed about those storms. Be prepared. And be transformed, by God's grace!

Notes

1. Nancy Switzer and her family are members of our congregation. My deepest appreciation to the Switzer's for their permission to share their story in the ministry of proclaiming the gospel.
2. Charles Spurgeon, *Daily Helps*, p. 13.

COMMENT

Storms in life. Who hasn't faced them? Addressing them is a sure-fire way to engage the attention of almost any person in church on Sunday morning. Sometimes I look out at the congregation I lead and wonder how the floor can hold the weight of the troubles people bring to church with them. Maybe it's just that I'm finally becoming more in touch, or maybe it's the time in which we live. It seems as if there are more and more crises confronting all of us. Does the Bible have a word for us as we deal with the storms of life?

Dennis Kizziar answers with an emphatic "Yes!" This sermon is his way of answering the universal question of how to cope with the situations in life that challenge our faith at the very core of our being. As we look more closely at the sermon we will see how he uses a well-known story in the life of the disciples to illustrate how Jesus helps us face the crises we are sure to encounter.

PROBLEM

Kizziar begins with a first-person story that sounds like something out of an idealistic early 1960s "Brady Bunch" television episode. What could be better? A daughter off to college to become a doctor calls home to tell her family she loves them and is having a wonderful time. There is a note of dissonance because it becomes clear she is talking to a mother—so the male preacher is obviously not the recipient of this almost sentimental slice of the good life. Can things really be this carefree?

The proverbial "other shoe" drops with the next phone call. I don't think we are surprised. We have come to expect bad news. Good times never last. Problems are sure to arrive—generally sooner than we hope. Life is difficult and no one escapes the pain. As a culture we have become increasingly pessimistic. Perhaps it is because there is so much empirical evidence to support our expectations that while good things may happen, "trouble comes in threes."

This is part of the problem we have as Christians. We are influenced by our media-saturated culture to buy into the pervasive hopelessness that drives daytime television shows and creates a general atmosphere of corporate depression. If we cannot expect to escape the same storms that hit non-Christians, then what good is it to be a follower of Jesus Christ?

TEXT

Kizziar moves from the poignant crisis of the Switzer family into a transition that contains his primary thesis: When storms happen, we can survive by the power of the Holy Spirit. He takes us right into the Gospel story without further introduction. While many preachers use this text to focus on the person and power of the Incarnate Creator of nature, Kizziar highlights the image of the storm and the disciples' response to it.

After the opening personal story, the preacher follows a teaching outline that leads the hearers to consider a conclusion that might seem obvious to many but difficult for most people to experience. His traditional three-point outline is easy to follow and remember: be informed, be prepared, be transformed by the storms. While it may be predictable, it is also a good preaching technique to lead people in a direction they expect you to go so they can follow without undue resistance.

Given the external pressures and stresses of modern living, we are in need of constant reminders of the timeless truth of biblical principles for hope-filled living. It is not demeaning to a congregation to remind them of what many already know so that they can live out those truths during difficult days.

Assuming people know the story of the storm, Kizziar explains some facts about the situation the disciples face as a way of understanding how we can apply the text to our lives. He doesn't elaborate but lets the story unfold and speak for itself. Kizziar also refers to other passages of Scripture, again with little elaboration, to underscore his main point: You can survive.

PROCLAMATION

It is reassuring to know that our struggles do not escape God's attention. We are not left on our own to cope as best we can using our own resources. We don't have to be surprised by storms. Nor do we have to be overwhelmed by them. While they are difficult to navigate, storms can actually work for our benefit and growth. God allows storms to come into our lives to help us become more Christlike. These are meant to be encouraging words to people who may be afraid to step into the future knowing that storms do lie ahead.

I wonder how encouraging this teaching might be, however, to those who are in the middle of a storm and are ready to scream in terror just like the disciples did. When people are weak and trembling, feeling like life is out of control and the pressures are too great to bear, it's important for us in preaching not to sound like Marine Corps drill instructors: "Buck up! Be tough! Have faith! This is good for you. You're goin' to thank me when this over. Don't be like those weak-kneed, namby-pamby disciples!" People in our congregations on a given Sunday are at many different places in their joys as well as crises. Preaching must always seek to minister to all the need of the congregation.

Our proclamation of the gospel must include the weak and the strong, the bold and the fearful. We resemble the petrified disciples more than the resolute Christ more often than we care to admit. But that is a key point of the good news. God's power to survive the storms of life is available to anyone willing to place their lives in Jesus' hands. When we admit life is out of control, when we can acknowledge that we can't handle the storm, when we are at our weakest and most fearful extremity, Jesus can do for us what he did for the disciples at their greatest point of need. He can give us peace in the middle of the storm and hope for the future.

We can survive, not by our power, but by the power of the Holy Spirit. We may be afraid as we face the storm, but when we awaken the Savior through tearful entreaties, we can watch him do what we are incapable of doing. That is how God has dealt with people of faith over the centuries.

And we can trust that God will be faithful to carry us through our life's storms as well.

RESPONSE

This sermon is short on practical action steps. It is spoken in the imperative. "Be prepared. Be convinced. Be aware. Be transformed." In one sense, the actions are called for throughout the sermon. As we think, so shall we act. That may be true for some, but I'm not sure it's true for everyone.

When we preach we need to be cognizant of the fact that we are a "minority report" to many of our listeners. They may not be hearing the "Word of the Lord" on a regular, daily basis. They are bombarded by self-help messages that would encourage them to trust anything by God to carry them through life's storms. It may be difficult for many to actually comprehend the magnitude of the message that Jesus' power is available to them by faith. They may be unable to comprehend the majesty of God's grace that can give people a capacity to actually thrive despite adversity. "Practicing the presence of God" in practical, everyday situations may be virtually unknown to many.

We have the privilege of proclaiming the good news of God's personal power for bad days and good days—for the storms as well as the sunshine days of life. Perhaps the best part of the gospel is that we don't have to "qualify" before Jesus will hear our cries for help. He has already done everything necessary on the cross to make it possible for us to live "in cooperation" with God. We can be transformed through life and look forward to what God has in store for the future.

And this is part of our ministry of reconciliation to the world facing storm after storm. Instead of caving in to fear and hopelessness, we can help people discover the Lord of nature and the Lord of our lives. We can help ordinary, weak and trembling people find the Master who can give them strength for extraordinary living.

This sermon is a challenge to each of us to uncover the secret pockets of fear and pessimism in our lives and to turn them inside out to be filled instead with courage and hope by the power of Jesus' love. Then to people tossing and turning in life's storms, we can say with conviction, "Peace, be still! Jesus will help you through the storm into the safe harbor of his love."

SUGGESTIONS

- Develop a sermon on Mark 4:35–41 focusing on what this passage says about who Jesus is. What does the story proclaim in terms of Christology? How does the story function in Mark's narrative? Focus on vv. 39 and 41 of the pericope. How can you relate the Christological meaning of the story to your congregation?
- Kizziar's sermon utilizes a traditional three-point teaching outline. How would you preach this story using a *narrative* preaching method, that is, building the sermon almost entirely around the biblical narrative and illustrative stories from your experience and the experiences of your people?
- What "storms" have you personally experienced in life? Have you related them in your preaching? How can you do so?

Gary W. Downing

COMMENT

WHAT'S THAT MEAN?

JOHN 13:1–17

REV. DR. CURTIS W. FREEMAN
WEST END BAPTIST CHURCH
HOUSTON, TEXAS

WHAT'S THAT MEAN?

JOHN 13:1–17, NRSV

C ajun humorist Justin Wilson tells the story about two boys who lived next door to each other. They were best of friends on Monday, Tuesday, Wednesday, Thursday, Friday, and Saturday, but on Sunday they were enemies because one was a Catholic and the other was a Baptist. Their parents didn't like the fact that these religious differences were producing such uncongenial relations, so they agreed to have their sons visit each other's church services so that a mutual understanding might foster a more tolerant attitude.

On the first Sunday, the Baptist boy visited the Catholic church. When they walked in, just before they sat down, the Catholic boy genuflected. "What's that mean?" the Baptist asked. All through the mass, the Baptist boy wanted to know what this and that meant, and the little Catholic boy explained everything very nicely.

The next Sunday it was the Catholic's turn to visit the Baptist church. When they walked in the building, an usher handed them a printed bulletin. The little Catholic boy had never seen anything like that before in his whole life. "What's that mean?" he asked. His Baptist friend carefully explained. When the preacher stepped into the cockpit (as the Baptists called it), he carefully opened his Bible, and he very conspicuously took off his watch and laid it on the pulpit. "What's that mean?" the Catholic boy asked. And the Baptist boy said, "Not a darn thing!"[1]

As we gather tonight for this ecumenical Maundy Thursday foot-washing service, you may find yourself turning to a Methodist, or Presbyterian, or Baptist friend and asking, "What's that mean?" I hope that we can do some explaining to one another. Unfortunately, the Baptist and Free Church suspicion of things sacramental has found us pointing even to such things as the Lord's Supper and baptism to ask, "What's that mean?" To which we have replied in effect, "Not a darn thing!" Only our way of putting it has been to say something like, "Remember that these are *just* symbols. They don't mean anything." But the truth is they *do* mean something. Whether we call them "ordinances" or "sacraments" they are *very* real.

My task is to direct our attention to the gospel, the good news, so that together we can ask one another "What's that mean?" With the guidance of the Holy Spirit, perhaps we will have a better understanding of what it might mean for the gospel to be displayed in the church of Jesus Christ today. In the interest of brevity and simplicity, I want to suggest that the Gospel passage for today helps us to answer two questions: one about who Jesus is and the other about who we are.

I.

Who is Jesus? No other Gospel contains the story of Jesus' washing the feet of the disciples. It is unique to the Fourth Gospel. In the Gospel narrative, as John tells it, the foot washing takes the place of the institution of the Lord's Supper. In the other Gospels, the narrative of the Lord's Supper interprets the death of Jesus. The bread and the wine are ways of remembering Jesus. So in John's Gospel the towel and the basin are ways of remembering him.

When we ask, "What does this story tell us about Jesus? How does it identify him? What kind of Savior does it show him to be?" we get quite shocking answers.

After having eaten with his disciples, Jesus "got up from the table, took off his outer robe, and tied a towel around himself. Then he poured water into a basin and began to wash the disciples' feet and to wipe them with the towel that was tied around him" (John 13:4–5). He was doing what a slave or servant should have done. How can this humble servant be one and the same with the Son whom the Gospel praises as the preexistent agent of creation and the incarnate message of revelation (John 1:1–18)?

The thought of the Lord Jesus at the feet of Peter (or one of us) is too threatening. If somehow we can't bring ourselves to utter the words, Peter does it for us, "You will never wash my feet" (John 13:8). Finally, Jesus tells Peter that foot washing isn't just something he does. What he *does* shows who he *is*. If Peter can't accept it then maybe he's just in the wrong place. Reluctantly, Peter lets Jesus wash his feet; just as reluctantly we take off our shoes.

Could it be that the true nature of the one who sits high in the heavens becomes most visible when he stoops low? The great Swiss theologian Karl Barth says that Jesus Christ is the *Lord who became a servant* by going into the far country and concealing his glory. But in his condescension into servanthood, the Lord does not disfigure himself. Instead he reveals to us his true nature as one who came not to rule but to serve.[2]

Let us not, then, rush so quickly to the empty tomb to celebrate the *servant who became Lord* that we forget to look at the towel and basin to find the *Lord who became a servant.*

> "Who, though he was in the form of God,
>> did not regard equality with God
>> as something to be exploited,
> but emptied himself,
>> taking the form of a slave,..." (Phil. 2:6–7).

II.

The Gospel raises for us the *christological* question, but it won't let go of us until we also ask the *ecclesiological* question. The story makes us ask, "What kind of Lord is this one who died to save us?" It also forces us to wonder, "What kind of church does such a Savior's death demand?" Who are *we?* Listen to the words of Jesus:

> You call me Teacher and Lord—and you are right, for that is what I
> am. So if I, your Lord and Teacher, have washed your feet, you also
> ought to wash one another's feet. For I have set you an example, that
> you also should do as I have done to you (John 13:13–15).

So, what's that mean? Better yet, why don't we do it? Good questions, for which there are not always good answers.

Through the centuries, foot washing has fallen out of liturgical favor. Not until the 1950s did the Catholic church, at the urging of Pius XII, restore foot washing to the Holy Week observance. Even then it was called the *pedilavium*, which if you don't know Latin sounds like something illegal, immoral, or unhealthy. So you probably wouldn't know what it means, and even if you did you wouldn't want to tell anybody. Most Protestants are happy to *observe* foot washing just so long as that means to *watch* without really doing anything, but we're even happier with a nice dignified meaning where we don't have to take our shoes off. Actually very few Baptists know what it means. Freewill and General Baptists are the only groups that ever practiced foot washing with any regularity.

As far as I can tell, the Anabaptists stand alone in the consistent practice of foot washing. Dietrich Philips has a discussion of the "Seven Ordinances of the True Church" written in 1560. Philips includes foot washing as the third ordinance. It is preceded by the ordinances of Word and sacraments (Lord's Supper and Baptism), and it is followed by separation from the world, fraternal love, commandment keeping, and suffering (just to make it clear that Christians aren't in control of the world). These ordinances mark the church of God. Philips says that the Lord commanded foot washing for two reasons:

> First, he would have us know that he himself must cleanse us, and that we must allow him to wash away the sins which beset us. The second reason why Jesus instituted foot washing is that we should humble ourselves toward one another.[3]

Following in the tradition of Philips, the old *Dordrect Confession* of Mennonites of 1632 speaks of foot washing like this:

> We also confess a washing of the feet of the saints, as the Lord Jesus did not only institute and command the same, but did also Himself wash the feet of the apostles, although He was their Lord

and Master; thereby giving an example that they also should wash one another's feet, and thus do to one another as He did to them; which they also afterwards taught believers to observe, and all this is a sign of true humiliation; but yet more particularly as a sign to remind us of the true washing—the washing and purification of the soul in the blood of Christ (Article XI).[4]

I take it that what this means is that the church of God is most truly the church when we follow our Lord's example by taking the towel and basin to become servants. "For we do not proclaim ourselves; we proclaim Jesus Christ as Lord and ourselves as your slaves for Jesus' sake" (2 Cor. 4:5). What's that mean? It means that God's true church is a servant community because the church's true Lord is a servant Savior.

John Wesley, the founder of Methodism, lived by this motto, which reminded him that the end of the Christian life is servanthood:

Do all the good you can,
By all the means you can,
In all the places you can,
At all the times you can,
To all the people you can,
As long as ever you can.

His whole life exemplified this spirit. He was ordained at the age of twenty-four and remained in active ministry for the next sixty-four years. He preached forty-two thousand, four hundred sermons, an average of fifteen a week for over fifty years. At the rate of two sermons a week, it would take the average minister today four hundred and twenty-four years to preach as many sermons as Wesley. He traveled two hundred and ninety thousand miles during the course of his ministry, which is the equivalent of going around the world more than twenty times. When you stop to think that he did it on horseback or by foot, it is all the more remarkable. His translations, abridgments, journals, and sermons fill over two hundred volumes. When he died at the age of eighty-eight, John Wesley left behind a worn coat, a battered hat, a humble house, a tattered Bible, and a Methodist church.[5]

What's that mean? I think John Wesley knew. Jesus said, "If you *know* these things, you are blessed if you *do* them" (John 13:17, italics mine). Old Dietrich Philips puts the matter so sharply that we, being unfaithful and disobedient, can only stutter and stammer. He says:

> Now, if they are happy or blessed who know and do this, how void of blessing those remain who profess to be apostles or messengers of the Lord and do not know these things; or, if they know, do not do them nor teach others to do them.[6]

What's that mean? It means that in the humble act of foot washing we remember Jesus our Savior, and we signify that we are a church of servants. By washing the feet of our sisters and brothers we give witness to an unbelieving world that we know what it means to be a servant, and only in so doing will we be truly blessed. Will we follow our Lord's example and command by taking the basin and the towel to wash one another's feet?

Notes

1. Justin Wilson and Howard Jacobs, *Cajun Humor* (Pelican Press, 1974).

2. *Church Dogmatics,* IV/1/59.

3. Dirk Philips, "The Church of God," in *Spiritual and Anabaptist Writers,* ed. George Huntston Williams, in *The Library of Christian Classics* (Philadelphia: Westminster Press), p.245.

4. "The Dordrecht Confession," article XI, in *Creeds of the Churches,* ed. John H. Leith, (New York: Doubleday/Anchor Books, 1963), p. 302.

5. See Paul Powell, *Go-Givers in a Go-Better World* (Nashville: Broadman Press, 1986), pp. 84–85.

6. Philips, "The Church of God," p.245.

COMMENT

Toe jam. Fuzz balls. Stinky socks. No wonder foot washing has fallen out of favor.

Through an outmoded social custom, Curtis Freeman brings his listeners face to face with two of the essential questions of the life, death and resurrection of Jesus Christ: Who is Jesus? And who are we? In the sermon "What's That Mean?" Freeman uses Peter's reluctance and our discomfort with a long-discarded practice both to proclaim the gospel and educate his listeners.

I've known Freeman since he was a doctoral student spending intolerable long hours in a library study carrel slogging through Augustine's *City of God* at a time when the Baptist denomination was rife with internal conflict. Knowing his passion for historical theology and his impatience with denominational rigidity, I find it no surprise that he would use an ecumenical opportunity to speak to the heart of what we as Christians—no matter what our denomination background—hold in common as we approach the cross. Preaching a Maundy Thursday service to an ecumenical gathering of Baptists, Methodists, and Presbyterians, along with a few other mismatched denominations thrown in, Freeman allows the text to speak to denominational diversity, sacramentalism, and the christological centerpoint of the narrative.

WEDDING HUMOR AND CHRISTOLOGY

Many sermons are christological—but few sermons *use* the term *Christology*, and even fewer use the term in a manner understandable to individuals without seminary degrees. Freeman does both.

Freeman knows that to preach from a lesser-known text (one found only in John) and to ask the congregation to consider the christological significance of the passage, is a perfect set-up for wandering minds, distracted listeners, and ineffective preaching. Freeman hooks his congregation at the beginning of the sermon with an illustration perfectly matched to the text and appropriately humorous for the occasion. The Justin Wilson story becomes the thematic springboard for the sermon—effectively introducing the question which Freeman returns to repeatedly. At least fourteen times Freeman uses the phrase, "What's that mean?" Again and again he calls his audience back to the pertinent question, using clear, simple language and effective repetition.

Freeman accomplishes two objectives by addressing the christological implications of the text: (1) he proclaims the Lordship of Jesus Christ, the good news of Christ's gift of himself to his followers, and (2) he manages to teach some significant historical theology at the same time.

Not bad for a twenty-minute sermon!

FOOT WASHING—A CHALLENGING TEXT

Foot washing. A retired custom, an awkward practice, a humbling intimacy. Not only is foot washing a nonexistent or seldom-practiced rite in many denominational traditions, but Freeman recognizes the Baptists attending this service may get a little fidgety with *any* sacramental subject. Just *preaching* about foot washing (not to mention actually *doing* it) makes modern-day congregations uncomfortable.

But we aren't the only ones uncomfortable with someone else washing our feet. Even when it was an accepted social custom, Peter was less than enthusiastic about allowing Jesus to wash his feet. Jesus' words and actions frequently surprised and baffled the disciples, yet few Gospel stories so clearly portray the disciples feeling uncomfortable, reluctant, and hesitant. As he frequently did, Jesus turns social conventions upside down in the story of the foot washing. A *servant* washes feet—a Lord and Master doesn't.

Stories in the Gospel of John are full of rich theological symbolism with multiple layers of meaning laced through the narrative. The story of Jesus washing the feet of the disciples has long been regarded as a narrative that functions in this Gospel *in place of* the Lord's Supper, dovetailing with the New Commandment which follows several verses later (John 13:31–35). Jesus' actions precede his teaching the New Commandment. In other words, he demonstrates what he later tells the disciples he expects of them, and in so doing, challenges the disciples to live their lives by a different standard.

Freeman deftly takes the listener into the theological depth of this text, moving easily from Johannine narrative to Johannine theology. The foot washing text isn't simply a series of actions; this is a story about who Jesus is. Freeman neither minimizes the significance of foot washing, nor discounts it as a practice no longer acceptable or appropriate. He encourages his listeners to see what these actions of Jesus have to say to us, today, in our culture. In keeping with the teaching and actions of Christ, Freeman challenges us to question *our* common acceptance of the social conventions of our day.

REFUSING TO "DUMB IT DOWN"

Christological. Ecclesiological. Pedilavium. Not exactly common terms for a dinner party conversation. Freeman refuses to preach to the lowest common denominator. He preaches with theological depth, and assumes his congregation can handle some fairly sophisticated theological vocabulary—and again, he does so with good humor.

While tracing the church's acceptance (or lack of acceptance) of the practice of foot washing, Freeman says, "Even then it was called the *pedilavium,* which if you don't know Latin sounds like something illegal, immoral, or unhealthy…. Most Protestants are happy to *observe* foot washing just so long as that means to *watch* without really doing anything, but we're even happier with a nice dignified meaning where we don't have to take our shoes off."

By structuring this sermon around the two essential questions (who is Jesus and who are we), Freeman begins with the meaning of this narrative for each of us individually, and then moves to the ecclesiological meaning—its meaning for us as a congregation and a church. He starts with the reality of our personal discomfort and moves beyond our corporate discomfort to the call inherent in this text when he says, "what this means is that the church of God is most truly the church when we follow our Lord's example by taking the towel and basin to become servants."

Throughout this sermon, Freeman weaves both figurative and literal meanings for contemporary listeners. He eases our discomfort with the unfamiliar with the effective use of humor. He challenges us to think beyond cultural norms while refusing to "dumb down" the biblical narrative and the theology in his preaching. "What's That Mean?" is a sermon of christological and theological integrity—and it works.

SUGGESTIONS

- Freeman builds this sermon around two simple questions: What does this text tell us about who Jesus is? What does this passage tell us about ourselves? Preach from a gospel narrative using those two questions as the sermon's infrastructure.

- Freeman touches on differing views of the sacraments in Christian traditions. Perhaps addressing "What do the sacraments mean for us?" is an appropriate and timely issue in your congregation. As Christians, what do we hold sacred? What is sacramental in our lives?

- Possibly the most obvious suggestion to come from reading Freeman's sermon is simply this: consider a Maundy Thursday foot-washing service for your congregation. Sometimes the rewards of moving beyond our comfort zones are surprising.

Debra K. Klingsporn

FAITH AT WORK

PHILIPPIANS 2:1–13

REV. DR. DAVID C. FISHER
COLONIAL CHURCH
EDINA, MINNESOTA

FAITH AT WORK

PHILIPPIANS 2:1–13, NRSV

You heard it! Right there in the Scripture lesson Paul said it, "Work out your own salvation with fear and trembling." New Testament scholar Edgar Krentz, commenting on this verse, says, "Now that sounds very American, doesn't it?" And it does! Work out your own salvation. We like that. We are, after all, a do-it-yourself culture, a nation of self-made men and women—or at least we'd like to think so.[1]

Krentz points to Bill Gates, owner of Microsoft Corporation, as a modern prototype of the American dream. Here's a man who dropped out of Harvard, started his own company and is now, according to *Forbes* magazine, the richest man in America. And he did it on his own. How admirable!

We modern Americans are the self-help generation. With nearly boundless optimism we figure we can fix most anything, including ourselves. With ingenuity, resources and hard work we solve problems, build companies and do it all ourselves.

I suspect part of the anger about politics and government that seems to lie so deep in the soul of our nation stems, in part, from our deep sense of impotence. Here's one thing, the government, we just can't fix. And it won't fix itself. That's un-American. Americans make things work.

We've never been a reflective people, nor has philosophy been high on our educational agenda. But we have a philosophy. It's pragmatism. We're practical people who figure out how to make things work. Blessed with abundant resources and amazing creativity, we make things work. We send our experts all over the world where they make things work there too. We know how.

The signs of that pragmatic optimism lie all around us. Take the super-market check-out line, for example. Waiting in line there this week, I checked out the tabloids and magazines conveniently displayed to amuse and amaze me as I waited. The cover of one popular magazine advertised its contents as follows: "Eight Truths to Base Your Life On," "Fifteen Things Never to Say to a Man," "How to Turn Ordinary Love into Adult Love," "Three Ways to Improve Your Sex Life." And on it went. (You don't want to know some of the other titles!) We know how to make things work. It's part of being American.

We know how to make religion work too. At least we Protestants do. For most of its history, this nation has been a righteous empire of sorts. Though we are currently out of power and no longer the dominant force in our culture, nonetheless we have the biggest churches in the world— maybe in all of church history. We have more churches per capita than any other country, and our churches work. We know how. We have techniques for making churches large or larger, revitalizing dead old churches, creat-ing new churches, organizing moribund churches, fixing broken churches, raising money for churches. You name it and we can make it work better.

We have organizations: parachurch organizations, intrachurch organi-zations, inner-church organizations, interfaith organizations, interdenomi-national organizations, added to evangelistic organizations, renewal orga-nizations, mission organizations, theological organizations, educational organizations.... If you organize, people will come! You will get members, followers, subscribers. Yes, we Americans do know how to make things work.

We are a nation of believers and behavers. Religious activism is part of our national character. Denominational distinctions and theological differ-ences tend to break down here. Liberals and conservatives, Baptists and Episcopalians, all of us believe that faith demands action. American Protestantism has always been active. Liberals feature social action and con-servatives favor spiritual action, but we're all in action. Our churches are open seven days a week. The lights are on most nights of the week. We march, we protest, we volunteer, we help, we give. Our faith works.

Whatever differing behavior codes we grew up with, that we measure our-selves—and others—by, we American Christians agree on a moral vision that demands activist behavior.

We Protestants work. We fix things, ourselves and each other. At least we think we can fix ourselves and others. I went to the local religious book-store this week to check that out. Sure enough, I found books to fix the soul, the mind and the body, books with titles like "Key(s) to…," "Guide(s) to…," "The Secret of…," "How to…."

No wonder our ears perk up when we hear Paul say, "Work out your own salvation." Here is an American Paul! Philippians is the epistle for Americans. I know it's my favorite of Paul's letters. Someone near and dear to me told me this week it's hers too. It's short, direct, simple and full of things to do. This little letter simply bristles with imperatives, quite a few of them in our text. We read this text, roll up our sleeves and go to work.

I suppose it's worth noting that the word *grace* appears just three times in this book: once in the introduction, "Grace to you and peace" (1:2), once in the conclusion, "The grace of the Lord Jesus Christ be with your spirit" (4:23), and another nontheological use in chapter one (1:7). How different from those long complicated epistles Romans and Galatians, where grace is the dominant theme. No, here we are confronted with things to do, imperatives to obey. In fact, our text is a long string of commands.

All of these imperatives, these things-to-do, point to a single command that runs from the beginning of this letter to the end: "Be one." Or, to put it another way, "If you Philippians, or Americans, want to fix something, fix this—live in unity!"

Interesting that Paul doesn't tell them to fix their organization. He doesn't tell them to form a committee to study how to make their congre-gation larger, more successful, or better run. All that may be necessary, but such attempts miss a Christian essential, indeed, a mark of the church. According to the apostles, unity is an essential part of the character of the Christian church.

The logic goes something like this. If sin by its very nature scatters people, pits us against each other and creates alienation everywhere, then salvation by its very nature reconciles divided people and destroys alienation everywhere. Therefore, the church by its very nature is a company of reconciled people living in community as a public sign of God's reconciling good news. From the very beginning the church has confessed its essential character as a unity.

The Nicene Creed, which has been used by Christians all over the world at Holy Communion for nearly one thousand, seven hundred years, confesses in its third article, "We believe in one holy catholic and apostolic Church." Note that "one" is the first essential of the church confessed. Nothing could be more apostolic! Paul uses all his skills as a writer to make just that point in our text. One commentator puts it this way:

> He uses words big in meaning, compacted into brief verbless phrases; rare words; and words never found anywhere else in the New Testament. He piles clause on top of clause, beginning each clause with the same word. He does all this as if searching for ways to make his readers both think and feel deeply about the essential nature of harmony and its necessity within the Christian community. Even the exalted solemn speech-pattern of this section adds to the magnitude of this idea.[2]

Paul begins his argument with a passionate call for the Philippians to remember their common life in Christ (vv. 1–4). *"Has your life together encouraged you?"* Paul asks rhetorically. Of course it had. Each member of the church could remember times their common life had encouraged them. And so can we. I recall events in this very room in which you encouraged me. Last February, I knelt on this platform while you laid your hands on me to set me apart to be your senior minister. It was a moving experience for me. In fact, I'll never be the same. You, too, can remember times in which people of this congregation laid hands on your soul and marked you for life. Yes, we can remember when this church has encouraged us.

Paul goes on to ask, *"Has love ever motivated you?"* Has God's love ever prompted you to do something you'd not do otherwise? Has the love of God displayed in God's people ever moved your heart?

Of course. God's people have been motivated by love for two thousand years. In the early days of the church, a plague broke out in Alexandria, in northern Egypt. A member of the church there remembered those terrible days:

> Most of our brothers [and sisters] did not spare themselves and held together in the closest love of their neighbors. [We] were not afraid to visit the sick, to look after them well, to take care of them for Christ's sake and to die joyfully with them. Many of [us] lost their own lives after restoring others to health thus taking their death on themselves.... In this way some of the noblest of our brethren died....3

I don't suppose many of us have experienced that kind of heroic love. But God's love is a powerful motivation and none of us is quite the same after knowing it. It's always been that way. God's love motivated Christians in Philippi and it motivates us here at Colonial Church.

Paul continues his passionate appeal to remember by asking the church at Philippi—and us—"Has the Holy Spirit ever prompted you?" Of course, they answered. They remembered. And so do we. That's what the Holy Spirit does in the church.

When the young English preacher Charles Spurgeon began his long ministry in London, God honored that ministry in a remarkable way. Years later Spurgeon remembered those days:

> Shall we ever forget...those...meetings when I felt compelled to let you go without a word from my lips, because the Spirit of God was so awfully present that we felt bowed to the dust. And what listening there was...where we scarcely had air enough to breathe! The Holy Spirit came down like showers which saturate the soil till the clods are ready for breaking; and then it was not long before

we heard on the right and on the left the cry, "What must we do
to be saved?"[4]

They remembered in Philippi how the Spirit had worked. And we
remember. Right here in this Meetinghouse, or in rooms in this building,
perhaps in a home, but we remember.

Finally, Paul cries out, *"Is there any compassion, any sympathy?"*
Hundreds of incidents, words, hugs, events and persons sprang to mind.
Oh yes! There's compassion and sympathy in Christ's church. And we
remember.

Then, Paul argues, if you remember any times that your common life
encouraged you, any moments when love motivated you, any prompting
of the Holy Spirit, any compassion and sympathy, "make my joy complete:
be of the same mind, having the same love, being in full accord and of one
mind." Concentrate on each other's interests, he goes on, not your own.
Abandon selfish ambition and live for the sake of one another (vv. 2–4).

I often read those verses at weddings. Though they are written to a
church, Paul's line of thought is certainly appropriate for all relationships,
and especially for marriage. In fact, a creative American Christian could
probably write a self-help book based on this text! It does sound like a
"how to" opportunity. We can live in harmony by increasing opportunities
for encouragement, developing love as a motivation, creating more places
for the Holy Spirit to work and deliberately fostering memories of sympathy
and compassion. If we do those four simple things, unity will be formed.

Paul isn't finished. He goes on to quote what is likely an early church
hymn. In most modern translations verses 6–11 are in poetic form to mark
the hymn off from the rest of the text. Perhaps it is a hymn Paul taught the
church. They'd sung it many times and Paul quotes the hymn to stir their
passions even deeper.

The hymn is a dramatic picture of Christ's descent to earth. Although
he had all heaven's perks and privileges at hand, Christ did not selfishly
grasp nor exploit his position. Rather, he emptied himself and took on the
form of a servant. And in human flesh he voluntarily died for us on the

cross. Therefore, God exalted him and gave him a name above all names,

> that at the name of Jesus
>   every knee should bend,
> in heaven and on earth and under the earth,
>   and every tongue should confess
> that Jesus Christ is Lord (10–11).

"Let the same mind be in you," Paul says (v. 5). Christian unity is the result of downward mobility and humble service. Just like Jesus.

Depending on the religious tradition in Philippi, I suppose the church was ready to respond. After all, Christians always respond to the example of Jesus' life and death. If Paul gave an altar call, the front of the church would be full. Sign-up sheets in the foyer would overflow. A Lenten series, "The Way of the Cross," would be packed out.

Paul's point is simple. Work out your own salvation. Or, in other words, *"Fix your church."* Everything else is secondary. *Be United!*

We've been working on that unity for nearly two thousand years. The church stubbornly resists unity and all attempts to bring it to unity. Find a church, any church, large or small, local or national, and you'll find issues that divide, persons who are divisive and incidents that alienate. So long as humans make up the membership of churches, that's the way it will be. We bring all our human stuff to church with us, the good, the bad and the ugly.

Perhaps we're not so good at fixing things after all. Oh, there *are* things we humans can fix—organizations, institutions, corporate structures, for example. But when it comes to human souls and the soul of the church, we're pretty helpless. Oh, we try to fix each other and the church, but we soon learn we're in over our heads.

Memories, the very best of them, fade before harsh realities. Excellent theology recedes before human experience. Work out your own salvation, Paul argues. Fix your church. We try, but when it comes to unity, real unity, we simply cannot make it work.

The text has good news, though, and I bring it to you this day. Paul saves his real point for the end of this long plea for unity. I think he wants us to feel the dramatic tension between God's demand and our inability to make it work.

In a dramatic shift of syntax and language that cannot be adequately translated, Paul suddenly writes, "For it is God who is at work in you" (v. 13). Literally translated, the text goes something like this, "Work out your own salvation with fear and trembling, for God, the one energizing, is among you."

You see, it's not that God gives us divine energy to help us muddle through. No, God gives us himself. "God, the energizer, is among you." Everything necessary for unity has already been done. All we do is receive the gift from the Giver. We cannot in our best schemes and finest plans create Christian unity. But God can. In fact, God already has!

This text is supremely a church text. Worship is the center of the life of the church. Here in worship God is uniquely present among the people. Here God transforms his people. Here we find unity. "God, the energizer, is among us."

When I was growing up my mom told me at least a hundred times, "Don't just stand there, do something!" Here in the Meetinghouse, God tells us again and again, "Don't just do something, stand there!"

God is among us "to will and to work for his good pleasure" (v. 13).

I've seen God create unity. Years ago, I looked out from my pulpit chair and saw one of the richest men in town seated between two women. One was his wife, decked out in fur and looking good. The other was a poor woman, a former barmaid who'd spent some time as a prostitute. Both the rich man and the woman were new Christians. I'll never forget it. The rich man took the hymnbook, opened it and shared it with the poor woman. The only place that kind of thing can happen is in the house of God. God was there. And nothing was ever the same.

It's happened to me personally. When I was a graduate student, the senior professor in the department was after me, at least I thought so. He was hard on all of us, but it seemed he really went after me. Perhaps I deserved it, but it hurt. He was not my favorite person.

One day, by God's grace, not by my choice, I found myself seated next to him in chapel. We shared a hymnbook and sang to the God we loved. We knelt together to pray to the God we served. We read from the Psalter in the back of the hymnal and listened to the word of God.

I don't know about him, but the ice in my heart melted—and it's never come back. God was there.

God is here. And nothing is ever the same.

Notes

1. Edgar Krentz, "Work out your own salvation," *The Christian Century,* (September 11-18, 1996), p. 847.
2. Gerald F. Hawthorne, *Philippians,* Word Biblical Commentary, Vol. 43 (Waco, TX: Word Books, 1983), p. 64.
3. Quoted in John R. Hendrick, *Opening the Door of Faith* (Atlanta: John Knox, 1977), p. 96.
4. Charles Spurgeon, *The Early Years,* Reprint edition (Banner of Truth, 1962), p. 328.

COMMENT

"I did it my way…" Frank Sinatra proudly sang in his hit song a few years ago. Few of us in American culture would admit how deeply that philosophy is etched in our souls. We live by it more than we know. We like to *do it,* and we like to do it *our way.* In his sermon, "Faith At Work," David Fisher puts good old rugged American individualism and pragmatism alongside the Christian gospel and comes up with much more than "tension." He finds deep antithesis between *"I did it my way"* and *"God is at work among you."* That antithesis constitutes the soul of this sermon.

In reading the sermon, notice that it takes us a while to get to the gospel and to the antithesis. In the early going, we have the sense that being a do-it-yourself culture and having boundless optimism are not so bad after all. They bring results, don't they? It's only toward the end of the sermon that we finally realize the profound contradiction—that the gospel challenges our idolatry of doing-it-our-own-way.

This is a sneaky sermon on a tricky text. Much like Jesus' style of teaching in his parables, this sermon sneaks up on us with the gospel. Just when we thought we were pretty good folks after all—into our self-help, our doing, and our boundless optimism—Fisher reminds us of grace, and of the God among us, who alone gives us life, gives us himself, creates unity, heals our souls. So much for *"I did it my way."*

CREATING TENSION

Fisher wastes no time in this sermon. In the opening lines he goes directly to Paul's much misunderstood phrase, "Work out your own salvation with fear and trembling." We don't realize it, but the preacher begins setting up a profound tension from these opening lines of the sermon onward. When we hear the words, "Work out your own salvation," spoken out of context, it taps into our do-it-yourself-mover-shaker-fix-it mentality. Most of us are ready to kick into gear: "Okay, preacher, I'm ready!" I can do this. Just tell me what to do and how to do it, and I'll get on with it!" But as we soon discover, this text, when heard in its full context, no longer legitimates our individualism or our activism. The gospel, rightly understood, turns upside down our usual assumptions about life.

Notice that Fisher doesn't take us to a full hearing of the gospel until the end of the sermon. Instead, throughout the sermon, he creates a tension—a wanting-to-know how to work out our own salvation. He taps into our shadow side and leads us along. We keep thinking that at the end of this sermon there is something for us to do. We listen for how to grow, shape, organize and fix our own salvation. Is it through study, prayer, more good deeds, spiritual or social action? But we never learn how, because the gospel is not about American pragmatism.

Instead, in this sermon we discover again that the gospel is a strange word of mystery that challenges most of our common human assumptions. When grace finally comes into the discussion, as it does toward the end of the sermon, if we're honest, we sit back and say, "You did it again, God! Just when we rolled up our sleeves and were ready to go to work, you told us there's nothing to do!" We are brought out of our assumptions to stand under the text as Word of God. And there, we encounter again the God whose thoughts are not our thoughts and whose ways are not our ways.

PROBLEM & TEXT

In many sermons, the introduction slowly leads us into the problem of the human condition and eventually into the biblical text. Not in this sermon. Fisher puts the text right up front in the opening lines: "You heard it! Right there in the Scripture lesson Paul said it, 'Work out your own salvation with fear and trembling'…. Now that sounds very American, doesn't it? [Krentz]…We like that. We are, after all, a do-it-yourself culture, a nation of self-made men and women—or at least we'd like to think so."

With this opening, Fisher lets the biblical text itself define the problem and create the tension in the sermon. As listeners, we don't sit through any cute stories or jokes to entertain us and ease us into the sermon. Instead, we're confronted immediately by a number of questions: What's wrong with being a do-it-yourself culture? What does this "work out your own salvation" mean? Where is this sermon going? By opening the sermon in this way, Fisher lets the text get our attention. A conversation has begun. We just don't know where it's going.

As Americans, we pride ourselves on figuring things out, making things work, fixing things, and doing it all our way. As the sermon develops, however, we are soon reminded that our philosophy doesn't always work. In the places in life where it matters most, we're often powerless and helpless. Individualism and pragmatism become sources of hubris and idolatry. They are certainly not what the Christian gospel is about.

In identifying this problem, Fisher reminds us of familiar examples of pragmatic optimism all around us. Bill Gates did it his way and made millions. The supermarket tabloids tell us we can too. Even our churches know how to build, organize, and do the faith in an active way.

Notice the refrain Fisher repeats throughout the early portion of the sermon: *We know how.* There's truth in that. Culturally, we identify with it. We do know how to build, organize, fix, and figure a lot of things out. That's why Fisher says we love this text from Philippians. "'Work out your own salvation.' Here is the American Paul.... We read this text, roll up our sleeves and go to work."

But the problem is that it finally doesn't work. We know how, and we don't know how. We find it exceedingly difficult, especially in the church, to accept our own limitations when things don't work and we don't know how to fix them. We can't do it all on our own. No amount of trying harder, being better and doing more will ever save us, or make us whole, or bring us unity.

The point of this biblical text and of Philippians as a whole, is the call for unity among God's people. Even there, we think we can do it on our own. But again, Fisher says, that's the problem: "When it comes to human souls and the soul of the church, we're pretty helpless. We try to fix each other and the church, but we soon learn we're in over our heads....We try, but when it comes to unity, real unity, we simply cannot make it work."

So there's the tension between our own world and the world of the biblical text: We think we can do it on our own, but we can't.

"EXEGESIS, EXEGESIS, EXEGESIS!"

On the occasion of his formal farewell to his students in Bonn, just before his expulsion from Germany in 1935, Karl Barth said, "Listen to my piece of advice: exegesis, exegesis, and yet more exegesis! Keep to the Word, to the Scripture that has been given to us" (quoted in Eberhard Busch, *Karl Barth: His Life from Letters and Autobiographical Texts,* Fortress Press, 1976). Solid, disciplined exegesis on a regular basis is absolutely essential to preaching. The task of determining as accurately as we can what the text meant back then (for its first-century hearers or readers) is essential for making that word a living word for a twentieth-century audience.

Serious wrestling each week with the meaning of the biblical text is critical. Yet, under the pressures of pastoral ministry—administration, budgets, committee meetings, hospital visits, appointments, weddings, funerals and social events—we all know how easily serious exegetical study becomes shortchanged or eliminated. Sometimes we stop doing it because of the pressures of ministry. Sometimes we stop because the text and preaching have become too familiar. We think we know what the text says because we've heard it so often. For whatever reasons, when we stop giving the time to careful exegesis, our preaching suffers. We no longer "keep to the Word" that has been given us. And in time, the Word no longer speaks with power and clarity. Our people suffer; the church suffers; and we lose vitality in ministry. Barth's appeal is timeless: "Exegesis, exegesis, and yet more exegesis!"

CONTEXT IS KEY

Fisher's sermon is a good example of the kind of careful exegesis which should underlie every sermon. The phrase "work out your own salvation" is easily misinterpreted if taken out of its historical and literary context in the Philippian letter. Fisher's study of this phrase leads him to establish at least three important points in the course of the sermon.

1) *Literary context.* The phrase, "work out your own salvation," is part of a larger section of the Philippian letter which must be interpreted as a whole. It is obvious that Fisher has asked one of the most basic but essential exegetical questions: What is the point of this whole section (Philippians 2:1–13) and how does "work out your own salvation" fit into the logic of the section and the overall thought of Paul's letter? Determining the literary context is absolutely essential to a proper interpretation of Philippians 2:12b. When one does that, it is clear that these words occur in the context of Paul's appeal for unity among the believers in the church at Philippi.

2) *Call for unity.* Fisher has done his homework when he says of Paul's exhortations in Philippians: "All of these imperatives, these things-to-do, point to a single command that runs from the beginning of this letter to the end: 'Be one...live in unity!'" In its literary context, Philippians 2:1–13 is therefore about unity. Fisher traces Paul's call for unity down through the text in Philippians 2:1–11: Remember how your common life together has encouraged you. Remember how love has motivated you. Remember how the Holy Spirit has prompted you. Remember the compassion and sympathy in Christ's church (v. 1). At each point, note how Fisher asks his listeners to reflect on how these things have been true in their experience in the church.

Then Fisher traces the call for unity in 2:2–11. Remembering these things, "make my joy complete: be of the same mind, having the same love, being in full accord and of one mind, concentrating on each other's interests and not on your own" (vv. 2–4). Let the same mind of "downward mobility and humble service be yours, just like Jesus" (vv. 5–11). The whole text leading up to and including vv. 12–13 is about unity in the church. Fisher concludes: "Paul's point is simple. Work out your own salvation. Or, in other words, '*Fix your church.* Everything else is secondary. *Be united!*'"

3) *A church text.* The context makes it clear that the words "work out your own salvation" are to be understood in a corporate sense (plural verb and plural reflexive pronoun) and are addressed as an exhortation

to the entire church at Philippi. In this passage Paul is not focusing on the individual at all, but on the community of believers. In its wider literary context, the term "salvation" (v. 12) is used in a non-eschatological sense, referring to the church's ongoing life, unity, spiritual health and vitality.

By this point in the sermon, Fisher's exegesis has established that the text is not about *me* but about *us*, and it's not about *my salvation* but about *our unity as the one church—the body of Christ*. Now he comes to the most basic problem of all:

> We've been working on that unity for nearly two thousand years. The church stubbornly resists unity…Find a church, any church,…and you'll find issues that divide…. We bring all our human stuff to church with us…. Perhaps we're not so good at fixing things after all…. When it comes to human souls and the soul of the church, we're pretty helpless…. We soon learn we're in over our heads…. We try, but when it comes to unity, real unity, we simply cannot make it work.

PROCLAMATION & RESPONSE

At the beginning of this sermon we had our sleeves rolled up ready to go to work on a problem. By the end, we learn that the text is not even about the problem most of us first imagined (being better Christians), and it's certainly not a problem we can fix on our own. Unity in the church—how? We all know it doesn't work. The sermon has developed a tension that we do-it-yourself-fixers cannot resolve. So where to now?

Fisher turns to the only place we can turn for ultimate help and healing. Notice how he announces the proclamation of the gospel: "The text has good news, though, and I bring it to you this day. Paul saves his real point for the end of this long plea for unity. I think he wants us to feel the dramatic tension between God's demand [for unity] and our inability to make it work."

This is the turning point in the sermon. Now we finally hear the gospel: "Work out your own salvation with fear and trembling, for God, the One energizing, is among you." Fisher explains: "You see, it's not that God gives us divine energy to help us muddle through. No, God gives us himself. 'God, the energizer, is among you.' Everything necessary for unity has already been done. All we do is receive the gift from the Giver. We cannot in our best schemes and finest plans create Christian unity. But God can. In fact, God already has!" In that phrase, "We cannot...but God can," we experience the antithesis between the gospel and all our self-made attempts at doing and fixing.

Grace has spoken. Fisher concludes with two real-life stories about how the God at work among us transforms lives and creates unity among his people, the church. In these stories, grace is not something anyone does. Grace happens as a gift from the Giver.

Our response? "Don't just do something, stand there!" In other words, receive the gift! How countercultural. How subversive of all our doing.

"I did it my way"? No. God is at work. Grace has spoken. And we are never the same.

SUGGESTIONS

- Develop your own sermon on Philippians 2:1–13. What misunderstandings of v. 12b do you think your congregation may have? How does this text apply to your listeners in your local context?

- What process of sermon preparation do you follow each week? Do you have a set routine for the discipline of exegesis? How do you move from exegesis of the text to address the needs and issues of your people? There are many good resources available on the task of exegesis. For a refresher or first-time study of the principles, read Gordon D. Fee, *New Testament Exegesis: A Handbook for Students and Pastors* (Westminster, 1983).

- If you haven't done so, read Eugene Lowry's *The Homiletical Plot: The Sermon as Narrative Art Form* (John Knox, 1980). Then review the above sermon along with Fisher's sermons in Volumes 2 and 3 of this series. How do Fisher's sermons reflect Lowry's approach to preaching? If you have not done so, consider using Lowry's method of formulating a sermon.

Gary W. Klingsporn

TOPICAL INDEX

Scripture Index